The International Behavioural and Social Sciences Library

SYSTEMS OF ORGANIZATION

TAVISTOCK

The International Behavioural and Social Sciences Library

ORGANIZATIONAL BEHAVIOUR
In 10 Volumes

SYSTEMS OF ORGANIZATION

The Control of Task and Sentient Boundaries

E J MILLER AND A K RICE

First published in 1967 by
Tavistock Publications Limited

Reprinted in 2001 by
Routledge
11 New Fetter Lane, London EC4P 4EE

Transferred to Digital Printing 2002

Routledge is an imprint of the Taylor & Francis Group

Printed and Bound in Great Britain

British Library Cataloguing in Publication Data
A CIP catalogue record for this book
is available from the British Library

Systems of Organization
ISBN 0-415-26467-7
Organizational Behaviour: 10 Volumes
ISBN 0-415-26513-4
The International Behavioural and Social Sciences Library
112 Volumes
ISBN 0-415-25670-4

SYSTEMS
OF ORGANIZATION

The control of task and sentient boundaries

E. J. Miller and A. K. Rice

TAVISTOCK PUBLICATIONS

London · New York · Sydney · Toronto · Wellington

First published in 1967
by Tavistock Publications Limited
11 New Fetter Lane, London EC4
This book is set in 12 point Monotype Bembo, 1 point leaded
and was printed in Great Britain
by Ebenezer Baylis & Son Ltd
The Trinity Press, Worcester and London
© The Tavistock Institute of Human Relations, 1967

Distributed in the United States of America
by Barnes & Noble, Inc.

Contents

*Part V: The Elimination of Organizational Boundaries
within Enterprises*

CONTENTS

Figures

Preface

We try in this book to develop a theory of organization that reconciles tasks, human activities, and organization within one general framework. In doing so, we draw on our experience with a variety of enterprises and also build on earlier theoretical approaches of colleagues and ourselves.

In previous studies we used an open-system theory of organization and the concepts of the primary task and the socio-technical system to provide tools for the analysis of different kinds of enterprise.[1] Then, as now, we were hoping to extend our understanding and control of the inter-dependence between the social and technical variables of organization. To do so, we tried to provide a framework within which the independent values of these variables could be studied.

Our conception of organization as a tool designed primarily for task performance required that human needs – for satisfaction and for defence against anxiety – should be regarded as constraints on task performance. It has been amply demonstrated that they are significant constraints. For example, Trist and his colleagues have shown that, in the coal-mining industry, if the technical demands of task performance completely deter-mine the social organization, human needs can be so frustrated that task performance suffers.[2] Many other writers have been concerned with the discrepancies between human and enterprise objectives and with the need to modify 'task-centred' organizations in the interests of human need.[3]

When it was applied to practical organizational problems, in particular to situations in which either social or technical changes had to be accom-modated, this conception inevitably led to solutions that compromised between the technical requirements of the task and the human needs of

---

[1] Rice (1958, 1963, 1965); Miller (1959); Emery & Trist (1960).

[2] Trist & Bamforth (1951); Herbst (1962); Trist, Higgin, Murray & Pollock (1963).

[3] Among the more important and recent: Argyris (1962, 1964); Bennis, Benne & Chin (1961); Brown (1960); Likert (1961); McGregor (1960); Sayles (1964); Schein (1965); Sofer (1961); Zaleznik & Moment (1964); Katz & Kahn (1966) (which appeared as this book was going to press).

those performing it. The assumption was made that the 'right' organization would satisfy both task and social needs. Put in another way, the inference was that in the 'right' organization the human groups required for task performance were always identical with those required to satisfy the social and psychological needs.

The search for this optimum has been productive. Experiments in the Indian textile industry and the research in coal-mining, for example, have shown that forms of work organization can be discovered which provide a better match between task and human need and, correspondingly, procure significant improvements in both human satisfaction and productivity (Rice, 1958; Trist *et al.*, 1963). More recently, however, we have come to realize that there are settings where elegant solutions of this kind cannot be found or where, if found, they introduce new and intractable constraints.

A major difficulty in reconciling 'task-centred' and 'person-centred' views of organization is that organization for task performance is a co-ordination of activities – whether carried out by human or mechanical agencies: 'the object of co-ordination is activities not people' (Schein, 1965). But people are more than the activities they participate in, and, as has been pointed out many times,[1] only some of the activities of any given human being are relevant to task performance as such. Thus which particular human being carries out which particular part of a task, provided he has the technical skill required, may be quite irrelevant to theories of task organization; though his other activities, and the attitudes and beliefs they represent, may clearly be relevant to the way in which he helps or hinders task performance. In other words, task organization can exist independently of those who man it and can survive changes in membership. Moreover, at any given time, it is the needs and activities of existing role incumbents that determine the attitudes of working groups towards change, and hence may generate resistance to change. The painful consequences for future incumbents are too familiar to need elaboration.

The struggle to accommodate 'whole' human beings in organizational theory has led to the formulation of concepts of 'formal' and 'informal' organization: formal organization being the co-ordination of activities for task performance; and informal organization the relationships, both internal and external, of those who carry out the activities. A problem in any enterprise is the relative strengths of the formal and informal systems

[1] In particular, Barnard (1948).

and the discrepancies between them. When formal and informal systems are in opposition to each other, task performance inevitably suffers.

Divergence between task and human needs, and hence between their associated organizations, perhaps mattered less when the rates of development of technology and of understanding of human affairs were comparable; the integration of task and human needs could keep pace with changes in both. But the rapid social and technical changes of recent years, and the many more scientific and technical resources now available for task performance, have seriously disturbed not only the social organizations related to task performance, but wider political, social, and economic systems as well.[1] Those enterprises that have been engaged in competitive activity, but have not adopted the newer technologies, have foundered. They have then satisfied neither task nor human needs – present or future. And those non-industrial enterprises that have had no competitive criteria by which to judge task performance, and have thus been able to subordinate the need for change to the demands of their senior members that they should avoid it, have usually become outdated monuments to what is alleged to have been a happier and more productive past.

One theme of this book is that those enterprises in which task performance and organization so satisfy human needs that the recognition of a differentiated social organization is unnecessary, or, more precisely, in which the boundaries of task systems and of *sentient* systems[2] coincide, are particular cases of a more general proposition: that any enterprise requires three forms of organization – the first, to control task performance; the second, to ensure the commitment of its members to enterprise objectives; and the third, to regulate relations between task and sentient systems.

---

[1] The consequences of the introduction of modern industrial technology into developing countries are only too well known. We are now also witnessing, both in those countries and in Western Europe, a widespread dislocation in enterprise organization, caused by the introduction of new 'social technologies' – for example, economic planning at national and supra-national levels.

[2] We have considered many different words – commitment, identity, affiliation, cathexis – to denote the groups with which human beings identify themselves, as distinct from task groups, with which they may or may not become identified. We have chosen *sentient* – 'that feels or is capable of feeling; having the power or function of sensation or of perception by the senses, 1632' (*Shorter Oxford English Dictionary*) – as expressing most clearly what we mean without using the specialized vocabulary of psycho-analysis. We shall therefore talk of *sentient system* and *sentient group* to refer to that system or group that demands and receives loyalty from its members; and we shall talk of a *sentient boundary* to refer to the boundary round a sentient group or sentient system. We shall also use *sentience* to mean 'the condition or quality of being sentient' (*Shorter Oxford English Dictionary*).

The earliest manifestations of the struggle between task and human needs were the bitter fights for the recognition of trade unions and of their rights to defend their members against exploitation in the interests of task performance. Progressive employers of the late nineteenth and early twentieth centuries tried to reconcile the two needs through the introduction of welfare activities: housing, sickness and retirement schemes, sports clubs, and other benefits for their employees. The difficulty was, and is, that none of these activities is necessarily relevant to task performance and some are frequently opposed to it. We therefore add a corollary to the general proposition above: an effective sentient system relates the members of an enterprise to each other and to the enterprise in ways that are relevant to the skills and experience required for task performance.

Our earlier concepts and theories of organization were based, for the most part, on studies of manufacturing industries. In them, adaptation to technical change was intermittent. Between such adaptations task organizations were relatively stable, and it was these conditions that made possible the discovery of 'optimum' forms of organization in which the task groups themselves could provide some satisfaction and some defence against anxiety for their members.

We began to experience some difficulty when we used the concepts to deal with problems of reorganization of the top management of large complex enterprises that were facing rapid changes in their social, economic, and technical environments. We had to produce a culture in which continuous reorganization, with its consequent changes of role and group membership, became a 'steady state' (Rice, 1963). We experienced still more difficulty when we studied the organizations appropriate to sales-force activities and to research and building operations. In the former we were concerned with transactions and hence activity systems that crossed enterprise boundaries; and in the latter with tasks that were inherently temporary. In both, the nature of the task made it impossible to set up organizations in which task and sentient boundaries could coincide. We had to differentiate them organizationally. The development of a system theory of organization based largely on factory production systems had obscured the contribution of the exchanges that are the essence of boundary transactions; and the attempts to seek accord between technical systems and human social and psychological needs had hindered the recognition of boundary regulation as the essential managerial control in any enterprise, industrial or non-industrial.

Our second theme, therefore, is the importance of boundary definition and of associated control systems both within enterprises and between enterprises and their environments.

In Part I we outline the conceptual framework that we employ to analyse the examples given in the remainder of the book. It defines what we mean by the boundaries of activity systems and their control, presents briefly a theory of human behaviour in terms of the individual and the group, discusses the concept of the primary task, and relates all to a system theory of organization. In Part II we give examples of activity systems that cross enterprise boundaries and examine their effects on enterprise organization. We describe a sales force and a service industry for this purpose. In Part III, as a contrast to the organizational consequences of trans-boundary activities, we take the example of a family business to illustrate the problems that occur when inadequate attention is paid to the coincidence of multiple task- and sentient-system boundaries. In Part IV we use the building of a new works, the organization of research work (both industrial and non-industrial), and the development of the organization of a transport undertaking in an attempt to establish the proposition that temporary and transitional activity systems, and their equivalent *project-type organizations*, form the most appropriate basis for a general theory of organization. In Part V we return to the internal organization of an enterprise and consider the effects of the introduction of computer control systems on the organizational boundaries between sub-systems that are both technically and socially differentiated from each other. In this part, in which the automation of a steel works serves as our example, we discuss the organizational problems involved when continuous monitoring processes are substituted for established and traditional boundary controls. Part VI summarizes the findings, and further illustrates the two themes of the book with brief examples from the theatre and from professional, educational, and religious institutions.

Though our intention is that Parts II to V of the book should have each its own theme, we recognize that in terms of the theories we outline in Part I, they all overlap; and each example could be used to illustrate different aspects of our two main themes. Thus, although we take the task of a representative in a sales force as evidence of the problems involved in transactions across enterprise boundaries, we could also have looked at it as an instance of a temporary and transitional activity system. In effect, no one example is a simple exposition of one theme. This arises from two causes: first, we have drawn only on studies in which we have both been involved, on the ground that if we write about our own experience we, at least, can feel more certain of our interpretations; and second, and more importantly, we believe that the comprehension of complexity is essential for the understanding of organizational problems. We shall do no service, we feel, either to practitioners or to students, if we appear to give simple answers to what are essentially very complex questions, or if we speculate about enterprises and situations of which we have no direct first-hand experience.

Acknowledgements

In the autumn of 1964, we began an organizational study in an airline. For us this was an unfamiliar industry (apart from our experience as consumers), and its very unfamiliarity was a major reason for choosing it as a research setting. But what we did not foresee was the extent to which some of our findings on airline organization would illuminate previous work we had done, as consultants and research workers, in a variety of other enterprises. We suddenly saw a pattern that linked these experiences together, and we began to write this book.

We therefore owe a special debt to the Social Science Research Council,[1] who are sponsoring this project, and to British European Airways, who gave us action research opportunities and financial support. The Chairman of BEA, Sir Anthony Milward, the Chief Executive, Mr Henry Marking, and the members of a co-ordinating committee of the airline who collaborated with us on the project – Mr Cyril Herring (Chairman), Dr W. S. Barry, Mr Brian Brough, and Dr Jack Grumbridge – have all contributed greatly to our thinking and commented on drafts of Chapters 15–18. Mr Brough read the entire book in manuscript and made many constructive criticisms. Our expression of gratitude to them is, of course, accompanied by the usual disclaimer: the responsibility for the published result is ours, not theirs.

Some of the other organizations with which we worked previously, and whose members have helped at various times to sharpen our ideas, will have to remain nameless; but we are glad to be able to acknowledge our debt to Richard Thomas & Baldwins Ltd, who financed the project from which much of the material in Chapters 11, 12, 19, and 20 was derived, and to Mr W. G. Ellis, who was previously associated with another of the companies that provided data. We also wish to thank the James Marshall Fund, Inc., of New York for a contribution to the cost of writing about earlier work, some of which has been incorporated in this book.

[1] This project was first sponsored by the Department of Scientific and Industrial Research and was taken over by the Social Science Research Council.

We are grateful, too, to Mr David Armstrong and other colleagues at the Tavistock Institute who have been actively involved with us in some of the work described here. The genealogy of concepts is always hard to trace; but they and many other colleagues certainly feature in this tree.

We wish also to record our debt to the editor, Miss Rosamund Jackson, who has done painstaking work to prepare the manuscript for publication.

We express our appreciation to our secretarial staff, particularly Miss Fiona Hunter Russell and Miss Margaret Pavitt, who bore the load of typing and re-typing successive drafts of the manuscript. They were a good deal less protesting and more supportive than we deserved.

Finally, acknowledgements are due to John Murray Limited and to Houghton Mifflin Company for permission to reproduce some lines from *Summoned by bells* by John Betjeman.

Centre for Applied Social Research   E.J.M.
Tavistock Centre   A.K.R.
London N.W.3.

PART I

A Conceptual Framework

Introduction

Any enterprise may be seen as an open system which has characteristics in common with a biological organism. An open system exists, and can only exist, by exchanging materials with its environment. It imports materials, transforms them by means of conversion processes, consumes some of the products of conversion for internal maintenance, and exports the rest. Directly or indirectly, it exchanges its outputs for further intakes, including further resources to maintain itself. These import-conversion-export processes are the work the enterprise has to do if it is to live.

One intake of a biological organism is food; the corresponding conversion process is the transformation of food into energy and waste matter. Some of the energy is used up in procuring further supplies of food, some in fighting, or in securing shelter from, hostile forces in the environment, some in the functioning and growth of the system itself, and some in reproductive activities. In the same way, a joint stock company imports capital through the sale of shares or the raising of loans, converts the capital into income by investment in commercial and industrial enterprises, uses some of the results to maintain itself and to grow, and exports the remainder in the form of dividends and taxes. A manufacturing enterprise imports raw materials, converts them into products, and sells the products. From its returns on the sale it acquires more raw materials, maintains and develops the enterprise, and satisfies the investors who provided the resources to set it up.

Other kinds of enterprise have different intakes and different conversion processes, and the returns they obtain from the environment in exchange for their outputs take different forms. An educational enterprise, for example, imports students, teaches them and provides them with opportunities to learn; it exports ex-students who have either acquired some qualification or failed. The proportion that qualifies and the standard the individuals are perceived to have attained determine the extent to which the environment provides students and resources to maintain the enterprise. In a learned society the primary pay-off may not be expressible in monetary terms or in terms of securing further material or human intakes

3

but rather in prestige and self-esteem. Such pay-offs, however, are important for educational enterprises and may not be unimportant for profit-making enterprises as well.

Just as the study of living organisms requires the integration of many different theories, so the study of enterprises requires scientific theories corresponding to the anatomical, physiological, and ecological disciplines of the biologists. Organizational anatomy is concerned with the nature and structure of the resources through which the enterprise carries out its tasks; organizational physiology with the processes of task performance, including the interrelations of different internal processes; and organizational ecology with the place of the enterprise in its physical, social, cultural, and economic environment.

But we are concerned in this book not merely with developing theories that will help us to understand the structure and functioning of enterprises; we have also to bear in mind that enterprises and human beings, unlike other living organisms, need theories to apply to the solution of their own practical problems of organization.

Accordingly, in presenting our theoretical framework in Part I, we start in Chapter 1 with an examination of the systems of activity through which the enterprise carries out its import-conversion-export processes. We attempt to use concepts at a level of abstraction that makes them applicable to the functioning of all types of enterprise.

Activities, however, require resources to produce them and all enterprises have to employ some human resources. Any theory of organization therefore entails a theory of individual and group behaviour. An outline of such a theory is presented in Chapter 2.

Organization is the means through which the enterprise secures the performance of its tasks. In Chapter 3 we discuss a method of analysing task priorities and of determining the resources needed for, and the constraints on, task performance.

In Chapter 4 we put forward a system theory of organization and discuss model organizational forms through which resources can be deployed in systems of activity. We then examine the types of regulation that are required to relate people to tasks and to take into account the constraints that are imposed by the employment of human resources.

CHAPTER I

Systems of Activity and their Boundaries

In this chapter we shall first consider the enterprise in terms of the systems of activity through which the import-conversion-export processes are carried out. We shall distinguish between operating activities and maintenance and regulatory activities, and we shall then discuss the definition of the boundaries of systems of activity and the control of transactions across them.

THE PROCESSES AND ACTIVITIES OF AN ENTERPRISE

A process *is a transformation or a series of transformations brought about in the throughput of a system, as a result of which the throughput is changed in position, shape, size, function, or some other respect.*

An activity *is a unit of work. The transformations that contribute to a process are brought about through interaction of the inherent characteristics of the throughput and* operating *activities, which are carried out on the throughput.* Activities may be carried out by people or by mechanical or other means. We call the producers of activities *resources*.

An enterprise relates to its environment through a variety of import-conversion-export processes, which require a corresponding variety of activities. A manufacturing company, as we have said, imports raw materials, converts them into products, and acquires a pay-off from selling the products. But it also recruits employees, trains them, assigns them to jobs, and sooner or later exports them by resignation, retirement, or dismissal. It imports and consumes stores and power. It also collects intelligence about its market and its competitors, analyses this information, makes decisions about design, quantity, quality, and price of products, and issues communications of different kinds as a result of the decisions taken.

In the analysis of an enterprise, or of a unit within an enterprise, we reserve the term *operating activities* for those activities that directly contribute to the import, conversion, and export processes which define the nature of the enterprise or unit and differentiate it from other enterprises or units. Thus in a shoe-manufacturing company the operating activities are those that procure the leather and other raw materials, convert these materials into shoes, and sell and dispatch the shoes to customers. Similarly, in an airline the operating activities are those that directly contribute to the process of transforming potential travellers into ticketed passengers and of transporting these passengers from a departure point to a destination. If the unit of analysis is an accounts department, then the operating activities will be those through which the relevant data are acquired, processed, and exported in the form of invoices, cheques, cost reports, payrolls, and accounts of various kinds.

Besides operating activities, two other types of activity may be identified: maintenance and regulation.

Maintenance activities procure and replenish the resources that produce operating activities. Thus not only the purchase, maintenance, and overhaul of machinery, but also the recruitment, induction, training, and motivation of employees come under this heading.

Regulatory activities relate operating activities to each other, maintenance activities to operating activities, and all internal activities of the enterprise (or unit) to its environment.

Maintenance and regulatory activities can themselves be analysed in import-conversion-export terms. In regulatory activities, for example, the intake is information about the process being regulated, the conversion process is the comparison of the data against objectives or standards of performance, and the output the decision to stop or to modify (or not to stop or modify) the process, or the decision to accept or to reject the the product. Similarly, to take the selection procedure for new employees as an example of a maintenance process, import activities procure an applicant, conversion activities apply the procedure through which comes the decision to select or to reject, and export activities place the new employee or dispose of the rejected applicant.

SYSTEMS OF ACTIVITY

A system of activities *is that complex of activities which is required to complete the process of transforming an intake into an output.*

A task system *is a system of activities plus the human and physical resources required to perform the activities.*

The term 'system', as we use it here, implies that each component activity of the system is interdependent in respect of at least some of the other activities of the same system, and that the system as a whole is identifiable as being in certain, if limited, respects independent of related systems.

Thus a system has a boundary which separates it from its environment. Intakes cross this boundary and are subjected to conversion processes within it. The work done by the system is therefore, at least potentially, measurable by the difference between its intakes and its outputs.

But a measurable difference between output and intake does not of itself imply that the boundary so identified is the boundary of a system of activities. For example, in an automatic transfer line a component passes through a succession of machines, each of which performs a distinct operation, the output/input ratio of which can be measured; yet the machines are so interconnected that all either operate together or stop together. Even if variable-feed devices are introduced between the machines, the output/input ratio that is significant is that of the whole line. A system boundary implies a discontinuity. We make the hypothesis that the discontinuity at the boundary constitutes a differentiation of technology, territory, or time, or of some combination of these (Miller, 1959).

In a simple system there are no internal system boundaries either between one operating activity and another or between operating activities on the one hand and maintenance and regulatory activities on the other. A complex system contains such internal boundaries. In a large complex system there may be several orders of differentiation: major operating systems themselves being differentiated into bounded sub-systems, which in their turn may also be differentiated, and so on until simple undifferentiated systems are reached.

Most enterprises have the characteristics of complex systems: they include a number of identifiable sub-systems of activities through which the various processes of the enterprise are carried out. These constituent systems, like the enterprise as a whole, are open systems which acquire intakes from the environment, transform them, and export the results. Thus one department in a manufacturing process may have as its intakes part-processed products which are the outputs of departments preceding it in the process. In its turn, it exports to succeeding departments the same products at a later stage in manufacture. The total enterprise is therefore a significant part of the environment for its component systems of activity.

When maintenance activities are carried out in differentiated component systems of an enterprise they too can be treated as systems of activity

7

with their own operating activities and related maintenance and regulatory activities.

MONITORING AND BOUNDARY CONTROL ACTIVITIES

What distinguishes a system from an aggregate of activities and preserves its boundary is the existence of regulation. Regulation relates activities to throughput, ordering them in such a way as to ensure that the process is accomplished and that the different import-conversion-export processes of the system as a whole are related to the environment.

Most processes are in some measure 'self-regulating' in the sense that the nature or structure of the process imposes disciplines and constraints on the associated system of activities. Thus a given operation that is part of a series of operations is 'regulated' by preceding and succeeding operations. Similarly, in parts of the chemical industry, once chemicals have been mixed, and heating, flow, and other processes started, technology takes over and for the most part determines quantity, quality, and speed of output. Important though these inherent constraints and disciplines are, they are not regulatory *activities* as such.

In the analysis of systems of activities two types of regulatory activity can be identified: monitoring and boundary control.

Whenever an operating activity is stopped, for however short a time, to check that it is achieving its purpose, a regulatory activity is introduced: operating activity/check/resumption of operating activity. Thus when a carpenter, sawing a piece of wood, pauses to make sure that his cut is in the right direction, he is changing his activity from operation to regulation. An example of a less perceptible change of activity occurs in the task of a salesman. In his transactions with a potential customer the salesman is carrying out a regulatory activity whenever he monitors what he has said already, assesses what effect this has had on the customer, and on this basis decides whether to continue the same approach or to adopt a different mode of attack. We use the term *monitoring* to refer to such intra-system regulatory activities, which are different in kind from, and not directly related to, the controls activated at the boundaries of the system.

Regulatory activities that relate a system of activities to its environment occur at the boundary of the system and the environment and control the import and export transactions across it. Boundary regulation is therefore external to the operating activities of the system. The important implication is that the boundary round a system of activities is not simply a line but a region with two boundaries, one between the internal activities of the system and the region of regulation, and a second between the region of regulation and the environment. For this form of regulation we use the term *boundary control function*.

BOUNDARY CONTROL FUNCTION

The relation of a boundary control function to the import-conversion-export process is shown in *Figure 1*. *Figure 2* depicts the system of activities in topological form and shows the relation of the boundary control function to the operating activities.

FIGURE 1 *Regulation at the boundaries of a process*

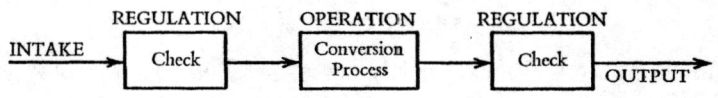

FIGURE 2 *The boundary control function of a system of activities*

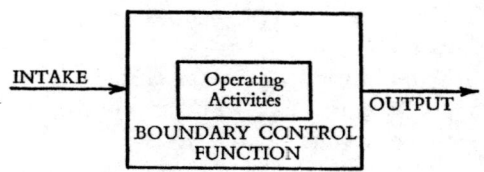

The boundary of a system of activities therefore implies both a discontinuity and the interpolation of a region of control. We shall see that difficulties arise if an organizational boundary is imposed at a point in a process which does not satisfy these two criteria of the boundary of an activity system. Unless there is a discontinuity, there can be no boundary region and thus no sense in which activities carried out within the supposed system are insulated from other activities 'outside'.

We have pointed out that regulation can itself be analysed as an import-conversion-export process: import activities are the collection of data from measurement or other observation; conversion activities, the comparison of these data with objectives or standards of performance; and

9

export activities the decisions to stop or to modify the process or to pass the product. Simple examples are the inspection functions of manufacturing enterprises, by which raw materials are tested before being accepted and products inspected before dispatch. In most large factories inspection functions are also interposed between departments. Provided the inspections occur at boundaries between the enterprise and its environment or between differentiated constituent systems of the total enterprise, there are few problems of boundary confusion. The problems increase when we consider the organizational effects of the introduction of continuous automatic controls, particularly those that incorporate feedback and self-correcting devices, and hence eliminate the need for the pause for checking between one system of operating activities and the next.

MONITORING ACTIVITIES

A simple form of automatic regulation can be illustrated by contrasting the sawing of a piece of wood by a carpenter, who pauses to check the direction of his cut, with the same operation performed on a mechanical saw, when the direction of the cut is determined by a pre-set jig. In the mechanical operation the saw-minder regulates the quantity, and probably the quality, of the intake, but the conversion activity is controlled automatically. The saw-minder's task is to monitor; the actual sawing is carried out by the machine.

The next step is the introduction of mechanical devices to link the sawing operation with the preceding and succeeding operations. By these devices raw materials are acquired, checked, sawn, and transferred without pause to the next operation. The devices make and implement decisions about adjustments to these operations without halting the process.

The consequences of introducing a continuous monitoring function are illustrated in *Figures 3* and *4*. *Figure 3a* shows the simple interposition of checks between three consecutive processes, and this is contrasted in *Figure 3b* with a continuous monitoring function. When there are pauses for regulation, each part of the conversion process is potentially, at least, carried out through a differentiated system of activity, each with its own boundary control function. But when there are no pauses for check the boundaries between the operating systems are removed and the different operating activities are carried out in a single operating system. *Figures 3a* and *3b* are shown in topological form in *Figures 4a* and *4b*. The boundary control function shown in *Figure 4b* both regulates the transac-

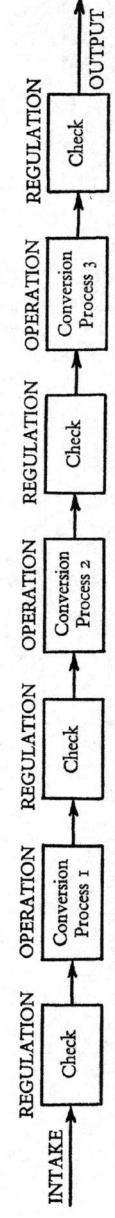

FIGURE 3A *Checks between consecutive processes*

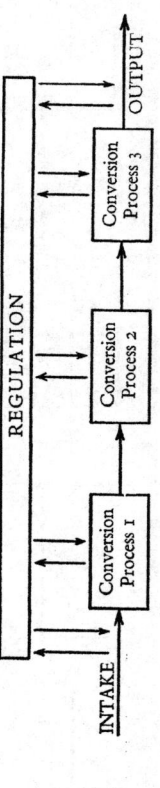

FIGURE 3B *Continuous monitoring function*

FIGURE 4A *Three consecutive activities: independent regulation*

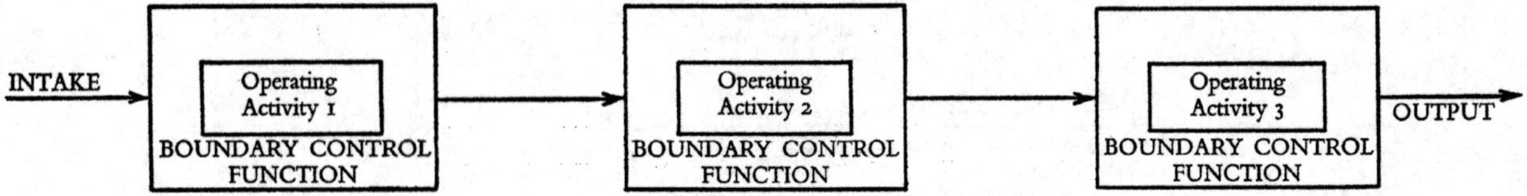

FIGURE 4B *Three consecutive activities: integrated regulation*

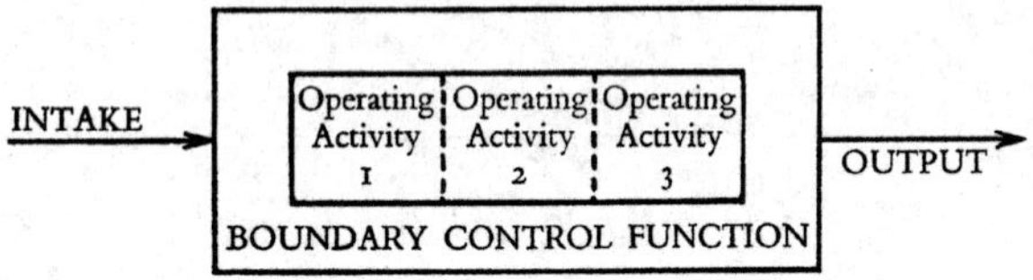

tions of the three operating activities with the environment and monitors the intra-system transfers between the operating activities.

We shall return later in the book to the organizational implications of such developments. The general point to be made at this stage is that it is possible to construct a scale or hierarchy of regulatory activities as decisions are required at progressively higher levels of abstraction, or as new variables have to be taken into account in the decision-making process. The simplest regulation is that carried out by an operator who halts an activity to check that it is fulfilling its purpose – the carpenter who pauses in his sawing; at the next level an operator monitors a single activity or a simple series of activities – the saw-machine operator; at the next, the data used for regulation are abstractions read from dials and gauges – as by the process operator in a chemical works; at the next, the data are read and processed automatically, and the decisions themselves are implemented as self-correcting devices – computer-controlled production from an automatic plant. A new level in the hierarchy of regulation is introduced whenever the data required for control purposes are beyond the data-processing capacity of the available regulatory resources.

However sophisticated the technology, there nevertheless comes a point at which regulation cannot be mechanized and automated, and at which there has to be a pause to check the output of the system against the requirements of the environment. At this point a boundary region is introduced and an organizational discontinuity occurs.

CHAPTER 2

Individuals, Groups, and their Boundaries

Every enterprise requires resources to produce the 'units of work' – the activities – through which its processes are carried out. And, besides the resources that actually produce activities, there are those that provide an environment within which the activities can take place. Thus the physical resources of a manufacturing company will include factories and the relevant machinery and equipment, all of which represent a major capital investment. If the enterprise is a partnership of general practitioners, the investment in physical resources will be more modest: surgeries and their equipment, waiting rooms, and receptionists' offices. Both in extent and in kind, the physical resources employed vary between one type of enterprise and another and between the different parts of any one complex enterprise.

Common to all enterprises, however, is the deployment of human resources. Regardless of the extent of automation, there are always some activities in an enterprise that must be carried out by human beings. Moreover, human beings do not exist simply as individuals; they are joined together in groups, small and large, and they interact in these groups both as individuals and as groups. Further, individuals can belong to many small groups in any large group and to many large groups in any environment. Indeed, an individual cannot exist in isolation, but only in relation to other individuals and groups. Even when he is alone, what he is and what he does are in large part a product of past relationships and of anticipated relationships in the future. Any theory of organization requires, therefore, not only a theory of systems of activities and their boundaries, but also a theory of human behaviour.

The theories of human behaviour and of activity systems are in many respects analogous. Like a system of activities, an individual or a group may be seen as an open system, which exists and can exist only through processes of exchange with the environment. Individuals and groups, however, have the capacity to mobilize themselves at different times into many different kinds of activity system; and only some activities are relevant to the performance of the tasks of the various enterprises to which they belong.

Within our conceptual framework, the individual, the small group, and the larger group are seen as progressively more complex manifestations of a basic structural principle. Each can be described in terms of an internal world, an external environment, and a boundary function which controls transactions between what is inside and what outside.

The personality of the individual is made up of his biological inheritance and the experiences through which he passes, particularly those of early infancy and childhood. In a modern industrial society ordinary men and women have three overlapping areas of conduct – family, work, and social activities – through which they can work out their own development. Through these areas of conduct they satisfy their physiological and psychological needs and defend themselves against the stresses and strains of having to come to terms with the realities of their environment. They grow to maturity through the relationships they make in them. A baby is dependent on one person – his mother. He gradually assimilates into his pattern of relationships his father and any brothers and sisters. As he grows into childhood he includes other members of the extended family and of the family network. The first break with this family pattern is usually made when the child goes to school and encounters for the first time an institution to which he has to contribute as a member of a wider society. It is his preliminary experience of what, in later years, will be a working environment.

The hopes and fears that govern the individual's expectations of how he will be treated by others and the beliefs and attitudes on which he bases his code of conduct derive from these relationships and are built into the pattern that becomes his personality. They form his internal world. This contains his primitive inborn impulses, and the primitive controls over them that derive from his earliest relationships with authority, usually represented by his parents. His internal world embodies the part of himself that longs to do what was forbidden or made impossible, and the part that is composed of the images of those who both excited the impulses and forbade them.

A useful contribution to our understanding of the development of personality is made by object-relations theory. According to this theory, the baby can make no distinction between what is inside himself and what is outside. He has no 'ego' that can differentiate his feelings and their causes. What he feels about an object that is outside becomes an attribute of the object itself. He 'projects' his feeling onto it. So far as it excites him and gratifies him, it is a 'good object' which he loves and on which he lavishes his care; so far as it frustrates or hurts him, it is a 'bad object' which he hates and on which he vents his rage. In his struggle to deal with these contradictory attributes he splits objects into good and bad, which represent their satisfying and frustrating aspects. But he has to learn that in reality it is the same object that sometimes satisfies and sometimes frustrates, that is sometimes good and sometimes bad. Both what later appears as protective love and what appears as destructive hate may originate in one confused and violent feeling that is inherently unstable because, in his very need to take in what is good, the individual also takes in what is bad, and hence threatens to destroy what he wants most to preserve. From this violent confusion of feelings for the same object come the later tendencies, on the one hand to idealize those who are felt to be protective and loving, and on the other to execrate those who are felt to be antagonistic and obstructive.[1]

In the mature individual, the ego – the concept of the self as a unique individual – mediates the relationships between the internal world of good and bad objects and the external world of reality, and thus takes, in relation to the personality, a 'leadership' role. The mature ego is one that can differentiate between what is real in the outside world and what is projected onto it from inside, what should be accepted and incorporated into experience and what should be rejected. In short, the mature ego is one that can define the boundary between what is inside and what is outside, and can control the transactions between the one and the other.

Diagrammatically, the individual may be represented on the pattern of a system of activity: see *Figure 5*. The ego is the equivalent of the boundary control region that mediates between the inner world and the environment.

The tendency for most human beings to split the good from the bad in themselves and to project their resultant feelings onto others is one of the major barriers to the understanding and control of the relationships between human resources and the tasks to which they contribute. And the difficulties of accepting that love and hatred can be felt for the same person are intensified in the relations between managers and the members of the

[1] For a fuller account of this theory see Klein (1959).

FIGURE 5 *Individual personality*

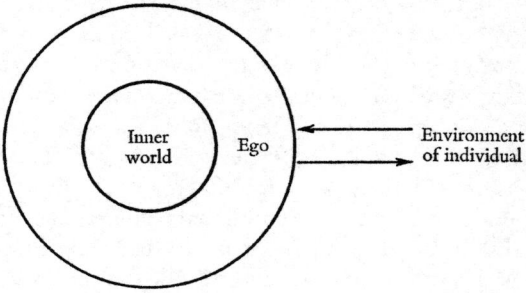

enterprise they manage. The members of an enterprise depend on their managers to identify their tasks and to provide the resources for task performance. A manager who fails, or even falters, as inevitably he sometimes must, deprives his subordinates of satisfaction and thereby earns their hatred. But the leadership role of management is a lonely role and leaders must have followers; any hanging back or turning away is a threat to their own fulfilment. This inevitable, and mutual, dependence increases the need of both leaders and followers to defend themselves against the destructive power of their potential hostility to each other.

THE GROUP

We have described the internal world of the individual as made up of objects and part-objects derived from the relationships he has made. An individual has, therefore, no meaning except in relationships with others with whom he interacts. He uses them and they him, to express views, take action, and play roles. The individual is a creature of a group, the group of the individual. Each, according to his capacity and his experience, carries within him the groups of which he has been and is a member. His experiences as infant, child, and adolescent within his family, at school, and at work, and the cultural setting in which he has been brought up, will thus affect, by the way in which they are moulded into his personality, the working relationships he makes with superiors, colleagues, and subordinates.

Every group, however casual, meets to do something. In this activity the members of a group co-operate with each other; and their co-operation calls upon their knowledge, experience, and skill. Because the task for which they have met is real, they have to relate themselves to reality to perform it. For task performance they have to behave as rational human beings. As such, they have to have methods of communication between themselves and with the external environment about their task. In so far as they develop attitudes towards and beliefs about each other and about the group that transcend the purpose for which they have met, they are making assumptions about themselves as individuals and about the group as a group.[1] These assumptions, together with their attitudes towards their purpose, provide the emotional climate in which they meet.

The internal world of a group is made up, then, first of the contributions of its members to its purpose and, second, of the feelings and attitudes the members develop about each other and about the group, both internally and in relation to its environment. At the level of task performance, members take part as rational mature human beings; at the level of assumptions they make about each other and the group, they go into collusion with each other to support or to hinder what they have met to do. The resulting pattern is one of co-operation and conflict between the members as individuals and between them and the group culture they produce.

The external environment of the group includes other individuals, groups, and institutions with which group members interact as individuals and as members of the group.

The two levels of the internal world of the group are depicted schematically in *Figure 6*. As members of a work group, individuals contribute overtly and consciously to the task of the group; simultaneously, they project into and out of the group, in ways of which they are unaware, their assumptions about themselves, about one another, and about their environment. Thus the group, behaving as if it had made assumptions about itself (the 'assumption' group), invades the boundaries of individuals; and, similarly, the external affiliations of individual members breach the boundary of the group.

A group, by definition, must consist of more than one individual; but groups of different sizes have different characteristic patterns of behaviour. Thus pairs and trios obviously have different properties as groups; and, so far as we can tell at present, there are characteristic changes with

[1] Cf. Bion (1961). Bion identifies three 'basic' assumptions: dependence, pairing, and fight-flight. Thus groups, whatever their overt task, behave, according to Bion, *as if* they had met: to depend on one person to provide all physical or spiritual nourishment; to reproduce themselves; or to fight somebody or something or to run away from somebody or something.

FIGURE 6 *The two levels of the internal world of the group*

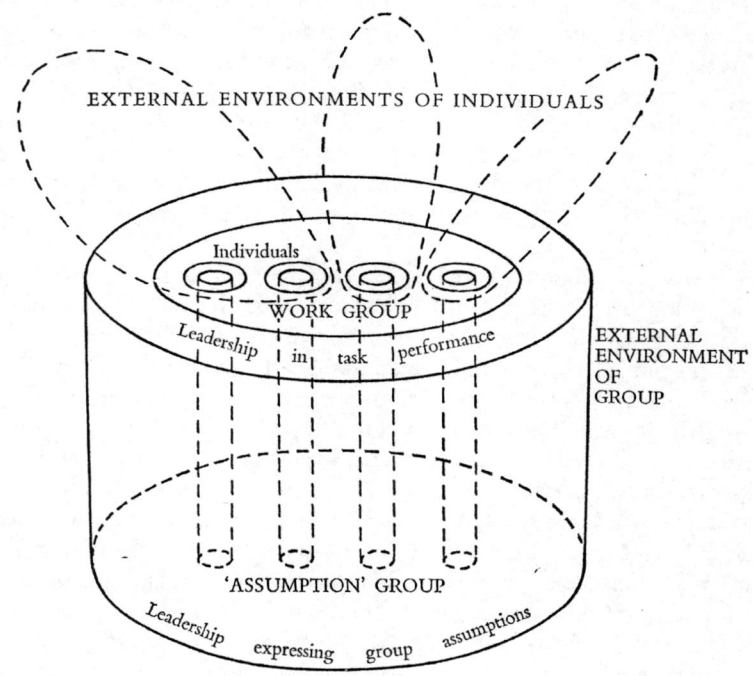

each additional member up to five, six, or even seven. Thereafter, as the group grows from seven to between eleven and sixteen members, though changes take place, the essential characteristics are those of the small face-to-face group. In such a group there are not so many members that they cannot sustain close and continuous personal relationships; but neither are there so few that the defection of one member can jeopardize the group's security. The small face-to-face group provides a boundary within which the member can be known and can feel secure; within which, as an individual, he can seek reinforcement and help; in return, however, he has to conform to the patterns of behaviour imposed by the group, and contribute to the different assumptions that make up the group culture.

Larger groups may or may not be internally differentiated. Undifferentiated large groups are usually very short-lived. Lacking the controls imposed by structured relationships at the work-group level, they are correspondingly more prone to be dominated by irrational assumptions. Thus the members of a demagogue's audience or of a rioting mob shed their individual boundaries and are submerged in the group.

Beyond a membership of twelve or thereabouts, groups tend to split into subgroups. Since many enterprises require more human resources than can be provided by a small face-to-face group, they have to take into account the phenomena not only of small groups but of large groups as well.

The large group is composed of individuals and of the small groups to which they belong. The small groups may be 'formal', in that their membership and purpose are consistent with the requirements of the enterprise; or they may be 'informal', directed towards other ends. The individual may be related to the large group through membership of more than one small group. The internal life of the large group consists, therefore, of the relationships between individuals and of the relationships within and between the groups to which they belong. Individuals have their own overt needs and unconscious strivings, and small groups their tasks and assumptions which identify them and hold them together. Moreover, individuals and groups interact at conscious and unconscious levels and at work and assumption levels simultaneously.

Whether a group is large or small, leadership, the equivalent of the ego function of the personality, is required to relate what is inside the group to its environment; that is, leadership of the group, like that of the individual, is a boundary function that controls transactions between inside and outside. Leadership is not a function necessarily or even usually exercised by one individual; at different times and in different circumstances various members may act on behalf of the group. In our terminology, therefore, it is activities that define leadership, not the verbal designation of someone as 'the leader'. 'The leader' of the work group may indeed have to contend with the behavioural reality that leadership activities are a function of the 'assumption' group and may be in conflict with work-group requirements. Wherever they are located and whoever performs them, however, leadership activities express and confirm the distinctive identity of the group as against other groups, and differentiate between membership and non-membership.

The existence of a group presupposes some emotional investment by its members in the identity of the group and hence in the preservation of the boundary round it. Groups vary in the extent to which they invest emotionally in their boundaries; in other words, some groups are more important to their members than others are, or, to use the terminology introduced in the preface, some groups have more *sentience* than others. Such variations are manifested through the transactions across the boundary – the control of which is the function of leadership. Whether this function is filled by one individual or by a number, the extent to which transactions across the boundary display consistency is one measure of the extent to which the members are emotionally committed to their group.

But, as we have said, individuals belong simultaneously to many different groups of different sizes. This is illustrated in *Figure 7*, which shows that C, a member of Small Group I, is also a member of Small

FIGURE 7 *The large group*

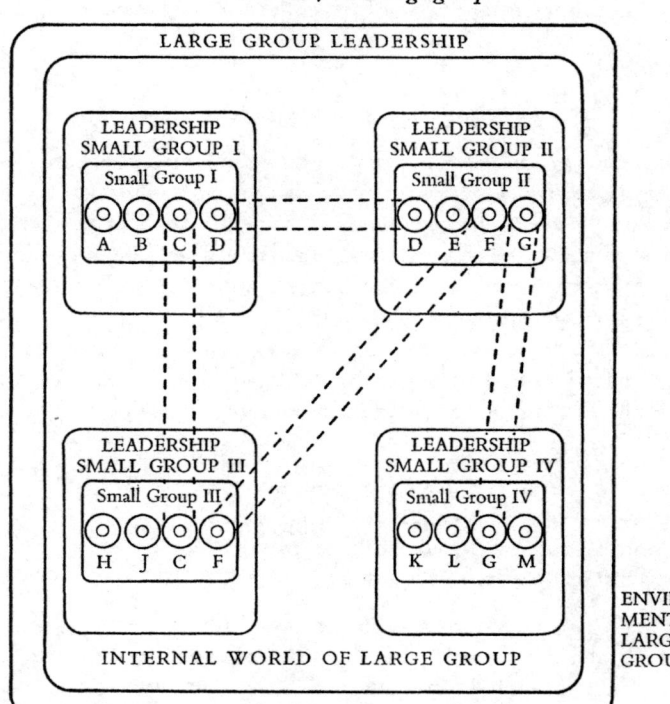

21

Group III, and that G is simultaneously a member of Small Groups II and IV, and F of Small Groups II and III. (This diagram does not show external affiliations; nor does it depict the two levels of the internal world of the group: cf. *Figure 6*.) Thus, for C, one of these small groups may have more sentience than the other; and the boundary of the large group may have more, or less, sentience for him than has either of the small groups.

Although our diagrams suggest similarities between the leadership of groups and the boundary control functions of systems of activity, it would be a mistake to press the comparison too far and to regard individuals and groups as simple activity systems. As we have said, individuals and groups can mobilize themselves at different times and even simultaneously in many different activity systems; and individuals can belong simultaneously to many different groups of different sizes. Indeed, in any hierarchical structure, every member of the enterprise except those at the very top or at the very bottom must belong to at least two groups simultaneously – that of his subordinates, and that of his colleagues and superior (Likert, 1961).

INTERGROUP TRANSACTIONS

Any form of intergroup relations involves transactions of some kind across group boundaries. But for transactions across group boundaries, a group has to have some means of speaking as a group. It has to have a 'voice', and for the 'voice' to be coherent and understandable, not only outside the group but inside as well, some mechanism, some 'political' machinery, has to be devised. In other words, the group either has to speak in unison or has to be 'represented'. In the simplest case, in which Group A communicates with Group B through a representative (a), a new boundary and four new dimensions of relationships are automatically involved (as shown in *Figure 8*):

   (i)   between Group A and its representative (a);
   (ii) between representative (a) and Group B;
   (iii) within Group B with the addition of (a);
   (iv) within Group A with the loss of (a).

The initiating group has to come to terms with what is being said or done on its behalf; and the representative has to reconcile his own views with the group policy he has to communicate. The receiving group's boundary is also crossed and the group has to come to terms with the intrusion from

FIGURE 8 *The boundaries of representative activity*

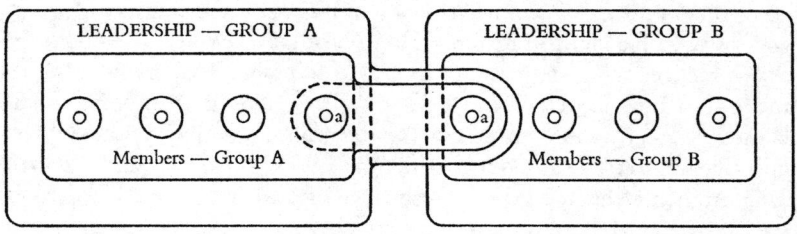

the environment and with the addition, however temporary, to its number.

When representatives from several groups meet together to establish intergroup relations between all their groups, still another boundary is added and another set of relationships: between the representatives as a group and the groups from which they come. This is shown in *Figure 9*. It is not uncommon for representatives to be disowned by the groups they represent because they have transferred, or are suspected of having transferred, their allegiances to the groups they visit or to the 'group' of representatives.

The sending out of any member to represent a group also reduces the power of a group as a group. If, while the representative is absent, the group is inactive, this means that all group activity is vested in the representative; and the group as a group is rendered impotent. Its leadership is being exercised by the absent member. If, on the other hand, the group remains effectively active while the representative is away and as a result of its activity grows and develops, then this means that the representative represents only the past, and his 'leadership' as expressed in relation to the environment is diminished. He no longer represents the group as it is, but only as it was.

In general, the setting up of any intergroup relationships involves the drawing, temporarily at least, of new boundaries. And the drawing of new boundaries contains the possibility that the new boundaries will prove stronger than the old – that the new boundaries will enjoy a greater sentience than the old.

Potentially, therefore, the setting up of any intergroup transactions has destructive characteristics since the relationships involved may destroy, or at least weaken, familiar boundaries. But any open system, in order to live, has to engage in intergroup transactions. The members of any group

23

are thus inevitably in a dilemma: on the one hand, safety lies in the preservation of its own boundary at all costs and the avoidance of transactions
across it; on the other hand, survival depends upon the conduct of transactions with the environment and the risk of destruction.

In practice, any enterprise has multiple transactions with its environment, and thus has to defend itself by the conditions it imposes on the
nature, variety, and consistency or inconsistency of its transactions.
Clearly, the more numerous the members who 'represent' an enterprise
to its environment, the greater the chance of inconsistency; and hence, as
we have postulated, of reducing investment in the enterprise boundary.

FIGURE 9 *The formation of the representatives' group*

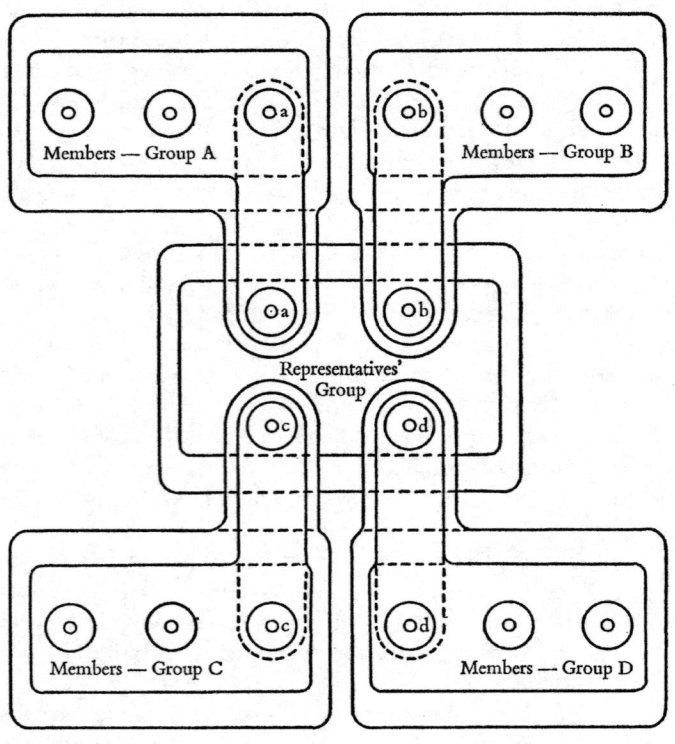

CHAPTER 3

Task Priorities and Constraints

In Chapters 1 and 2 we have outlined concepts of activity systems and their boundaries, and of human behaviour. In this chapter we shall be concerned with task priorities: that is, with the priorities of the activities through which an enterprise is related to its environment and the parts of an enterprise are related to each other and to the whole. The concept of the primary task allows us to explore the purposeful nature of these relationships.

We have said that any enterprise may be considered as an open system, that exists, and only can exist, by exchanging materials with its environment. It imports materials, converts them, and exports some of the results. Its outputs enable it to acquire more intakes, and the import-conversion-export process is the work the enterprise has to do to live. The task of any enterprise can be defined in the most general way, therefore, as to secure a pay-off by converting intakes into outputs – the minimum pay-off being the postponement of death.

But even simple enterprises, as we have shown, have multiple intakes and outputs and hence perform multiple tasks. They correspond to the operating, maintenance, and regulatory activities we have identified. We postulate that at any given time an enterprise has a *primary task – the task that it must perform if it is to survive*.[1]

THE CONCEPT OF THE PRIMARY TASK

The primary task is essentially a heuristic concept, which allows us to explore the ordering of multiple activities (and of constituent systems of activity where these exist). It makes it possible to construct and compare different organizational models of an enterprise based on different definitions of its primary task; and to compare the organizations of different enterprises with the same or different primary tasks. The definition of the primary task determines the dominant import-conversion-export system,

[1] See also Hutton (1962); Rice (1958, 1963).

and the operating, as distinct from the maintenance and regulatory, activities. It specifies the resources required and hence determines the priorities of constituent systems.

One implication of this is that there may be conflict between the way in which a constituent system defines its primary task and the way in which the superordinate system defines it. For example, the internally defined primary task of a factory department might be to maximize the output of a particular product; from the perspective of the enterprise, however, a greater pay-off might be secured by limiting the output of this department and increasing that of another, or even by requiring from it a different kind of output and modifying its resources accordingly. On a larger scale, the definition of the primary task of medical services as to save life can, in developing and overcrowded countries, lead to tragic consequences when what is required to sustain the inevitably increased population – food, housing, and other resources – is not also made available.

Similarly, environmental definitions of the primary task of an enterprise may differ from and impose constraints on its own definition. A community, for example, may define the primary task of the largest company in the district as that of providing essential employment for the local population. Such a definition may contradict the policy of the company, which, to improve performance of the primary task as defined by its own management – to carry out a profitable manufacturing operation – may require a more mechanized production process and a correspondingly reduced labour force.

In most industries, however, the general 'public' definition of the identity and purpose of an institution assigns long-term priority to a particular task and hence to a particular import-conversion-export system. Thus an educational enterprise must export some trained students and a manufacturing enterprise must produce some goods; and unless they secure such a return from their outputs that they are able to procure fresh intakes – of students and of raw materials, respectively – they cannot survive.

But tasks that are in the long-term ancillary to the primary task may temporarily become primary. For example, in a factory, the production system that converts raw materials into finished products has long-term priority, and the primary task is the conversion of raw materials into products. But if the machinery breaks down the primary task of the conversion system shifts from producing goods to repairing machines. The maintenance system of activities (which 'imports' malfunctioning machinery and spare parts and 'exports' repaired machinery) has priority. Similarly, an educational institution's primary task is jeopardized if it cannot procure staff, so that at certain times the primary task may shift from education to recruitment.

Such a temporary shift of the primary task may, however, lead to a permanent redefinition of the primary task of the enterprise and hence of priorities among the multiple tasks performed. To attract staff, it may be necessary for an educational institution to expand its research activities, in which staff can participate and from which they can earn academic prestige. As the ratio of research activities to teaching activities increases, so the definition of the institution's primary task may become, whether explicitly or not, progressively modified. The behaviour of the enterprise may then indicate that its primary task is no longer the production of trained students but the production of research publications.

In some enterprises there is no settled order of priority. A teaching hospital provides a classic example. To survive, it must import medical students, train them, and export an acceptable proportion of them as qualified doctors; and it must also import patients, treat them, and export an acceptable proportion of them as convalescents. At any one time, one task or the other has priority, and in the operating theatre the primary task may shift from moment to moment according to the progress of the operation. The prison service of the United Kingdom has three tasks: to punish the wrongdoer on behalf of society; to confine the socially dangerous; and to rehabilitate the delinquent member of the community. Given our present knowledge and resources, rehabilitation, which requires an open prison, and confinement, which by definition requires a closed prison, are not easily reconciled within the same system.

In the analysis of organization, the primary task often has to be inferred from the behaviour of the various systems of activity, and from the criteria by which their performance is regulated. One may then be able to make such statements as: 'This enterprise is behaving as if its primary task were . . . .'; or: 'This part of the enterprise is behaving as if the primary task of the whole were . . . .'. Such formulations may be compared with explicit statements by the leaders of the enterprise and of its parts about their definitions of the primary task.

The primary task is not a normative concept. We do not say that every enterprise *must* have a primary task or even that it must define its primary task; we put forward the proposition that every enterprise, or part of it, *has*, at any given moment, one task which is primary. What we also say, however, is that, if, through inadequate appraisal of internal resources and external forces, the leaders of an enterprise define the primary task in an inappropriate way, or the members – leaders and followers alike – do not agree on their definition, then the survival of the enterprise will be jeopardized. Moreover, if organization is regarded primarily as an instrument for task performance, we can add that, without adequate task definition, disorganization must occur.

RESOURCES AND CONSTRAINTS

Resources provide, or facilitate, the activities through which intakes are converted into outputs. The resources required for any task performance are human and physical. In some enterprises, such as highly automated factories, the majority of activities are carried out by machines; in others, such as educational institutions or the selling departments of manufacturing companies, they are carried out by people. Yet, even in completely automated factories, the design of the process, and its maintenance and regulation, depend on people, with their scientific and technological knowledge, their skill and their experience. The extent to which resources exist or do not exist constitutes the major internal constraint on task definition and performance. The social, political, economic, and legal conditions of the environment constitute the major environmental constraints.

Thus, while the general definition of the primary task of any industrial or commercial enterprise is 'to make a profit', how it may be made, how much, and what can be done with it, are constrained by law, by custom, and by taxation. In addition, in most cases the human resources available for an enterprise come from the society in which it is located. The members of the society create its culture and hence bring to the enterprise in which they work the cultural constraints of their society. Environmental constraints are therefore inevitably built into enterprises and thus become a part of their internal culture. When an enterprise is itself valued both by its employees and by its society, the constraints on task definition and performance attract value as well, and become for this reason difficult to change. Both definition and performance are therefore constrained by the external environment and by the internal culture, and the interaction of the enterprise and its environment strengthens and confirms the constraints. Consequently, new knowledge, fresh experience – in general, new resources – are frequently difficult to introduce.

Constraints arising either from the environment or within the enterprise itself need, therefore, to be kept under constant review to determine whether they are in fact inviolable. Less than perfect task performance always has to be accepted because of known constraints; this performance is, of necessity, standard performance. A relaxation of constraints – a new invention, the development of a new skill – could lead to new tasks, or the better performance of old ones; but if there is no corresponding re-examination of task definition and of criteria for the judgement of performance, what was standard can become substandard.

In enterprises with more than one task and no adequate determination of priority, the performance of one task acts as a constraint on the performance of another. The teaching hospital has already been mentioned: given existing levels of knowledge and skill, patients may be necessary for the training of doctors; but this does not always mean that those patients who are attended by apprentice doctors get the best treatment. Large enterprises are differentiated into constituent systems, each of which has its own discrete primary task. In this sense, any large enterprise carries out multiple tasks. Further, the environment of any constituent system is comprised of other constituent systems and the whole, and the constraints on definition and performance in constituent systems include, therefore, those imposed by other constituent systems. The greater the differentiation of a large, complex enterprise, the more numerous the constraints imposed on each constituent system by the others and the whole; and the more subsidiary the constituent system, the greater the force of constraint on task definition and methods of performance.

THE CONSTRAINTS IMPOSED BY THE EMPLOYMENT OF HUMAN RESOURCES

More generally, once the primary task has been defined, and the definition accepted, other activities, however necessary and important, are subsidiary and can become constraints on primary task performance. Except in very primitive communities in which work, play, and family life are all integrated community activities, the members of an enterprise carry within themselves memberships of many different groups with many different activity systems. However positively they accept the definition and the methods of performance of an enterprise's primary task, it is unlikely that values derived from all their other different memberships will always be in harmony with those attached to work.

Therefore, a major constraint on the efficiency of any activity system is that technology has not eliminated, and never will entirely eliminate, the need to mobilize human resources, which bring with them into the enterprise more than the activities they are required to contribute. In the assignment of activities to roles and of roles to task groups, human needs may modify task requirements. On the scales of task-system efficiency are superimposed scales of human satisfaction and deprivation.

An individual may therefore be seen as experiencing satisfaction or deprivation in his work arising from:

(i) the interpersonal and group relationships directly involved in the activity system;

(ii) the harmonies or disharmonies of these relationships with other group memberships.

To these we must add a third: the satisfaction or deprivation experienced in the activities themselves. The satisfaction obtained by a craftsman is frequently contrasted with the deprivation experienced by an assembly-line worker on repetitive work. Some tasks, by their nature, offer greater possibilities for intrinsic satisfaction than others; though not all individuals would agree about what was satisfying and what depriving. Moreover, some tasks offer not only greater possibilities for intrinsic satisfaction, but at the same time greater possibilities for deprivation. Menzies, in her study of hospital nursing services, says:

'Nurses are confronted with the threat and reality of suffering and death as few lay people are. The work situation involves carrying out tasks which, by ordinary standards, are distasteful, disgusting, and frightening. The work situation arouses very strong feelings in the nurse: pity, compassion, and love; guilt and anxiety; hatred and resentment of the patients who have aroused these strong feelings; envy of the care given the patient' (1960, p. 98).

She showed that, given such a task, nurses had to have defences against the stresses and strains they had to endure. She showed also, however, that the usual defences, provided through the hospital organization, led to ineffective task performance:

'There is nothing more painful, more productive of anxiety, depression, and despair, than not being able to succeed in a task which has deep psychological significance for oneself' (1961).

In short, the nature of the task and of the activities involved in its performance can provide the individual with overt satisfactions – reward, prestige, accomplishment – or with overt deprivations – low reward, disrepute, boredom; it can also provide satisfaction and deprivation by reciprocation with his inner world of unconscious drives and needs for defence against anxiety.

Satisfaction and deprivation derived from the nature of the task, from relationships directly involved in the activity system, and from the harmonies and disharmonies with other group memberships, appear to be conceptually distinct, though in specific cases they merge: for example, satisfaction and deprivation derived from the nature of the task and from relationships directly involved in the activity system may be virtually indistinguishable in the salesman's job. For some tasks it is sometimes possible to construct organizations in such a way that not only do workgroup boundaries coincide with task boundaries, but membership of the resulting work group provides considerable satisfaction for its members. Experimental changes in work organization in an Indian textile mill, for example, have shown that, where a task can be assigned to a small group, internally led, so that group leadership is coterminous with regulation of the system of activities, both system efficiency and human satisfaction are likely to be higher (Rice, 1958). Studies of British coal-mining have produced similar findings (Trist et al., 1963).

These findings are important in demonstrating that work organization is not uniquely determined by the technical system and that alternative organizational models are often available. Even so, the organizations in which it is possible to match sentient groups to tasks – and so make task and sentient boundaries coincide – are the exception rather than the rule. What is more, a group that shares its sentient boundary with that of an activity system is all too likely to become committed to that particular system so that, although both efficiency and satisfaction may be greater in the short run, in the long run such an organization is likely to inhibit technical change. Unconsciously, the group may come to redefine its primary task, and behave as if this had become the defence of an obsolescent system. The group then resists, irrationally and vehemently, any changes in the activities of the task system that might disturb established roles and relationships.

In this book we attempt to separate the concepts of task group (the human resources required for an activity system) and of sentient group so that we may explore their interrelationships in a variety of organizational settings. In this way, it should become possible to see more clearly the consequences of different compromises made in different enterprises, and perhaps to foreshadow novel forms of organization that may be required in the future.

CHAPTER 4

Organizational Model-Building

So far in Part I we have been describing a conceptual framework for the analysis of enterprises of different kinds. In this chapter we attempt to show how we apply these concepts to build organizational models.

Organization is the patterning of activities through which the primary task of the enterprise is performed. Thus the optimum form of organization is that which best fits the requirements of primary task performance. But the organizational form must also take account of the human and physical, scientific and technical resources available for task performance, and of the human, political, economic, and social constraints on both definition and performance.

Our starting-point, then, is a definition of the primary task for the performance of which the organization is required. To build an appropriate organizational model this definition should be precise. However, we have to recognize that the gradual course of enterprise growth may lead to imprecision. Thus in a textile company that has diversified and now produces chemicals as well, one definition of the primary task could be, 'to make a profit from producing and selling textiles and chemicals'. But an alternative definition could be, 'to make a profit from investing in a variety of manufacturing and selling operations'. In the second definition, textile and chemical operations would be current examples. Or, to enlarge on an example we have already used, and to which we shall return in Part IV, the definition of the primary task of a university may start as 'to train undergraduates and to export graduates', and may change imperceptibly into 'to train postgraduates in research work and to export, on the one hand, research publications and, on the other, postgraduates who have acquired doctorates'.

DISCONTINUITIES IN THE DOMINANT PROCESS

The primary task identifies the dominant import-conversion-export process. In the first example just quoted, the first definition implies a dual throughput of textiles and chemicals in first-order constituent systems. The second, on the other hand, defines the overall enterprise as a holding company with a throughput of money, and the textile and chemical operations become the tasks of second-order constituent 'sub-enterprises'.

The dominant process in turn identifies the nature of intakes, the activities required to convert these into, and dispose of, outputs, and the human and physical resources needed to provide or facilitate these activities.

The next step is to discover the discontinuities in the process which mark the boundaries of systems of activity. Several orders of differentiation may be entailed in a large enterprise. To take again the example of a textile-cum-chemical manufacturing company, *prima facie* six constituent operating systems of activity can be identified. They are shown in *Figure 10*.

This framework offers the possibility of two technological differentia-

FIGURE 10 *Six constituent systems of a textile and chemical enterprise*

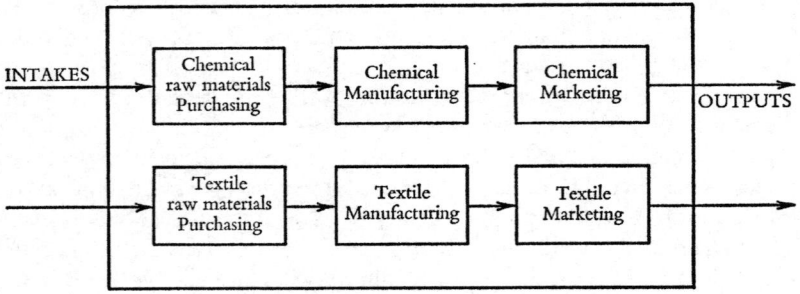

FIGURE 11 *First-order chemicals and textiles*

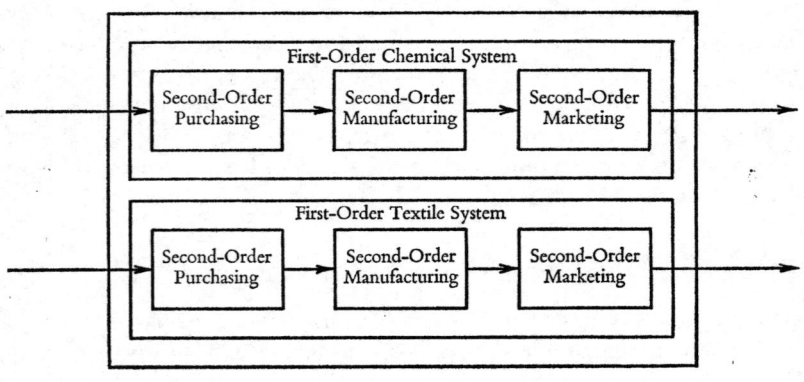

34

tions: one between chemicals and textiles (with a second-order differentiation between purchasing, manufacturing, and marketing), as shown in *Figure 11*; the other between purchasing, manufacturing, and marketing (with a second-order differentiation between chemicals and textiles), as shown in *Figure 12*. Again, it would be possible to conceive of a first-order differentiation into a combined purchasing system (with a second-order differention between chemicals and textiles), two separate manufacturing systems, and a combined marketing system, as shown in *Figure 13*. Factors such as the overlap between the two markets, the size of the investment in raw

FIGURE 12 *First-order purchasing, manufacturing, and marketing*

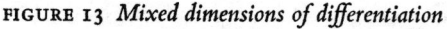

FIGURE 13 *Mixed dimensions of differentiation*

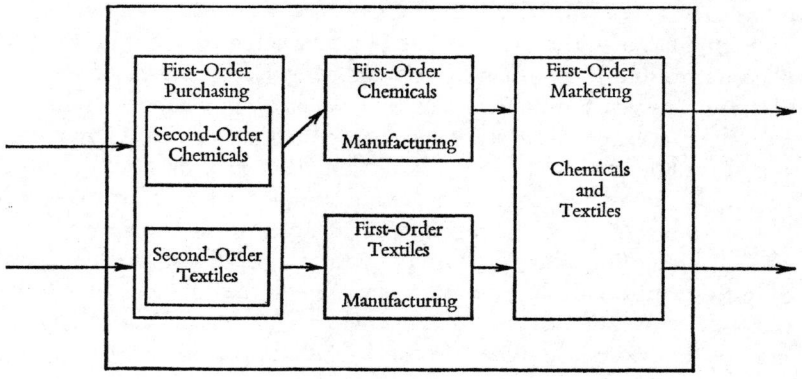

materials, similarities between these materials, the care with which they have to be stored, and the location of the factories will usually point towards one or other kind of differentiation.

The types of control that are required provide a means of judging the efficiency of the solution. A system boundary, as we have seen, implies a boundary control function. If a boundary is imposed at a point of substantial discontinuity in the process, intra-system and inter-system regulation will be simpler and, because there will be a 'pause' to check previous performance, more efficient. (The interacting development of operational research techniques and of computer technology has improved the tools available for logical systems analysis and for the determination of criteria of efficiency for task systems.) If the discontinuity is slight, a more elaborate apparatus of regulation will be required, first, to preserve the differentiation between the two systems, and, second, to secure co-ordination between them. If there is no discontinuity there can be no control region, and hence no boundary control function. And, without boundary controls, there can be no realistic way of determining what is inside and what outside. In practice, however, an organizational boundary may have to be drawn at a point where there is no discontinuity because existing regulatory mechanisms cannot span the system (the 'span of control' of classical theories of organization); but it is important to recognize that such a boundary is determined by constraints, and not by task requirements. It is the result of compromise, not of activity system differentiation.

Even with discontinuity, however, the kind and nature of the regulation required depend on the differences between the regions across whose boundaries the transaction is taking place. That is, the kind of 'conversion' process required in the control region depends on the extent to which the throughput that is being regulated is passing from a system with one set of characteristics to a system with a completely different set of characteristics. Between the departments of a factory, for example, little but inspection to standard criteria may be needed as a product passes from one department to another; but at the launching of a ship or the first flight of a prototype aircraft, far more elaborate and complex controls are necessary. In the same way, the kind and extent of the control that has to be exercised by leadership in interpersonal or intergroup relationships depend not only on the nature of the transaction, but also on the different cultures on each side of the boundary. The regulation of selling activities in a buyers' market, for example, is quite different from that in a sellers' market.

With the delineation of the boundaries of activity systems and of the nature of the regulatory and maintenance activities required, we can now set up a model organization for task performance.

MANAGING SYSTEMS

When a complex enterprise is differentiated into constituent systems we have used the term *operating systems* for those systems of activity through which the dominant import-conversion-export process is accomplished. With such differentiation, regulation of the relationships between the constituent systems, and between the whole enterprise and its environment, cannot be contained in any one constituent system, and a system external to the operating systems is required. This we have called the *managing system* (Rice & Trist, 1952; Rice, 1958, 1963). It is this system that provides the regulatory and maintenance activities to keep the operating systems going. Where regulation and maintenance are differentiated as discrete activity systems, they will thus be contained in the managing system. If a first-order operating system is differentiated into second-order systems, then they too will need regulation and maintenance, and a second-order managing system will be required which, in its turn, may contain differentiated systems for regulation and maintenance.

If we now return to the differentiated system shown in *Figure 11* and imagine two differentiated regulation and/or maintenance systems in the first-order managing system and two in each of the second-order managing systems of chemicals and textiles, the diagram of activity systems would appear as in *Figure 14*. The double boundaries round each constituent system represent the control regions within which regulation of inter-system activities takes place; and the double boundary round the whole represents the region of control of transactions between the total enterprise and its environment.

It will be appreciated that, to depict adequately more than one order of differentiation, a three-dimensional diagram would be required. The horizontal co-ordinates would represent operating systems and the vertical co-ordinate the hierarchy of superordinate managing systems. The marketing constituent system, for example, conducts transactions between the enterprise and its environment through representatives who may not, in a large organization, be reached until the fourth, fifth, or even sixth order of differentiation. The transactions, though carried out by activities at the sixth order of differentiation, are nevertheless still controlled through

37

FIGURE 14 *Operating, regulating, and maintenance systems*

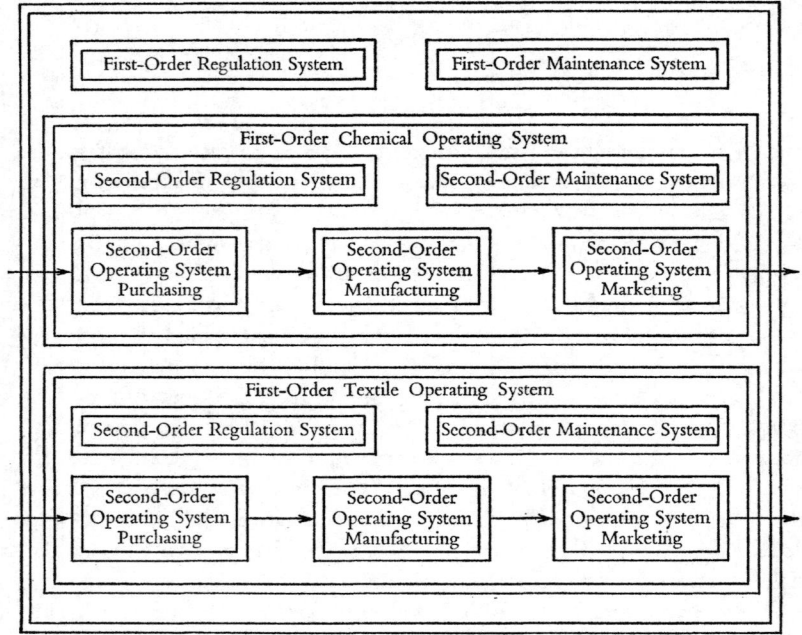

successive systems of higher order. The control at the sixth order is a delegated control.

In practice, therefore, in a large complex enterprise, there are far more orders of differentiation and far more differentiated regulating and maintenance systems than we have shown. To simplify future diagrams, the boundary control function of each constituent system and of the whole will be depicted not as a continuous region, but as a trans-boundary region at one point of a single boundary, thus:

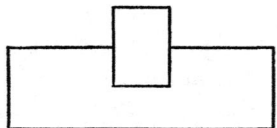

The organizational diagram corresponding to *Figure 14* is given in *Figure 15* which, while sacrificing some accordance with the diagram of

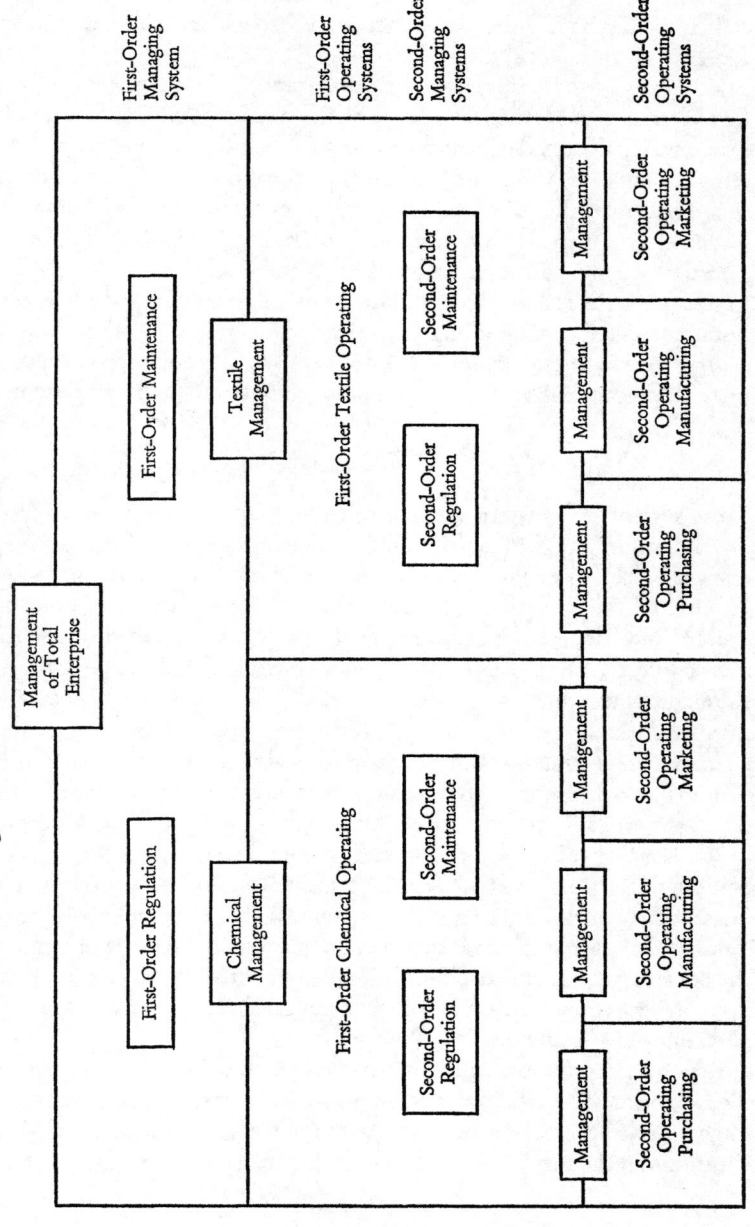

FIGURE 15 *Organizational boundaries showing management commands*

the two import-conversion-export systems through which the primary task is performed, does allow successive orders of differentiation to be represented more easily.

In *Figure 15* the boundaries are organizational boundaries; they therefore define management commands. In the example we have given, organizational boundaries and the boundaries of constituent activity systems coincide. If, for any of the reasons mentioned earlier, an organizational boundary has to be drawn where there is no process discontinuity, it would appear in the organization diagram but not in the diagram of the activity systems. For organization model-building, therefore, it is essential to start with the process flow, and move on to systems of activity and their boundaries before examining organizational boundaries, lest boundaries arising from constraints become prematurely incorporated, without adequate appraisal of the need for them in the context of activity systems.

ACTIVITIES, ROLES, AND ORGANIZATION

Most systems of activity include some human activities; some systems depend entirely on human resources. When an enterprise imports human resources, it is inevitably taking on more than the specific activities it requires of them. Without human creativity enterprises could not exist. One of the strengths of a human group is its capacity to turn itself into many different kinds of activity system in pursuit of different tasks. At one moment its task may be to design a strategy; at another, to execute it. It may then monitor its performance, remuster, procure reinforcements, and execute a fresh strategy. But this very adaptability can, as we have shown, be a major constraint in an enterprise in which the contribution required by an activity system from individual or group is limited and specific.

We have used the term *role* to refer to the activities that the individual contributes to a particular activity system and to the interrelations involved in carrying out those activities. Thus the role of a machine operator may require him to receive material from a preceding operator, to monitor the performance of the machine (a regulatory activity), to pass material to a succeeding operator, and also to accept instructions from a foreman affecting the rate and quality of output.

Beyond the activities and interactions inherent in the activity system, the individual acquires membership in the enterprise and in one or more formal and informal groups within the enterprise and perhaps outside. Merton uses the term *role-set* to refer to the 'complement of role relation-

40

ships which persons have by virtue of occupying a particular social status'. He gives the example of the medical student:

> 'the single status of medical student entails not only the role of student in relation to his teachers, but also an array of other roles relating the occupant of that status to other students, nurses, physicians, social workers, medical technicians, etc.' (Merton, 1957, p. 369.)[1]

The role-set of a salesman will relate him not only to customers and to the supervisor who controls his selling activities, but also to fellow salesmen of his own company and to competing salesmen from other companies. Similarly, the role-set of an industrial worker, whose task activities lie within the organizational boundary of an enterprise, may relate him to trade union members and officials outside.

Through its organization an enterprise assigns activities to roles and roles to individuals and groups; but the enterprise cannot always predetermine the consequential role-sets. These are nevertheless highly relevant to its effectiveness.

Management of an enterprise requires, therefore, four kinds of boundary control:

   (i) regulation of task-system boundaries (i.e. regulation of the enterprise as a whole as an import-conversion-export system, and regulation of constituent systems of activity);

  (ii) regulation of sentient-group boundaries (i.e. the boundaries of the groupings to which people belong either directly through their roles in systems of activity, or indirectly through their role-sets);

 (iii) regulation of organizational boundaries;

 (iv) regulation of the relation between task, sentient, and organizational boundaries.

Task, organizational, and sentient boundaries may coincide. Indeed, they must coincide to some extent at the boundary of the enterprise if it is to continue to exist. The enterprise may also be differentiated into parts, which are similarly defined by coinciding boundaries. But there are dangers in such coincidence. We have already suggested in an earlier section that one danger is that the members of a group may so invest in their

---

[1] Merton distinguishes between 'role-set' and 'multiple roles'. The latter concept refers to 'the complex of roles associated, not with a *single* social status, but with the *various* statuses (often in differing institutional spheres) in which individuals find themselves' (*loc. cit.*).

identity as a group that they will defend an obsolescent task system from which they derive membership. We can now add the possibility that the identification of change in task-system boundaries, and even the identification of the boundaries themselves, can be made difficult by the existence of group boundaries that are strongly defended. The representative who identifies more with his customer than with his own company, the politician who identifies more with his party than with his constituents, are not unfamiliar figures.

In general, we can say that, without adequate boundary definitions for activity systems and groups, organizational boundaries are difficult to define and frontier skirmishing is inevitable. It is perhaps a major paradox of modern complex enterprises that the more certainly boundaries can be located, the more easily formal communication systems can be established. Unless a boundary is adequately located, different people will draw it in different places and hence there will be confusion between inside and outside. In the individual this confusion leads to breakdown; in enterprises, to inefficiency and failure.

PART II

Transactions across Enterprise Boundaries

Introduction

Classical theories of organization drew heavily on experience of industries engaged in large-scale batch production. Joan Woodward's research has demonstrated that the organizational models and principles of management derived from this early work were over-determined by the particular type of technology which begat them and do not fit the needs of, for example, the process industries or factories engaged in unit production (Woodward, 1965). Similar findings have emerged from the work of the Tavistock Institute in this field. There remains a tendency, however, among theorists and practitioners alike, to look upon the organization of production operations as central and typical, and to assume that the principles of delegation and control that have emerged constitute general laws of organization. The organization charts of sales or research departments with their traditional chains of command often appear to be designed more on aesthetic grounds to harmonize with the corresponding chart for the manufacturing department than to facilitate task performance.

In this book, we draw most of our major examples from outside manufacturing industry. One good reason for approaching organization from this standpoint is that the proportion of the working population employed in production operations is steadily declining, whereas the proportion in distribution and services is rapidly growing.[1] Organization of non-production activities therefore deserves more attention in its own right than it has received. In addition, however, we believe that examination of non-production organization can help us to see production organization in a new light and to question some prevalent assumptions. Indeed, we shall argue later that in the context of a general theory of organization the conventional factory situation, far from being prototypical, is a special case.

For the moment, it is sufficient to draw attention to the point that

[1] Between 1955 and 1965, of the total population in civil employment in the United Kingdom, the manufacturing industries' share fell from 40·3 per cent to 36·2 per cent, while the share of service industries rose from 43·3 per cent to 48·9 per cent (source: *Ministry of Labour Gazette*).

conversion systems – the systems of activity through which production processes are carried out – differ in certain key respects from import and export systems.

A conversion system implies a unidirectional sequence of activities through which the raw materials are transformed into the finished products. Sequences may be complex. They may entail divergent systems of activity through which one input is converted into a variety of outputs (for example, crude oil being refined into a broad gamut of products, ranging from bitumen to pure alcohol), or convergent systems through which multifarious inputs are converted into one type of output (for example, parts being assembled to produce a motor car); and, in both, different sub-systems may operate in parallel or successively. The basic process flow is nevertheless in one direction.

More importantly, a conversion system is contained within the boundaries of the enterprise. The resources of the conversion system – the equipment and the people whose activities contribute to the process – are related to each other and to the throughput within a bounded structure that has some degree of permanence. Practically, this implies that the individual employee, day in and day out, works in the same setting and experiences the same pattern of relationships with the same people.

The import and export systems of an enterprise do not share these features. They are systems of activity that cross the boundaries of the enterprise, in that they involve transactions with suppliers and customers; and, in addition, since these transactions are the means through which the enterprise, as an open system, exchanges materials with its environment, they are two-directional. Export involves both disposing of an output and obtaining a pay-off for it; import involves making a payment to procure an intake. That selling requires a transaction with a potential buyer and buying a transaction with a potential seller hardly needs to be said; organizationally, the critical point is that the activities are such that they must involve members of different enterprises.

This part of the book addresses itself, then, to the problems of organization and boundary control that arise when the boundary of a system of activities cuts across enterprise boundaries. Innumerable instances could be given. Doctor-patient relationships and the diplomatic activities of an embassy abroad display the same basic phenomenon. We have chosen here two examples from fields in which we have worked. And, indeed, in carrying out our studies, which were not primarily to collect research data but to collaborate with clients in tackling their problems of management and organization, we ourselves were involved in an activity system of this kind.

The first example comes from selling. We concentrate mainly on the role of a manufacturer's representative selling non-durable consumer goods, but also draw some contrasts between this role and that of the 'speciality' salesman. Chapter 5 examines the nature of the task and the relations between representative and buyer within the activity system. Chapter 6 is concerned with the problem of managing transactional activities of this kind and proposes a model organization.

The second example is taken from a service industry – dry cleaning. In Chapter 7 we show that the two apparently simple transactions across the boundary – one when the cleaner receives the dirty clothing from the customer and the other when he hands the clean clothes back and takes payment – are suffused by the attitudes of customer and employee in a way that complicates the definition and control of the enterprise boundary. Chapter 8 describes the effect on the customer transaction, as well as on internal organization, of an apparently simple change in the technology of cleaning.

CHAPTER 5

The Selling Task and the Representative

We have chosen sales-force organization as our first illustration of the concepts outlined in Part I because, though the technology of marketing and the conditions under which it has to be carried out have both changed considerably in the last twenty years, the technology of the selling task itself has changed little. It has not suffered, if that is the right word, from the invention of mechanical and electronic devices that have made human skill redundant; nor have the skills themselves – the capacity that differentiates a good salesman from a bad one – yet been made very explicit, in spite of the claims of many sales-training organizations. Nevertheless, this chapter is written against a background of continuous change. The change has led, in the consumer goods industries especially, to a shift of the focus of top management attention from production to marketing; and, within marketing, from selling to advertising, promotion, packaging, and other forms of merchandising. At the same time, the growing affluence of the community has led, on the one hand, to a proliferation of competing products to take advantage of the greater spending power; and, on the other, to a revolution in the retail trade that has resulted in a sharp decrease in the number of independent traders and a corresponding increase in the number of multiples and chains.

The material for this chapter is taken from work with many different kinds of sales-force organization: consumer-goods distribution through the retail trade, direct selling to consumers through van-salesmen, the retail trade itself, the sale of industrial components, and both the sale and rental of equipment to offices, shops, restaurants, and clubs. The main material will be concerned with the sale of non-durable consumer goods by a manufacturer to the retail trade, either directly or through wholesalers; but other information on sales-force organization will also be used, particularly that from 'speciality' selling. Data have been collected from interviews and group discussion with sales and marketing directors and managers, with advertising agency personnel, and with representatives of various kinds in various markets; from direct observation; and from the study of written records of marketing policies, sales, and company histories. The data were obtained for the severely practical purpose of helping clients to reorganize their sales forces and to devise selection procedures for sales managers and representatives.

We shall start in this chapter with a discussion of the background against which the selling task – the primary task of a sales force – has to be performed in a consumer marketing organization. We shall examine the larger task to which this primary task has to contribute and the environment in which it has to be performed. We shall then consider the special characteristics of the representative's task and the effects of the various changes in the environment on the manner of its performance. In the next chapter we shall be concerned with the organizational problems posed by discrepancies between task and sentient boundaries and we shall discuss the consequences for management and leadership.

THE PRIMARY TASK OF A MARKETING UNIT
IN THE CONSUMER-GOODS INDUSTRY

Marketing is the process through which an enterprise obtains returns for its products. The process entails moving products to consumers in such quantities and at such prices as will yield an adequate profit on the total activities of the enterprise.

The major strategic decisions of marketing in the consumer-goods industry are decisions about what products to make. Such decisions relate the actual and potential production resources of the enterprise to consumer needs. And it has to be accepted (however much one may deplore the fact) that such needs are not necessarily only those that are conscious and overtly expressed. At the level of unconscious needs, important forces affecting consumer behaviour can often be identified in association with each product or class of product. The forces may be related not only to the satisfaction of wholly or partly unrecognized needs, but also to protection against anxieties associated with specific products. It is likely that a successful product will be one that meets the obvious and conscious needs for which it is designed and, at the same time, satisfies unconscious needs and acts as a defence against anxieties of which the consumer may be unaware. Conversely, a product is likely to be less successful if, while it satisfies an obvious and entirely rational need, it nevertheless – by reason of its scent, name,[1] colour, price, shape, or other circumstance –

[1] Rolls Royce are reported to have changed the name of their new model from Silver

either disappoints an associated or unrecognized need or intensifies an unconscious anxiety. Thus, at the level of marketing strategy, the enterprise is concerned with translating overt and latent consumer needs into saleable products; and it follows that the modification of consumer behaviour, including the stimulation of such needs and the introduction of new or changed buying habits, is an activity integral to the marketing process.

Within the limits set by strategic decision-making, the marketing process is carried out through five major groups of activities:

(i) *Advertising:* using television, newspapers, films, posters, and other media to present the company's products to purchasers and consumers (not necessarily the same) with the object of creating such a demand that stockists will want to sell them.

(ii) *Merchandising:* packaging, offers, bargains, promotions, displays, and other similar activities, to encourage not only consumers to demand and purchasers to purchase, but stockists to become active selling agents for the company's products.

(iii) *Selling:* making sure that stocks are available to consumers, or the ultimate purchasers, at appropriate places and prices and in appropriate quantities. In effect, in most of the consumer-goods industry this means persuading wholesalers to stock and retailers to stock, display, and push company products.

(iv) *Distributing:* moving stocks from producer to customer.

(v) *Collecting payment.*

At one extreme it is possible to imagine a product which, by reason of its nature, scarcity, or price, is in such demand from purchasers and consumers that it needs little or no assistance from advertising, merchandising, or selling. It is also possible to imagine such advertising and other marketing techniques that there is no need to sell, only to distribute. (Mail-order enterprises depend on these techniques for the most part.) But neither of these conditions characterizes the normal consumer market: there are too many products of like quality and price and too many able advertisers. Indeed, whatever the real quality of different products, so many rival claims have been made that the effect of any one claim in determining purchasing behaviour is inevitably reduced. In most consumer markets, products not only have to be advertised, promoted, and otherwise merchandised, they also have to be sold.

Mist to Silver Shadow, when they discovered that, in German, *Mist* was the word for manure, trash, or rubbish (*Weekend Telegraph*, 15 October 1965).

The first three groups of activities are to be found, therefore, in almost all marketing units of companies in this industry. The activities in the fourth and fifth categories are sometimes included within the unit, sometimes organized into different commands. Copies of a salesman's order, for example, may be passed to a transport department, which delivers the goods, and to an accounts department, which sends an invoice to the customer and collects his payment. The responsibility delegated to a marketing unit also varies: if the unit is incorporated as a separate subsidiary company it may 'buy' the products of a manufacturing subsidiary and have the task of making a profit on the total activities of the parent company. But the primary task of any marketing unit can be defined in general terms as to secure customers for products.

Of recent years, new advertising media, inventions of new packaging materials and designs, developments in techniques of display, the extension of the bargain pack and the give-away offers, and other such promotions have all tended to obscure the fact that the primary task of a marketing unit is accomplished successfully only when an order is obtained from a credit-worthy customer. The other activities, however important, creative, or useful, are only means to this end. A major consequence has been that the selling task, the task of ensuring that an order is obtained, has tended to be denigrated and the denigration to be extended to those who, for the most part, ensure its performance – the representatives.

Thus, although the selling task itself has not been subject to technical change, it has been substantially affected by surrounding changes in the marketing process as a whole.

CHANGE IN THE ENVIRONMENT OF THE SELLING TASK

We have said that marketing activities are successful only when they culminate in the performance of the selling task – taking an order. This task is always performed through a relationship between a member or members of the manufacturing enterprise and a member or members of a customer enterprise. The relationship usually has the characteristics of a face-to-face pair relationship in which the members of the pair owe their primary loyalties to different employers. The boundary of the task system, in other words, cuts across boundaries of the two separate and discrete enterprises. It has the characteristic of the intergroup transaction outlined in Chapter 2. The task system is shown in *Figure 16*, which will be recognized as a simplified version of *Figure 8*.

FIGURE 16 *Selling-task-system boundary*

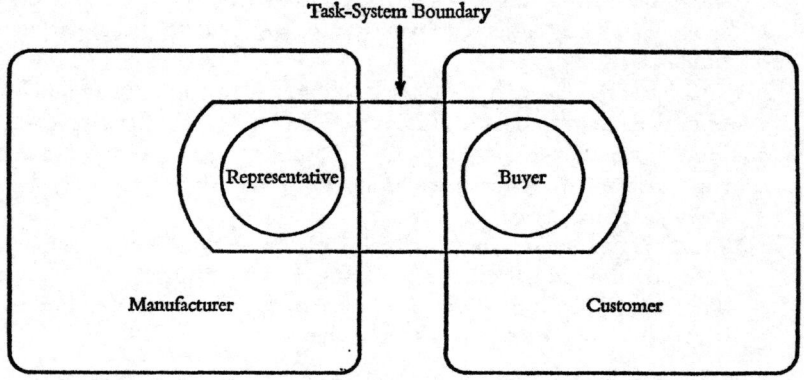

The human relationship within the task system may be friendly or un-friendly, collusive or conflicting, trusting or distrusting, but, because of the nature of the task performed within it, it must always contain some elements of manipulation. At one extreme this key relationship may be conducted through telephone conversations between clerks; at the other, through long protracted negotiations between principals. Usually, in the consumer-goods and many other industries, it is conducted on behalf of the manufacturing enterprise by a specialist – a 'representative'. His specialist skill is the 'management' of the relationship, and hence of the boundary within which the task is performed. (It is one of the paradoxes of competitive marketing that the selling task, without which no business can be accomplished, appears to be most denigrated when it is performed by a 'representative' whose expertise this is. Only when it is performed by a director, or manager of high rank, for whom selling is, at most, a very part-time occupation, does it appear to achieve dignity and status. We shall be examining this phenomenon from the organizational point of view in the next chapter.)

In effect, then, the task boundary contains two 'managers', one of whom 'manages' on behalf of the manufacturer, the other on behalf of the customer.

In the consumer-goods industry the pair relationship is 'managed' on behalf of customers by a wide variety of people in a wide variety of roles – owner, manager, buyer, assistant – and in a wide variety of retail and wholesale outlets. These outlets can be classified as:

53

(a) *Multiples:* which may be chains of small, large, or medium-sized shops of various kinds, in which buying is done either by local branch and departmental managers or by central, headquarters buyers.

(b) *Wholesalers:* who may be large or small and who may have their own dependent retailers, most of whom buy only centrally.

(c) *Large independents:* which may be grocers, self-service stores, supermarkets, or departmental stores, in which buyers may be owners or managers.

(d) *Retail buying groups,* in which, though buying decisions may be made by individual retailers, ordering may be central.

(e) The still remaining *smaller independents*, in which the buying is invariably done by the working owner.

Although there were some multiples in the past, and products have always been advertised, the major part of the turnover of a company in the consumer-goods industry used to come through independent traders. Selling to them was less dependent on promotions, bargains, and other merchandising activities than it is today. It was the representative who managed the relationships with the multitude of accounts on which the marketing organization so obviously depended for its success. More importantly, from both the representative's and sales management's point of view, there was a simple means by which the success of the representative could be judged – the size of his order book.

It is only in comparatively recent years that, following the lead, and reaching to the power, of large manufacturing companies, retail organizations have grown through mergers and takeovers. Today, the major part of the turnover of a company in the consumer-goods industry comes through relatively few large accounts. Marketing activities other than selling play a very large part in the total marketing operation. Because the accounts are large, and many more activities are involved, selling has a longer time-span, and order-taking is the resultant of more work by a greater number of people over a much longer period.

Many representatives still remember the era when, with less differentiated outlets and marketing activities, they could, to a large extent, plan their own work and use their own methods. So far as his own company was concerned, the representative controlled the key task boundary, and, provided his results, as measured by his order book, were good, he was left alone to conduct the relationships within it as he wished. Today, changes in the retail trade give less opportunity for the enjoyment of individual idiosyncrasy. The stakes are too high. Indeed, within the context of a complex marketing programme, the sequence in which the representative offers his wares and even the precise wording he is to use to present them are often predetermined for him. The individual order book is no longer the measure of success it used to be. The representative has now to try to get satisfaction from, and to be judged by, what is often a much less personal contribution to a total operation. He may be unaware of the full extent of the operation and of its boundaries; he may not even know the others involved in it.

In respect of the big accounts he has to be a negotiator, a contract manager, a businessman who can tolerate the uncertainties of waiting for his results while the marketing machine gets into action. If he still calls on branches of multiples and independents he may have to set up displays, carrying out the manual labour involved himself. The orders are placed elsewhere. Hard measurable evidence that what he does bears much relation to the success or failure of his company is scarce and thin.

In sum, when, to the changes in kinds of outlet and in kinds of roles taken by those with whom he does his job – the buyers, is added his partial responsibility for many of the ancillary marketing activities, the conclusion can only be that there is no one task that is the representative's task; rather, many tasks, of very different kinds and requiring very different skills, have been subsumed under the one title. Conversely, important representational activities are being carried out more and more by people who do not carry the title of representative.

THE QUASI-PERMANENT SELLING-TASK BOUNDARY IN THE CONSUMER-GOODS INDUSTRY: THE REPRESENTATIVE-BUYER RELATIONSHIP

In spite of the growing number and size of retail combinations, distributive outlets still differ in respect of the kind of custom for which they cater, the type of neighbourhood in which they operate, and the extent of their financial security and their buying power. Above all, those who buy – whether specialists or traders – differ as people. In every selling situation the representative has to try to adapt his company's overall marketing plan to the varying demands made upon him by the different buyers he meets. He reconciles the plan and the buyers' demands by the relationships he makes. Through them he translates a general plan into particular practice, and on them depends the success or failure of his contribution to the plan. (The representative who is required to recite a pre-rehearsed monologue is plainly precluded from acting as a real representative in this sense.)

Nevertheless, whoever the buyer and whatever the contributions of other parts of the marketing function, the essential task is carried out in a face-to-face relationship of two people, one of whom is not under the control of the marketing organization. Both representative and buyer make similar relationships with others: the representative with other buyers, the buyer with other representatives. Their meetings are short and recurrent, and take place at more or less regular intervals. Any meeting affects, and is affected by, the other meetings they have with each other and with other buyers and other representatives.

The representative-buyer relationship is seldom the only relationship between the two enterprises concerned. Although there are some van-salesmen who take orders, deliver the goods, and take the money, much more often these activities are organized separately and the representative is expected by the buyer to accept responsibility for delays in delivery or mistakes in invoices, which are outside the representative's control.

The relationship is also complicated by the number of linking relationships that separate it, on the one side, from the production/marketing boundary in the representative's company and, on the other side, from the ultimate transaction with the purchaser in the retail shop (and, beyond that again, from the consumer). For a given representative, of course, the first set of links is a constant, but his relationships may be with buyers who are variously located. At the one extreme is his relationship with the small, independent trader, in which he is talking to the owner who serves behind the counter and is thus in face-to-face touch with all his own customers. The representative's methods have to be related to the shopkeeper's direct personal knowledge of his customers. At the other extreme is the representative's relationship with the buyer for the large multiple, who occupies a central buying office and may not allow representatives to call on branches. The buyer knows about his company's customers in terms of statistical abstractions. If he is sophisticated, he is concerned primarily with the investment of working capital in moveable stocks. He calculates whether it pays to invest in larger stocks with attractive terms of trade at longer intervals or in smaller stocks at shorter intervals, with the consequent saving of storage and freedom from capital charges. At this extreme, selling is a commercial negotiation based on costs, margins, credits, and forecasts.

Though the owner-trader might be unlikely to forgo trading advantages through personal regard for a representative, he is in a position to let his feelings affect his judgement and he is accountable to nobody but himself when he does so. By contrast, the employee-buyer of the large multiple has no right – and certainly no obligation – to subordinate his company's profitability to his personal feelings for a representative. Both representative and buyer have to be conscious, unceasingly, of the other task boundaries within which they work – those of their employers, and those binding them to other buyers and other representatives. The complexity of these multiple, overlapping task boundaries is usually underestimated.

Some of the more obvious characteristics of the relationships within selling-task boundaries may be summed up as follows:

(a) Though personal, they are always about the sale of products in the 'value' of which the representative is supposed to believe, but about the quality of which, as compared with those of his competitors, he must sometimes be forgiven for being cynical – he has heard too many world-beating promises.

(b) The personal nature of the relationships differs with different buyers who themselves have different roles and different powers.

(c) The representative uses the relationships to perform a key task in a marketing programme over which he has little, if any, control and with which he may or may not agree.

(d) The representative is usually trying on behalf of his company to persuade buyers to do things they may not want to do – make special displays, become involved with coupons and other promotions.

(e) The representative is in competition with representatives of other companies selling similar products, offering similar inducements, and asking for similar concessions.

But, above all, the relationships are restricted, in the sense that feeling and warmth have to be subordinated to task performance, and neither liking nor disliking can have full expression. The representative cannot afford to discriminate in his behaviour towards his buyers on the basis of his feelings for them. He can do so only if by his discrimination he furthers his company's marketing effort. He must suppress, deny, or otherwise deal with his guilt at such manipulation and exploitation. He meets good and bad shopkeepers, good and bad buyers. He cannot help making comparisons, and he often knows better than those he meets what they should stock and how they should sell it. His perceptiveness must frequently be communicated to his customers, who then feel that judgements are being made about their managerial or trading competence. Some may welcome the implied help, but it would be surprising if others did not resent the inference and, consciously or unconsciously, resist both teacher and lesson. The representative may have to suppress both his desire to help, and his exasperation with, those he likes; and his superiority over, and his contempt for, those he dislikes. He may also have to deal with his envy of the competent and the successful.

Externally, as a representative he has to reconcile the inconsistencies between the many different roles he takes in his selling relationships, reflecting as they do the differential business and personal needs of his customers and the differential policies of his company towards them. As a person, he has to learn to manage, in a way that will cope with the inconsistencies, the transactions between his own inner world and his environment – an environment that comprises not only his working relationships but other areas of his life as well.

The representative is genuinely a part of his company, in that his opposite number in the task – the buyer – belongs to another enterprise. This can be satisfying. It can also be lonely. Whenever the representative is doing what he is paid to do, he is, as far as his company membership is concerned, on his own. In this sense he is isolated, and his isolation is not necessarily lessened by the thought of what he has behind him or of who is looking over his shoulder. As a representative he may experience power, prestige, and security. Equally, the responsibility can make him anxious and worried. The isolation is, of course, reduced by the making of a succession of pair relationships, perhaps the most satisfying, and certainly the most productive, of all human relationships. But the satisfaction can be diminished by the conscious or unconscious guilt that usually accompanies promiscuity. The ambivalence may be exacerbated when the one with whom he makes the relationship through which he does his job cannot give him some token of satisfaction at the end of the meeting – an order – but can offer only promises or hopes that an order may eventually materialize.

THE TRANSIENT SELLING-TASK BOUNDARY IN SPECIALITY SELLING

By speciality selling we mean such activities as the door-to-door sale of vacuum cleaners or encyclopaedias, the sale to shops of cash registers or scales, and the sale of office equipment. In this type of selling, in contrast to the kind we have been discussing, the goods are relatively durable and are for use by the purchaser (or his concern), not for resale.

One feature of this kind of selling is that the proportion of abortive to successful calls tends to be high. Generally speaking, the higher the cost of the commodity, the higher the ratio. For expensive items, many calls and much time may elapse between one order and the next. Another feature is that usually the successful call has the character of a 'one-off' operation. For complex equipment, such as computers, the 'one-off' may lead to a prolonged negotiation involving a study of the customer's needs, advice on the installation of new systems of working, and considerable follow-up to check that the equipment is doing what was promised. But in the majority of such operations the representative's job is to get an order and get out. Because the order is for durable equipment, repeat business is far less important than new. If there is any continuing relationship between the supplying firm and the customer, it is carried by service engineers or similar specialists.

The task boundary is the same as for the representative in the consumer-goods industry – it is drawn round a representative and his customer – but whereas the consumer-goods representative is going to make repeated calls at weekly, fortnightly, or other intervals, the speciality representative hopes to make only one call, or at most two, to convert a prospect into a customer. Multiple calls for one order are wasteful. Moreover, he may have some difficulty in getting to see a busy man, and he has therefore to make sufficient impact in his first meeting to complete his task. If he completes it successfully – that is, if he takes an order – he can get considerable satisfaction from it, a sense of achievement which, if repeated often enough, can earn him a lot of commission and approval from his own company. But closure also means the end of the relationship: 'Once the order is taken, the representative is finished with it; it is dead and he must move on to the next prospect.'

The task boundary, in other words, not only contains two people from different organizations, but is also transient. This continual change and impermanence can cause considerable strain, which for the most part goes unrecognized. There are times in most representatives' careers, at longer or shorter intervals, when the cumulative effect of the inevitable breaking of relationships and the unavoidable rebuffs in trying to make new ones piles up, until they seek to prolong relationships rather than break them, or find it impossible to start what, if made, must immediately be broken. The inconsistencies between task and personal boundaries become too great. It is common experience that all speciality representatives have 'bad patches'; these occur when the cumulative strain becomes too severe. They are the critical points in selling careers.

There is a major difficulty in detecting the beginning of the 'bad patch': to acknowledge a reluctance to effect closure or to make new relationships is contrary to all the salesman's training and to his experience of successful selling. Indeed, the skill of a good representative will carry him over the early stages of the bad patch and, if he get the right breaks, will often carry him through it. The implication is that by the time there is a noticeable falling-off in a representative's performance, the bad patch is already well advanced, and correspondingly greater effort is needed to pull out of it.

Our observations suggest that speciality salesmen, to get themselves out of the bad patch, not infrequently resort to getting out of their company. The successful representative can be defined as one who achieves a rapid turnover of 'sold' prospects. He engages their interest, takes their orders, and leaves them. He becomes accustomed to quickly made and quickly broken task relationships. The unremitting strain of repeatedly breaking relationships and striving to form new ones makes any real or imaginary falling-off in performance extremely worrying. One method by which the representative can seek reassurance that he can be successful again is to deal with his relationship with his company – the only one over which he has any real control – in the way that has previously brought success in his task relationships: he closes it. He resigns, and this closure, by giving him confidence that he can still achieve it, allows him, paradoxically enough, to continue his career as a speciality representative. Work records of many speciality representatives show that at fairly regular intervals, usually of a few years, they leave their job. The reason given is invariably 'for better prospects'; but, for the majority, the 'better prospects' seldom appear to be more than the taking of a similar job with a different company selling similar products.

THE REPRESENTATIVE AND HIS GROUPS

Whether secure or anxious, confident or unsure, the representative spends more of his working life with his customers than with his colleagues or superiors. And it is with his customers that he cannot, or should not, work out his own internal conflicts. So far as he needs people from whom he can get support and people with whom he can fight, he has to rely on other relationships: within his company, with salesmen of competing companies, and within his family and social networks.

The rate of turnover of speciality salesmen suggests that it is not easy for the representative to communicate his difficulties and needs to his company or for the company to recognize his needs and respond to them. Yet, for effectiveness in his job, the salesman needs to feel that he belongs to and receives support from the company he represents.

One common problem is that in his transactions with his company he is often the victim of inconsistencies between what is said and what he experiences. To take a simple example: in sales meetings he is often mobilized to identify himself with the company in its fight against competitors; he is encouraged to feel that he is at the front line in this battle and that the company relies upon him. Yet in the field there neither is nor can be much conflict with salesmen of competing companies. If he engages in anything that savours of sharp practice he knows that it will only attract retaliation, which will make a difficult job still more difficult. Instead, conventions provide what are, in effect, non-aggression pacts between competing salesmen. The representative who sees his opposite number from another company in a shop with a customer will normally wait outside until the transaction is finished. With this 'enemy', indeed, there is potentially a closer affinity than with anyone else, because they share the same kind of role with the same customers; and sometimes, albeit guiltily, they meet in cafes and public houses to exchange their experiences.

It is more often within the representative's company than in the field that the conflict finds expression. This is especially plain when the size of the order book or other apparently clear-cut measurements are used as criteria of performance. Somebody has to do less well than others. Unlike factory workers, representatives are not likely to be able to restrict their output so that nobody ever occupies the role of the 'man at the bottom'. In many discussions we have heard such remarks as:

'The man at the bottom is always a worried man.'

What may not be so manifest under such conditions is the importance for the others of having somebody else to fill this role. However they may be feeling about their own performance, they are all at least doing better than one other. The problem is that the filling of this significant role causes stress – stress which, if too prolonged, can become intolerable. And since there can never be any absolute standard of achievement, only a relative one, even those with previously good records are not likely to relish the prospect of that position:

> 'I don't know what I'd do if I ever dropped to the
> bottom, I'd get out; I couldn't stand it'

was, with minor variations, also a common remark.

Trainees can, to some extent, fill the role of the 'man at the bottom'. They cannot, of course, fill it very well, because as trainees they are not expected to do well; but equally, as trainees and for some time afterwards, they are protected from some of the consequences of being at the bottom. They can be accepted therefore as legitimate, if temporary, occupants of the role. They can, however, be only temporary occupants, since if their training period is unduly prolonged serious doubts must arise about their suitability. To fill this role, then, in what can be accepted as a legitimate if not very satisfactory manner, there must be a continuous supply of newcomers. But a continuous supply of newcomers when there are no obvious vacancies causes a different kind of anxiety, since if they are successful they will be presumed to be about to replace the less successful established representatives. There are two possible consequences: first, considerable forces are brought to bear to keep the newcomers' performance at a mediocre level; second, turnover in the early weeks is high. Neither process is conscious, and firm evidence is hard to elucidate, but it is surprising how many newcomers who start with a rush appear to fade away; and in many cases one cannot avoid the impression that some newcomers, at least, are selected not as potential representatives but as potential leavers.

Jostling for position within the group of salesmen cannot but reduce the capacity of the group to provide support for the individual in trouble. The overt goodwill of colleagues towards the man at the bottom is counteracted by the collusion of the group to keep him there.

Nevertheless, to be a representative, the individual must belong: he must be able to find some group, real or mythical, with which to identify. Salesmen often appear to deal with the ambivalence by a process of splitting, by exaggerating the goodness of X and the badness of Y. Such a phenomenon is, of course, by no means unique to salesmen, but in our experience it often occurs with particular vividness in sales organizations. The incompetence of the district superintendent is contrasted with the brilliance of the sales manager; and, higher up the scale, the ruthless power-seeking of the marketing director with the virtue of the managing director who has the welfare of all the employees at heart. The product is superb, the packaging dreadful; last year's promotions were brilliant, this year's trite. Such a mechanism of polarization enables the salesman to find some groups within the company in which he can invest, but only at the cost of rejecting others. So far as these mechanisms are used to deal with feelings of insecurity or dissatisfaction, their very use may add to the discomfort. Any tendency to idealize some managers and blame others has to contend with the knowledge that the company has appointed them all; any resistance to new ideas, dislike of changes, has to contend with the certainty that unless the company adapts to changes in its environment it will fail.

To the extent that the salesman cannot work out his conflicts and satisfy his needs for support within his relationships with customers or within his company organization, a greater strain may be thrown on other areas of his life. His home is, in any case, increasingly infiltrated by his work. Many wives of representatives complain that not only are their husbands married to their companies, but they themselves are rapidly being married to them too. The changes in the representative's task mean that he no longer takes only samples and an order book on his journeys but often whole stocks of goods, display material, and special equipment. All of this has to be delivered and stored, and it is the wife who has to deal with it. Her home is becoming an extension of the company's warehouse and office. Moreover, her husband's salary may or may not be increasing, but often his incentives take the form of gifts for the household, of clothes for both of them, of social functions, and even of holiday trips. She may like these things, but her liking can be tempered by a disinclination to have so many decisions made for her. Her home has already been invaded; her family life and social life are being determined for her as well.

The more working life overspills into, and gets mixed with, family and social life, the more its patterns of behaviour may carry over too. The more working life constrains the range of opportunities for the expression of real feelings, the more the constraints that arise in work can impair the quality of other relationships outside work. It is perhaps not surprising, therefore, that the representative sometimes finds it difficult to locate himself in society, to know with whom to identify. As a representative of a large and reputable company he may need no other working or professional sentient group. As a man whose task is changing with puzzling or even bewildering rapidity, and who has doubts about either his own or his management's ability, he may have to seek other sources of identification. There is some evidence to suggest that in such circumstances salesmen try to align themselves with the acknowledged 'professional' careers – banking, law, medicine, and so on. But this identification can bring little real comfort until society as a whole accepts the representative as a man whose conduct is regulated by a professional rather than by a commercial code; and society seems to be a long way from such acceptance.

In short, activities related to task performance take place within a boundary that is unlikely to satisfy completely any representative, unless he is an individual whose personality needs are best dealt with by a lonely, affectionless working life, in which pair relationships are promiscuous and transient. In the main, a sales-force organization has to provide constructive mechanisms to give representatives more stable and secure relationships than are available within the task boundary. We have suggested in this chapter that many companies fail in this respect. In the next chapter we shall go on to consider how far forms of organization can be devised that will provide a better fit for the needs of task performance and the needs of the individual salesman.

CHAPTER 6

Organization of the Sales Force

Forms of sales-force organization have to accommodate not only an accelerating rate of change – in products, in marketing techniques, in the social and economic forces operating upon consumers – but also an increasing diversity of customers. Major customers include sophisticated companies which, though they negotiate their main buying through headquarters, allow their own subsidiaries and branches to buy for themselves and, in addition, to determine their own needs for goods and services; they include others in which headquarters' policy and branch policy appear to be in conflict; and yet others in which branches are not allowed to accept visits from suppliers' representatives. Furthermore, besides the branches of the growing number of companies with regional or national networks of shops, there are still local wholesalers and independent retailers who owe allegiance only to themselves. Moreover, an equally important point is that changes of different kinds are taking place at different rates in different parts of the country. What works as a selling policy with one account may not work with others, and what works, indeed, with some branches of an account may not work with all of them.

Notwithstanding the effect of these overall changes in the market, at the point at which the representative carries out his task it is what is happening to a particular account at the moment he makes his visit that matters. However selling may be organized – and it must be organized in relation to a general trend – there can be no guarantee that any form of organization will necessarily help to improve the relationship between a representative and any given customer. Indeed, during a period of rapid and diversified change, the more far-sighted management is in preparing for the future, the more likely it is that the resulting policy and organization will give an inappropriate fit between the company, its representative, and some of his customers.

Markets today present an ever-changing array of opportunities; and an ever-changing array of opportunities requires a corresponding flexible range of methods of attack. Diversity in opportunity is already matched by diversity in product; it has to be matched also by diversity in the relationship made between the representative and his customer/buyer, at whatever level they both may be.

Any sophisticated marketing organization accepts, of course, that negotiation at a high level in a customer organization may have to be carried through by a member of corresponding rank in the marketing organization. And since 'representatives' seldom have the appropriate rank, the biggest accounts are usually managed by those who have acquired their status not necessarily from proved skill in selling, but from other skills and capacities, either in marketing or in enterprise management. Big customers who are 'lost' to representatives in this way are increasing in number. Within the relationships with the smaller customers left to him, the representative has to tolerate more and more intrusion from merchandisers and other specialist colleagues. Sometimes, as we saw in the last chapter, this intrusion extends to a detailed prescription and rehearsal of what the salesman must say and do in order to play his role with the customer in the context of an overall campaign.

Thus many companies are responding to diversity with diversity – but at the expense of diminishing the role of the representative. The inevitable result – and we have observed this in most sales forces we have known – is that the representative who seeks a higher status and a more certain future has to try to get promotion out of selling. He has to leave the job at which he is a specialist, and take one in which the skill that has earned him the promotion will probably turn out to be a disadvantage rather than an advantage. Even worse, those who fail to get promotion are often made to feel ashamed that they are still representatives. They find it difficult to admit, even to themselves, that they do not want 'to get on'. These attitudes are exacerbated by those who have been promoted and would rather be 'back on the road'. Because they feel they have to continue 'to get on' they cannot voluntarily apply for demotion, but have to pretend to be striving for still higher and still more unsuitable jobs. They frequently defend themselves by an unconsciously expressed contempt for 'the man who can do nothing but sell'.

The effect on those left in selling or on those moved back into selling cannot but be demoralizing. It may appear to them that only the less able get left; only those who have not made the grade elsewhere get moved back. But if the primary task of the company is finally performed only in the relationship made between a representative and a buyer, then it means that the most depressed part of the organization may be that part which is responsible for the task to which all other marketing activities are ultimately directed.

TOWARDS A BASIC ORGANIZATIONAL MODEL

Traditionally, sales management is the task of managing salesmen. And the recognition that a representative needs support has led to a proliferation of supervisors and of branch, district, area, and regional managers to provide it. Six- and even seven-tier hierarchies are not uncommon in large sale forces, and, in the smaller ones, the classical 'span of control' principles are usually rigidly applied. We question the tradition.

Our starting-point is the system of activities through which the selling transaction is carried out. This requires a role of representative whose task is to manage that system, that account, on behalf of his company. We distinguish between the management of the external environment – the management of accounts – and the management of the internal environment – the management of staff and the control of internal routines and procedures. In our view, sales management proper is the management of accounts; the member of the enterprise who carries out this function is, whatever his rank, a representative.

Management of an account requires a representative; but with rare exceptions the full-time representative is able to manage more than one account. Therefore the organizational problem is to discover a set of accounts that it is appropriate to assign to one representative, who can thus become the 'sales manager' in respect of these.

When most of the accounts with which a company had to make relations through its sales force were roughly the same – in the retail trade, independent traders, and in other kinds of selling, comparatively small (by present-day standards) undiversified companies – it was probably appropriate to assign a salesman to a territory. A territory could be defined as a set of accounts (and potential accounts) that was differentiated from other sets by geographical boundaries. It was an even more appropriate method of allocation if the territories were differentiated from one another by the economic and social condition of the consumer population – as were rural districts and conurbations, for example. This made the selling task different in different areas.

In the present day, however, when the marketing company's accounts range all the way from small local independents to major national undertakings, and when, at the same time, affluence and mass communication have diminished differences in consumption between urban and rural areas and between one part of the country and another, discrimination by type of account assumes much greater importance than territorial differentiation. Selling techniques have to vary according to whether the buyer is a businessman negotiating on investment and margin, a local shopkeeper satisfying local customers, or something in between. Negotiations conducted with a group headquarters will determine the kinds of relationship to be made in local outlets. Each account is affected in different ways by national and local advertising, by delivery dates and methods, and by after-sales service.

Since it is unlikely that one representative could command the whole gamut of skills needed for these very different types of negotiation, it follows that the set of accounts assigned to a representative should be as homogeneous as possible in terms of the negotiating skills required. In other words, technological rather than territorial differentiation needs to be the main criterion: the representative with his territory and the group of representatives with their district manager are organizational anachronisms. The number of accounts that any one representative can manage will be constrained by the time he has to devote to each, by the distances he has to travel, and by the amount of co-ordination that is entailed with other marketing specialists – in merchandising, display, and promotion – who operate within the boundaries of his accounts. Territorial task differentiation reinforces the technological only when selling in one territory is a different task from selling in others. All export selling may differ from selling in the home market, and, in addition, different techniques (and languages) may be called for in different countries; the north of England market may still differ in some ways from the southern one; regional television advertising may determine the incidence of marketing campaigns. At the point of task performance, however, the differentiation in a sales force will be made by putting together accounts that require the same marketing technology. Constraints that lead to specific territorial differentiation, as distinct from reinforcement of the technological, arise only from the number of similar accounts in a given territory. For example, in the consumer-goods industry, one man might be able to manage all the national accounts, whereas several might be required in each region to manage regional accounts, and a still larger number might be necessary to handle the many remaining local accounts.

In practical terms, this means that the primary operating system in a sales-force organization is the representative and a set of accounts that are relatively homogeneous in terms of the sales technology they require. The technological homogeneity may be sometimes reinforced, sometimes constrained, by territorial considerations. Each operating system is managed by a 'representative', whose rank, in traditional language, ranges all the way from a junior representative given his first 'territory' to a director managing the biggest and, from the marketing point of view, most valuable national or international accounts. All of these representatives are, as we indicated earlier, the real 'sales managers' of the organization. The implication is obvious, but awkward: if we depict the basic organization in the conventional 'line-management' diagram, junior representatives and directors of the company will be shown on the same level (see *Figure 17*).

FIGURE 17 *Sales-force organization: a basic model*

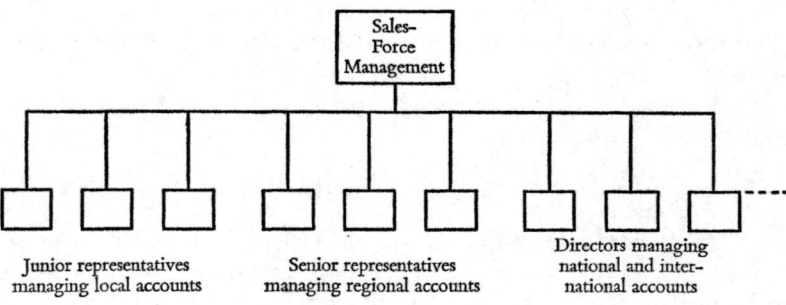

Awkward though this model may be, it appears to offer a better fit to the realities of the current market than do many existing organizations. A representative who negotiates at a high level in a customer enterprise may need to be at a high level in his own, but he should not be required to justify his status by part-time occupancy of some other – probably incompatible – role as well. Behind many existing practices of matching account size to organizational rank lies the implicit assumption that the skills required for managing accounts are the same as those required for planning a marketing strategy or for managing the internal environment of the enterprise. The evident differences in the content of these tasks make this assumption invalid. The planning of a marketing strategy and the creation of new marketing campaigns demand, among other things, a capacity to make judgements based on uncertain data reduced to abstractions in the form of trends, records of past performance, and the like; managing the internal environment entails a capacity to maintain sufficient control over routines and procedures to ensure implementation, and, above all, the capacity to manage fellow employees of the same company. By contrast, the major qualification for the management of accounts is the capacity to manage a series of pair relationships with different men, in different roles, in different companies, none of whom are fellow employees and all of whom have different loyalties. This fundamental requirement is shared by all accounts, regardless of size and complexity.

Figure 17 is thus closer to the realities of the task than are many existing structures; but there remains the problem of filling out this basic model to match the actual operational requirements of national marketing.

We have said that the dominant dimension for task-boundary definition is technological, in terms of accounts requiring similar techniques for their management; and that this will be reinforced by a territorial differentiation where it can be shown that different territories require different techniques. If we now imagine a company manufacturing and marketing products in the United Kingdom, and we make the assumptions that:

(a) managing local accounts is different from managing regional accounts;

(b) the incidence of television regions calls for regional managerial functions to co-ordinate television advertising, merchandising promotions, and sales campaigns, in all but national accounts;

(c) there are more national, regional, and local accounts than can be managed by one man;

then, in the terms we are using here, the second level of management in the United Kingdom sales force (counting the representative task as the first level – the management of accounts) will be the management of the sets of local accounts in any one region; the third level, regional management; the fourth, national management. The model organization for line management now looks something like that shown in *Figure 18*.

In such an organization the location of specialist functions – advertising, merchandising, brand management, personnel and training, and others – will be determined by the system to which they are technologically appropriate. The location of one or more advertising functions, for example, depends upon whether the sales force and marketing are differentiated as operating systems at national and regional levels, or whether advertising

FIGURE 18 *Model of a sales-force organization with technologically differentiated groupings of national and regional accounts*

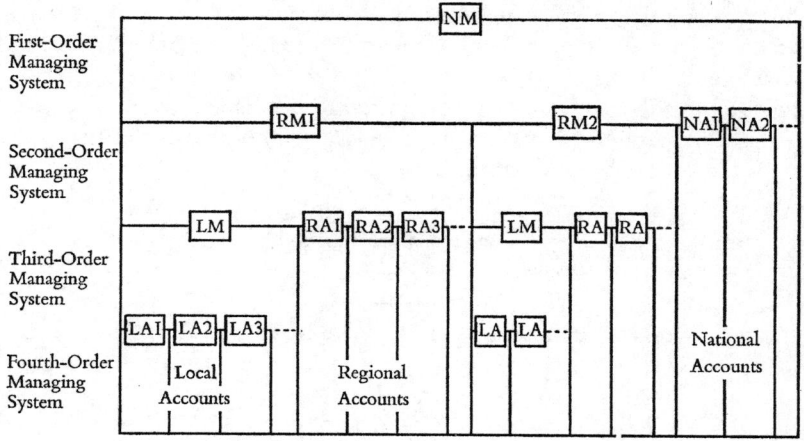

NM	:	National Management
RM1, etc.:		Regional Management, 1st Region, 2nd Region, etc.
NA1, etc.:		National Accounts Manager, 1st Group, 2nd Group, etc.
LM	:	Local Management
RA1, etc.:		Regional Accounts Manager, 1st Group, 2nd Group, etc.
LA1, etc.:		Local Accounts Manager, 1st Group, 2nd Group, etc.

is treated as a service function to selling. The former would locate advertising management as first- and second-order systems, parallel with national or regional management; the latter would locate it as a part of the existing first- or second-order systems. Similarly, personnel and training would be located nationally and/or regionally, depending on the need for national or regional policy-making; and specialist implementation and merchandising could be located in the second-order system for the conduct of regional campaigns, and in the third order for special campaigns directed to local accounts.

The important point is that the existence of any order of managing system or of any differentiated specialist function is determined first by technological differentiation only. Thus the existence of a third-order system for local sales-force management depends, from the task point of view, on there being sufficient difference between the techniques of marketing in local and regional accounts. If, as frequently happens in practice, there is little essential difference in this respect, or if, because of the constraint imposed by distance and hence the time taken in travelling, representatives have a mixture of local and regional accounts, then in task terms there is no need for a level in the hierarchy for the management of those who 'manage' local accounts. In the same way, if there is little technical difference in marketing between regional and national accounts, and the regional co-ordination of marketing activities is not technologically necessary, then there is no reason for regional management either. The corresponding organization would be as shown in *Figure 19*, which is essentially a redrawing of *Figure 17* in topological form, with the addition of specialist functions.

FIGURE 19 *Model of a sales-force organization in which accounts are not technologically differentiated*

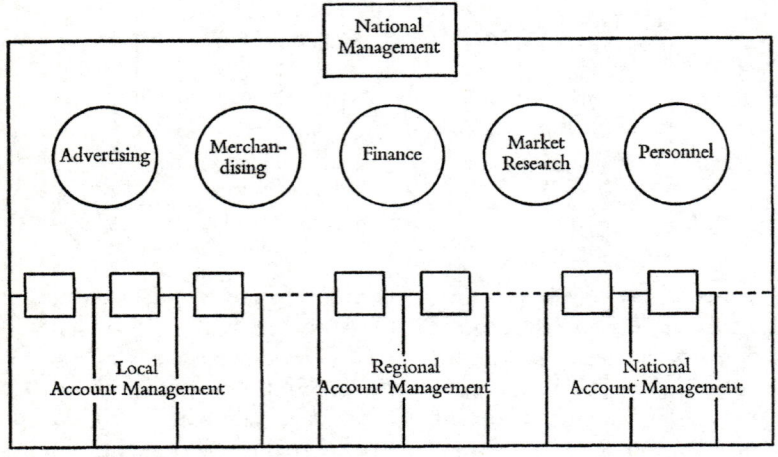

It can be seen that, where there was also an export side of the business, its organization would follow a similar pattern, but with added complications due to the number of different countries that had to be included. There would then be required a supra-order system to integrate home and export marketing.

These models reflect the reality that, in sales forces, simple hierarchies and simple consistent terms of reference for those in charge of representatives are unlikely to work. Even uniform terms of reference for representatives themselves are unlikely to be adequate. As a minimum it needs to be recognized that the representative's task is more than one task and may require more than one kind of person to perform it, and therefore more than one kind of management to control it.

It will also be seen that these organizational models provide for more than one line of promotion. There are still the 'vertical' lines for those who, after experience as representatives, find themselves, or are found, to have greater skills in specialist functions, or in the management of the internal environment; but, in addition, there is the 'horizontal' line for those who show a capacity to negotiate and thus to manage bigger accounts at higher levels in customer organizations.

ORGANIZATIONAL MECHANISMS FOR HANDLING COMPROMISES IN TASK-BOUNDARY DEFINITION

So much for the basic model to fit the primary task of the sales force. In practice, compromises are inevitable: first, because in a large sales force the numbers reporting to national or even to regional management would exceed a figure that could be adequately coped with, no matter how many members of management occupied the respective management 'boxes'; second, and more particularly, because the managing of national accounts may involve regular calling on branches spread throughout the country, and even abroad. Even if a 'box' labelled 'National Account Management' contained a team that could cover all branches, it might well be uneconomic for a member of such a team to make a special journey to call on a branch that would almost certainly be on the doorstep, so to speak, of one or other local accounts manager. In other words, local accounts managers will usually have to carry out some tasks on behalf of one or more national accounts managers, and hence task boundary controls will be breached. Furthermore, where an accounts manager's performance (and possibly his pay) is measured by what happens in the calls he makes, there can be complications if some of these calls are on behalf of accounts that he does not manage and for which, therefore, he cannot be held responsible. Within a region that has local as well as regional accounts managers, the same problems can arise, though on a smaller scale. It follows that we have to consider organizational mechanisms for dealing with these compromises.

If a region is geographically compact, compromise between a regional command and a local accounts manager's command should seldom be necessary. A regional accounts manager's team of assistant representatives (and clerks and porters if required) should be able to cover all branches of accounts in the region. If the region is large and such an arrangement is not commercially possible, then formal communications and even meetings have to be established between the regional accounts manager and those local accounts managers who are involved in his regional accounts. The difficulty about such communications and meetings is that they transgress the task boundaries of the local sales-force manager to whom local accounts managers are responsible. Nevertheless, the task boundary that is the subject of the communication is that of a regional account and hence under the control of the regional manager. If the local sales-force manager attends a meeting, he does so as holding a watching brief, as it were, over his own and his subordinates' responsibilities for local accounts. If conflicts between responsibilities cannot be resolved, the next formal meeting is between the regional accounts manager and the local manager as members of the regional managing system; if the difficulties persist, the regional sales-force manager has to be brought in.

If, in the attempt to avoid too many meetings, the bane of most modern enterprises, the majority of requests for service and of problems related to them are settled between the local sales-force manager and the respective regional accounts managers, or even through the regional manager's office, it has to be recognized that this is a further compromise and denies to the regional accounts managers access to those who work within their task boundary.

At national account level, distance and time wasted in meetings make compromise upon compromise almost inevitable; that is, requests for service and solutions of problems have to be dealt with between national accounts managers and regional sales-force managers, or through national management offices. If this were not done, national accounts managers would have to meet all local accounts managers, with the consequent breaching, far too often, of three successive task boundaries. The device of giving a national accounts manager a staff officer to maintain relationships, not only with the branches of his accounts but also with the regional and local services to the accounts, is, in our experience, rare; but then so is sales-force organization of the kind we have described. That it is feasible is shown by the regularity with which, when sales directors manage national accounts themselves, they invariably do use their personal assistants, or their line managers, in this way. The criticism is that those they do so use have seldom been chosen for this kind of task.

Mechanisms such as this do not avoid the breaching of boundaries.

This is inevitable in the complexity of a large sales organization. What matters is that the complexity is accepted and that the breaching is recognized when it takes place.

THE SENTIENT BOUNDARIES OF SALES-FORCE ORGANIZATION

We have said that task and sentient boundaries in sales-force organization cannot, by definition, coincide. Selling-task boundaries contain a pair, one of whom represents the customer. If sentient and task boundaries were coincident it would mean either that the representative was in the buyer's pocket or vice versa or that both buyer and representative had become more committed to their personal relationship than to the tasks of their different companies. Though such a situation could, in rare cases, enhance task performance and both marketing and customer enterprises might benefit, in the majority it could mean only that the representative was over-identified with his customer, or the buyer with his supplier – and the task from one of their points of view would inevitably suffer. Moreover, a representative has to make a task relationship with many buyers, and a buyer with many representatives. Thus even where, in rare instances, a representative has a supportive, task-oriented relationship with one buyer, he is very unlikely to have such a relationship with all the buyers he calls on; nor, for that matter, could a buyer have this kind of relationship with all the representatives who call on him.

In the previous chapter we have described some of the characteristics of the representative's task and their social and psychological consequences. We have referred to the transient nature of his task relationships, to the relatively long time he spends with his customers as compared with his company, and to his resultant isolation. We have also described some of the changes that are happening in his environment that have made him uncertain whether the skill and experience he has acquired will serve him in the future. Clearly, a representative has to make constructive use of his personality characteristics if he is to survive in his world of transient relationships. Equally clearly, not only the nature of the job, but the personality characteristics that match its task requirements do not make it easy for representatives to build the close, permanent face-to-face groups that can be found in research laboratories, in offices, and on the factory floor.

The obvious first identification for any representative is his company and its products; the second, his marketing organization; the third, the sales force. In companies in which the total sales force can be brought together frequently to hear about the results of past effort and about plans for the future, this source of support can perhaps suffice. It must be admitted, however, that such gatherings only too often tend to degenerate into parties of which the real objective appears to be to forget reality rather than to face it. They usually start with a rousing speech from the sales director, and end with everbody singing 'For he's a jolly good fellow'; leaving some other official to implement, in the following week, the difficult and unpleasant parts of the policy announced. Moreover, we have seen that there are often discrepancies between the verbal and behavioural communications that the representative receives from his superiors and colleagues in the sales force.

In a company in which the sales force is too large for regular and frequent gatherings, other smaller sentient groups have to be found. In an organization such as that shown in *Figure 18*, for example, the natural sentient groupings appear to be local managers with their local accounts managers; regional managers with their regional accounts managers; and a similar group of national accounts managers. With understanding and insightful management, such groupings can work reasonably well, but it has to be recognized that local, regional, and national managers are primarily responsible for operational performance and are thus not always the easiest persons to talk to about difficulties at work or elsewhere, particularly if it is the recurrent 'bad patch', or some other problem affecting performance, that is involved.

When any line manager is doing his job he has to organize his command to fight competition, and fighting must limit the consideration that can be given to those who are either temporary or permanent casualties in the fight. He has to make uncompromising judgements about the resources at his disposal, and his behaviour must be ruthless at least to the extent of not jeopardizing primary task performance out of sympathy for individual difficulty. His supportive capacity and his tolerance for rebellion must be constrained by his own role, however he may feel personally. The mechanism of district, area, and regional managers, each with their group of subordinates, is viable, therefore, only when a company can control its environment to the extent that it can ignore both the competition and the need to match buyer status with representative status. There are few companies left whose share of the market is large enough to satisfy these conditions.

To recapitulate: when a representative (whatever his rank) is doing his job he is trying to get results from a pair relationship. But to get those results he must fight unseen competitors who have been in before him and will undoubtedly come in after him, who will use every trick he can use and, he suspects, some he is not permitted to use. Some of the buyers he calls on he likes, and he can use his liking temporarily to allay his anxiety and to deal with his loneliness; others he does not like, but he has to submerge his feeling in the interests of his job. One thing he cannot do is use his task relationship to express his real feelings about himself, his partner within the task boundary, or his company. He needs people from whom he can get support, and people he can fight without jeopardy to his job. Convention, as well as the rules of normal social intercourse, precludes all-out fighting against his competitors, either indirectly through his buyers or directly when he meets them. He does not too overtly run down competitive products or personnel; and when he meets competitors' representatives he treats them, or tries to treat them, with professional politeness. He may even compare notes with some of them.

One organizational mechanism to provide support from within the sales-force organization is the appointment of one or more 'managers' in appropriate systems, with the specific task of helping various categories of representative. Their role needs to have a strong 'professional' component so that representatives can turn to them for help or advice, or to complain, without feeling that everything they say or do will be recorded in their official personnel file. It is unlikely that such a role could be taken by anyone for whom the representatives would not have high regard. The older representative for whom younger representatives have affection and respect, who accepts and can accommodate to current market changes, but for whom the frequency and type of calling now required are too onerous, can be an admirable candidate. Such 'managers' have to earn the right to representatives' confidence by their respect for confidentiality; and they have to earn their managerial status by the results they achieve. In effect, they have to create and control a boundary within which the representative feels 'safe', but one that will nevertheless enhance representative performance.

Another possible mechanism is the creation of pairs or small groups of representatives, to whom can be delegated the management of sets of accounts that would otherwise be divided between them. This arrangement allows representatives to assess each other's strengths and weaknesses and to share their work in ways that exploit the strengths and compensate for the weaknesses. In one organization that we have known, two representatives had separate territories in the west of England. One was a man who liked his material pleasures and loved his drink; the other was a puritan and had no vices. In the accounts in their territories the buyers were the usual mixture of hedonists and puritans. Both representatives were doing reasonably well, but the company suggested that they might combine and share out their accounts in a joint territory. As a pair they did very much better than they had done separately: that is, the level of orders from their joint territory was much higher than the sum of the orders from their previous and separate territories. To the surprise of the company and the representatives themselves, it was found that the pleasure-loving representative was managing most of the accounts with the puritanical buyers, and that the puritanical representative was managing most of those with the more hedonistic buyers.

CHAPTER 7

The Dry-Cleaning Receiving Office and the Customer

Although the relationship between representative and buyer is, as we have seen, one of considerable and growing complexity, there is at least reasonable clarity on both sides about the purpose and nature of the transaction. The buyer acknowledges that it is the representative's job to sell; the representative acknowledges that it is the buyer's job to decide whether and how much to buy.

Ostensibly, the transaction between dry cleaner and customer is equally clear: the customer wants his dirty clothes cleaned; the cleaner sells the necessary service. Like other selling, this involves a transaction across the boundary of the enterprise, between the customer who hands over the clothes and the employee who receives them and later hands them back. Such a system of activities poses the characteristic problems of control that we have already discussed: while the transaction is actually taking place, the representative is on his own – he is managing the relationship on behalf of the enterprise – so that the enterprise can control the transaction only indirectly by its management of the representative. It does this by prescribing or setting limits on what he may do and by giving him the kinds of training and support that make it likely that he will manage transactions with his customers in a way that really does represent the interests of the enterprise. Control of this boundary inevitably becomes much more difficult, however, if there are pressures from the customer to redefine the nature of the transaction and thus the role of the representative. And in dry cleaning, although there is overt agreement about the transaction and the role, there are strong covert pressures towards a different definition. This situation in turn affects control of the boundaries within the enterprise between the import-export system (the transaction with the customer) on the one hand and the conversion system (the cleaning activities) on the other.

Our work in the dry-cleaning industry was undertaken as part of our consultancy practice. The client company was one that offered all the usual services: cleaning, dyeing, pressing, repairing, eiderdown re-covering, renovating, and retexturing under a variety of trade names. It also offered different kinds and prices of cleaning, ranging from a cheap and crude method for boiler suits and overalls to an elaborate luxury service for cleaning, retexturing, and repairing suits and dresses. Active marketing was undertaken not only to bring in more business, but also to attempt, through special offers, to even out the flow of work through seasonal fluctuations.

At the time our project started the company had a chain of some two hundred shops known as receiving offices, from which all the clothing was sent to a central factory for processing. Two simultaneous and related events stimulated the company to approach us: increasing com-petition from other cleaners; and the technical innovation of compara-tively small, electrically driven, cleaning plants. The former led to a need to understand more about the nature of the service offered to customers; and the latter to a need for increased flexibility in organization.

In the course of our fieldwork we talked with consumers, both indi-vidually and in groups, in their houses and in shops; with shop and factory staff; and with managers.

This chapter is particularly concerned with the nature of the customer transaction and its consequences; the next with the effects of the technical innovation.

PRIMARY TASK, ACTIVITIES, ROLES, AND BOUNDARIES

The primary task of a dry-cleaning enterprise is to make a profit from cleaning, dyeing, pressing, repairing, and renovating clothing, bedding, and other soft furnishings. (In this context, as throughout the book, we use 'profit' as shorthand for the economic task of ensuring the long-term financial stability of the enterprise. Financially, this means ensuring that revenue exceeds expenditure so that there is, in the long term, sufficient capital and credit for growth, development, and the replacement of equipment; and, in the short term, adequate working capital to run the services provided.) Both the enterprise and its public would define the primary task in much the same way.

Similarly, there would be agreement that the intakes and outputs of the dominant import-conversion-export process, through which the en-terprise performs its primary task, are the clothing and other articles owned by and received from customers and returned to them after

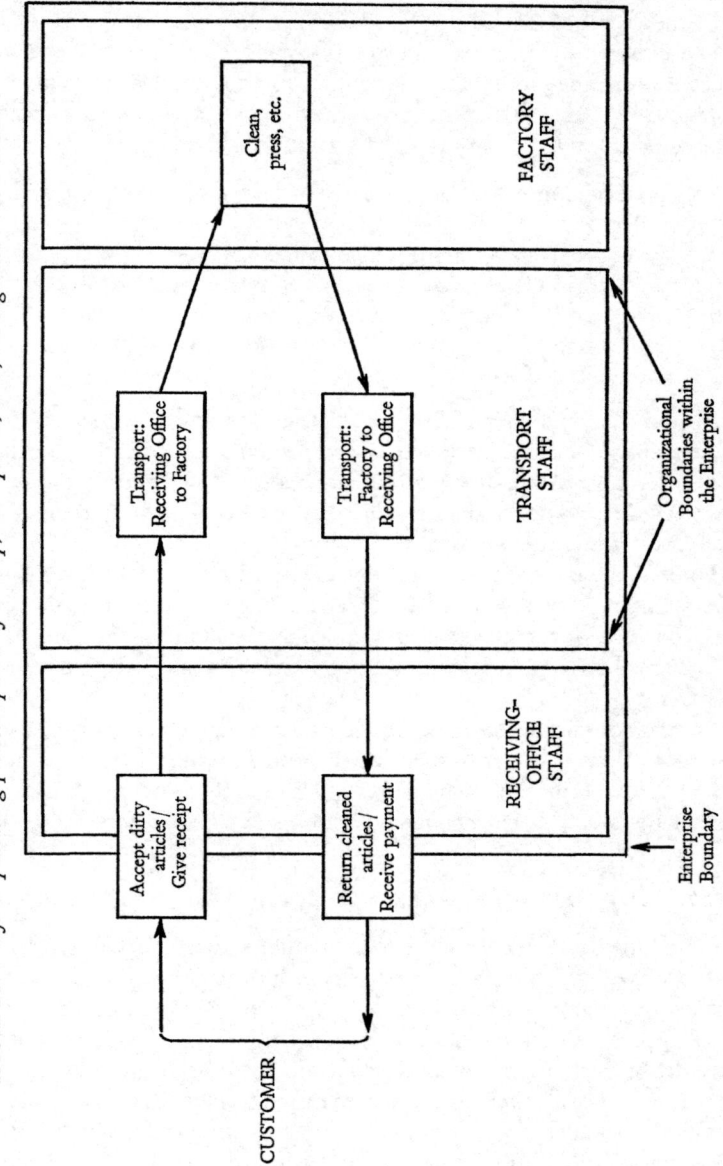

FIGURE 20 *The factory cleaning process: systems of activity, task systems, roles, and organizational boundaries*

treatment. The essential conversion processes are the cleaning, dyeing, and other work carried out.

The company concerned did not operate a customer service for the collection and delivery of dry-cleaning work, and, before plant shops were introduced, all treatment was carried out at the central factory. Consequently, five basic systems of activity could be identified:

(i) (at receiving office) accept dirty articles from customer and give receipt;

(ii) transport from receiving office to factory;

(iii) (at factory) clean, press, and otherwise treat the articles;

(iv) transport from factory to receiving office;

(v) (at receiving office) return cleaned articles to customer and receive payment.

Transport and factory activities are conversion systems, located within the enterprise boundaries. (Factory activities were further broken down into differentiated sub-systems, but these are not relevant to the present analysis.) Acceptance and return are import and export systems respectively, straddling the enterprise boundary.

These systems of activity are depicted in *Figure 20*, which also shows corresponding organizational boundaries. The enterprise boundary falls between receiving-office staff and customer; and the main internal task boundaries between receiving office and transport and between transport and factory.

Transactions across all these boundaries are inevitably affected by customers' attitudes towards their own clothes, which they continue to 'own' throughout the total process. We therefore have to consider a further boundary – that between clothing and the customer.

THE BOUNDARY BETWEEN CLOTHING AND THE CUSTOMER

To some men and women clothes are genuinely unimportant coverings – extraneous objects that have little to do with their personalities. To others, clothes are so much a part of themselves that they experience anything that happens to their clothes as if it were happening to them as well. The attitudes of the majority of adults fall somewhere between these extremes, but for most people their clothing is an important extension of themselves. The way in which they dress is the way in which they want to present themselves, consciously or unconsciously, to others. How they present themselves and how they are perceived may differ considerably, and both presentation and perception may vary with different people and at different times with the same people.

Moreover, style and fashion reflect not only individual choice and economic level, but also cultural factors. The relative status of men and women in any society is usually indicated by the clothing each group wears and for whose benefit it is worn. Who is chasing whom, and who is competing against whom, are certainly reflected in current teenage fashions in the United Kingdom. Individual and social attitudes are also shown by the care that is lavished on clothing or, in contrast, by its deliberate neglect. In many societies, including our own, different social classes have their own different practices in matters of dress and of cleanliness. What is correct and when it is correct; what is ostentatious and what modest; what is too formal or too informal – these points are frequently governed by strict, if unwritten and changing, social codes.

In short, those who make their living by working with clothing, be it in designing, manufacturing, or servicing, must not only take account of complex and largely unconscious social and psychological forces that permeate the individual and the groups to which he belongs, but also be aware of the often confused and unrecognized boundary between the individual and the clothes he wears.

CUSTOMERS' ATTITUDES TOWARDS CLEANING

The most remarkable feature of our work with dry-cleaning customers was their reluctance to talk about cleaning as cleaning. In neither group discussion nor individual interviews did customers ever talk spontaneously about the process as a cleaning process. They talked at length about pressing, retexturing, and repairing, and with animation about speed and price; but they always had to be prompted to talk about cleaning. Even when prompted, all customers without exception showed their reluctance by trying to change the subject. Indeed, most of them, particularly in group discussions, appeared embarrassed when faced with the reality that the main process of the industry removed dirt, stains, and other grime. The middle-aged and older respondents were, it is true, more embarrassed than the younger groups; but even these, though more matter-of-fact in their approach, preferred to concentrate on the ancillary services.

In one locality there was a well-known valeting service that was highly praised as 'the best *cleaner* in the district'. It was also the most expensive. The people we spoke to knew that this operator did not do any cleaning himself, but contracted it out to a much larger cleaning company which had a factory and chain of shops in the same district. Yet the same customers condemned the large cleaning company as 'cheap and garish':

'They never get things properly clean';

'I don't send things that matter to them, you never know whose dirty things they are going to be mixed with.'

Even when the obvious and indeed startling contradictions were pointed out, the valeting service was praised because:

'The clothes have such a beautiful appearance when you collect them', and

'But he gives such a personal service';

and the 'contamination' in the cleaning factory was ignored.

The idea of individual, personal service went so far with some customers that they displayed manifest guilt if they used more than one shop, or if they changed cleaners. Quite clearly, the feelings being expressed were about something other than a convenient utilitarian service. One respondent, middle-aged and partially infirm, complained of the difficulty she had been caused by the transfer of the manageress of her local shop to a more distant branch:

'I now have to go so far to get my cleaning done.'

When questioned more closely, she found it unthinkable that she could continue to use her own local shop now that the manageress had changed; her relationship was with a person, not with a company. Insistence on fidelity, or embarrassment at having to admit to using two cleaners, could not but suggest that the feelings aroused by going to more than one cleaner were a little like those aroused by an extramarital relationship – both guilt and pleasure. Certainly the feelings were much stronger than those usually expressed about most customer-trader relationships. Younger people found far less difficulty in discussing this aspect of their behaviour than did older married couples; equally, of course, young people find less difficulty in changing their boy and girl friends than do older people their husbands and wives.

In contrast to the reluctance to discuss cleaning itself, there was always lively discussion about ancillary services. Most of it, about pressing, dyeing, and retexturing, was usually rational and critical; that about speed of service and price was also lively but far less rational. Company policy was to sell two cleaning services: the more expensive one including a a special spot-and-stain removing service; the cheaper one offering cleaning only. In addition, there was a special speed service for which a supplement was asked. There was always frank disagreement about the significance of the different prices, and the reasons for them. Customers had apparently unshakable convictions that the actual cleaning processes were different, and that a fast clean was always a poor clean. It was irrelevant that it took time and skill to examine clothing after cleaning and to remove any stains left in: their own clothing never required special attention. Similarly, the explanation that the speed supplement had nothing to do with the time needed for the actual cleaning or spotting service but was to pay for the organizational costs involved in queue-jumping was hardly even listened to politely. Some customers went so far as to regard both the higher-priced clean and the speed supplement as a just punishment for dirtiness or lack of foresight:

'If I have to take the faster clean, it's my own fault for not thinking far enough ahead. And cleaners have to make a living, like anybody else, so I suppose I deserve it if I have to pay more and get less for it.'

Cleaning, it was felt, had to take some time: done quickly, it could not but be done less well.

None of these findings meant, of course, that the removal of dirt was unimportant. They suggested rather that it was so important and provoked so much anxiety that its necessity had either to be taken for granted or to be denied: either course avoided discussion of an embarrassing subject. Customers behaved as if they felt that the dirt in their clothes was an undesirable and dirty aspect of themselves. They relied on the cleaner to get rid of it without fuss (but not too briskly) so that they could start afresh. Moreover, they wanted to judge goodness by off-centre indicators that had nothing to do with the actual cleaning process, and to project their criticism of the cleaning process itself onto other related activities. To complain about stains left in after cleaning seemed tantamount to confessing that one was more than normally dirty to start with.

THE CUSTOMER/RECEIVING-OFFICE TRANSACTION

So far as customers were concerned, transactions across the enterprise/ environment boundary were not with a cleaner but with the particular staff of the branch shop to which they went. And the relationships they made with the staff of the dry cleaner were suffused with emotions and attitudes that were only indirectly related to the task that had to be performed.

It was remarkable how often criticism of the service would be followed immediately by denial of any criticism of the shop staff:

> 'It's not fair to blame the girls, it's not their fault. They are always so obliging. The factory gives them a lot of trouble.'

Such a comment seemed less remarkable, however, as it became clear in the course of our work how far the receiving-office staff shared and responded to their customers' attitudes and fantasies. To take one example: customers seemed to be unanimous in believing that the girls in the shops had 'nice, clean jobs'. (It was because of this that they were said to be almost invariably helpful, and the service they gave personal and individual.) Members of the staff, for their part, would in some cases even give cleanliness as one of the major reasons for their choice of job. When pressed they would mention the filthy state of some of the clothing brought in, but if they expanded their statements at all, it was usually to refer to their own washing facilities and the number of times a day they washed their hands.

The same identification of shop staff with customers was apparent when they were pressed – and they had to be pressed – to discuss the way in which the clothes were actually handled in the shops. This was a subject that caused manifest discomfort in all groups and interviews. Rationally, customers were prepared to say that when the clothes were dirty it did not much matter what happened to them, but we were always left with the impression that this was 'putting a good face on it', as one admitted. 'I'm not frightened' was an expression frequently used, though no suggestion was ever made that there was anything fearful in the transaction. Members of the staff, though more articulate, also spoke about receiving dirty clothes in ways that seemed far more extravagant than was warranted by the manifest operation involved. They would talk of 'chucking clothes on the floor and walking on them', and use words like 'horrifying' to describe what happened to clothes on their side of the counter. Perhaps naturally, neither customers nor staff appeared so bothered about discussing handing over the clean clothes; though even here we sometimes got the impression that it was an operation better carried out quickly lest what was handed over did not match expectations. In some discussions both staff and customers talked about the clothes being 'given a good bashing'; and the use of 'good' in that context, as in 'good' hiding, did mean that for some the bashing was felt to be good. The punishment was deserved and the staff obliged by administering it. Other customers clearly wanted reassurance that their clothes, and by transfer themselves, would be well cared for. Some just wanted their clothes cleaned. Most perhaps combined all three needs, but in different degrees.

ENTERPRISE/ENVIRONMENT BOUNDARY CONTROL

Many interpretations could be made about both customer and staff statements in these discussions; here we are concerned only with emphasizing that, from the company's point of view, the control of transactions across the enterprise/environment boundary for both intakes and outputs was vested in shop staff; and that the control depended more upon the human relationships the staff made with their customers than upon what really happened in the conversion process. Moreover, the human relationships were usually suffused with feelings that were deeper and stronger than was strictly appropriate to the manifest task.

The awkward point was that the primary task of the dry-cleaning enterprise was to make a profit from dry cleaning, and making a profit in the competitive environment in which it operated involved a careful calculation of what was given for what charge. Service and customer satisfaction were all-important musts, but they had to be on a strictly cash basis. In the shops, those who were good at their jobs, in the sense that they and their customers made mutually satisfying relationships, were unable to support, with wholehearted enthusiasm, management controls that were designed to ensure that they did not give anything away. Such controls were felt, at best, as unnecessary and, at worst, as exploitative.

The problem of control appeared at its sharpest when staff talked about the pricing policy. In spite of written policy statements and elaborate attempts by management to communicate their intentions, members of the staff frequently appeared as confused as their customers, and would give all kinds of reasons, except the right ones, for the differential prices. For some members of the staff the faster clean had to be a better clean, probably so that they could feel justified in charging more for it; others evidently agreed with their customers' assessment that no special attention was needed for *their* clothes, and would accordingly advise them not to have either the faster or the better clean.

Broadly speaking, the staff of the receiving offices dealt with their ambivalent feelings towards both their customers and their own company by identifying with their customers at the expense of the factory. They could then sell the two-price cleans and even accept the punitive implications of the more expensive one because it was the factory and not they who administered the punishment. They could also maintain the speed supplement with whatever rationalization suited them because, again, it was imposed by the factory and not by themselves. At least they could manage in this way with their ordinary customers; with pensioners, with mothers with children (who should always have the best, irrespective of price), and with other 'deserving cases', they were in more difficulty. Here they almost always became the customer's agent, advising him or her how to get the best out of the factory at the cheapest price.

But more significant than any of these attitudes in our view was the ability of the staff, because of their situation, to go into collusion with the customer to keep dirt and all its associated anxieties at a distance. In this they were greatly assisted by the interposition, between themselves and the factory, of the transport system.

BOUNDARIES WITHIN THE ORGANIZATION

Receiving offices were open at normal shop hours; the factory worked on a day shift only, except during the busy seasons when there was some overtime and part-time evening working; the transport system was a night-time operation.[1]

Van drivers loaded in the evening with clean clothing and during the night made their round of the receiving offices, delivering racks and parcels of clean articles and picking up bundles of dirty clothing. They had keys to the shops on their rounds and seldom met either shop or factory staff. In many ways it was surprising to find that the transport system was seldom blamed by the receiving office for what went wrong. Even if clothing was creased through having been crushed in transport

[1] With a few spare vans on duty during the daytime for urgent collections and deliveries.

or was wrongly delivered, it was the factory's fault for bad packing, or for giving the driver too much to carry.

'They have to come here in all weathers, in the middle of the night, night after night, and the factory expects them to run to a strict time-table, no matter how much they give them, or how much they have to pick up – it's not natural.'

Though the transport system was based on the factory, it 'belonged', in the eyes of the staff of receiving offices, to them. It was almost as if the drivers were regarded as taking away all the receiving-offices' problems and returning solutions to them. And if the solutions were inadequate, it was the factory's fault. By the nature of the task of the transport system – straightforward goods collection and delivery – and the time at which it was performed, it interposed a kind of insulating barrier between the receiving office and the factory.

The significance of this insulation will become still more apparent in the next chapter, where we shall show that the introduction of the 'plant shop', by removing an organizational boundary, modified trans-actions with customers. This will also illustrate the more general point that an organizational boundary which firmly separates an activity system and the associated group of people from other organizational units makes it very easy – and not only in the dry-cleaning industry – for the group to project its own 'dirt' – its negative feelings – into the groups on the other side. In this way members of the 'in-group' can feel more positively about each other. Removal of the boundary, however, confronts the group with the ambivalent reality of its own internal relationships.

CHAPTER 8

Effects of Technical Change in Dry Cleaning

The essential feature of the new type of small, electrically driven, dry-cleaning plants was that they took little space and could be accommodated in the back premises of any but the smaller receiving offices, or even in the shop window. In terms of the chemicals used and the treatment of the articles, the cleaning process is identical to that in the larger plants of the factory. Compared with the bigger factory machines the capital cost of the small plants is low, they are easy to install, transport time and costs are avoided, and it is possible to offer a much quicker service. On the debit side, less weight can be accommodated at one loading and rather more solvent is used because of the need to load and unload more frequently. Moreover, whereas for the removal of recalcitrant spots and stains the factory can call on the resources of a laboratory and a highly skilled staff, the plant shop cannot afford to carry the staff required. With the plethora of new materials now on the market, this means that the actual quality of service offered by the plant shop tends to be – at least by objective standards – inferior to that offered by a factory cleaner. Plant shops could nevertheless cope adequately with most of the work they were asked to do. On average, they could process some 85 per cent of the cleaning on the premises, sending only bulk cleaning and renovations to the factory.

Because the balance of advantages lay with these small autonomous units, the company introduced them quite quickly. Obviously, however, the greater the utilization of equipment that could be secured, the more profitable the new units would be. A start was therefore made by converting the large, city-centre receiving offices into plant shops. It was here that turnover was highest beforehand, and the introduction of the plant usually increased turnover substantially.

ACTIVITIES, ROLES, AND BOUNDARIES

As *Figure 21* shows, the activities entailed were the same as in the

FIGURE 21 *The plant-shop cleaning process (with subsidiary factory cleaning): systems of activity, roles, and organizational boundaries*

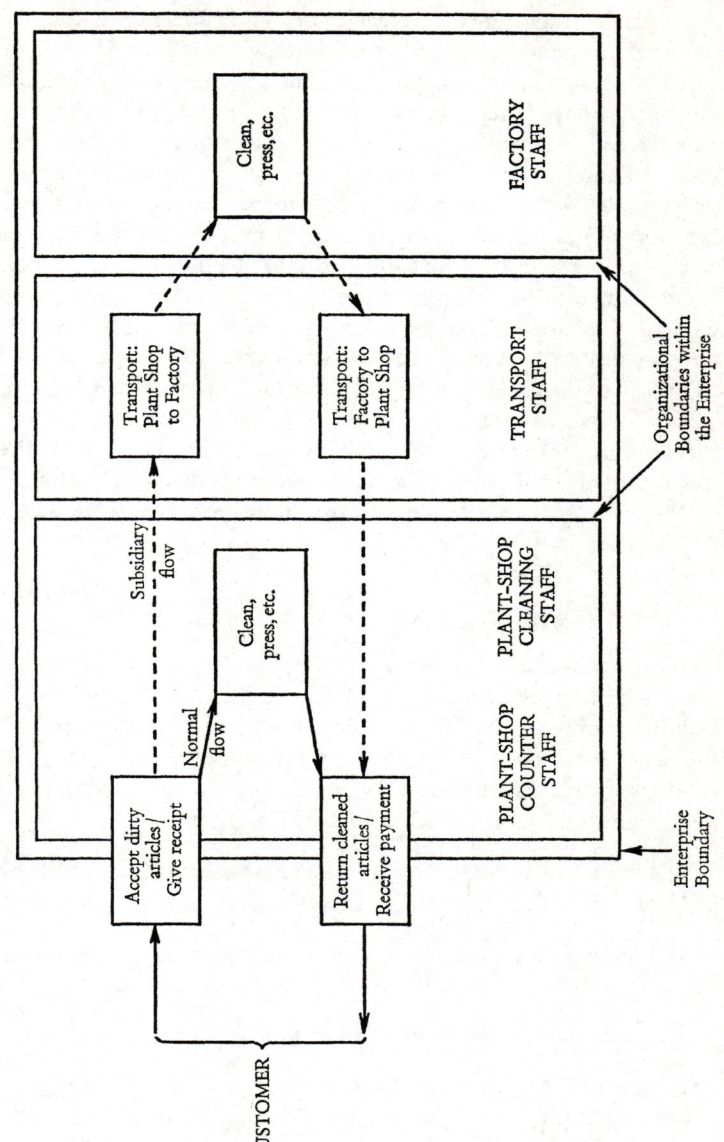

receiving shop/factory process. The essential difference, however, was the absence of an organizational boundary between the import-export activities and the great majority of cleaning activities.

All the plant shops we saw were, in our terminology, primary production systems. They were not therefore internally differentiated. Few employed more than eight people. Within this group there was some specialization of role: there were counter staff, sometimes under a counter manageress; cleaning staff, responsible for operating the machine, pressing, and spotting; and in larger shops a cashier. But the shop manager was usually a working manager, able to deploy himself as a machine operator if need be or occasionally as a counter hand, and the staff as a whole constituted a single working group which carried out the total import-conversion-export process. Moreover, in some shops interchangeability of role was developing: in particular, counter staff were learning how to press and spot.

A minority of cleaning was still sent to the factory, being picked up and returned by night by the same transport that served the receiving offices. We shall return later to the utilization of the factory and to attitudes towards it.

THE CUSTOMER AND THE PLANT SHOP

Customers of plant shops expressed the same general views about the services offered, and showed the same reluctance to discuss the process as a cleaning process, as did customers of receiving offices. But there were some attitudes that were specific to plant shops.

Shops in which the plant was in the window or in full view behind the counter seemed to cause particular difficulty:

'It's terrifying to think of your clothes being pushed around like that. They shouldn't do it.'

One customer came into a newly converted plant shop, stopped in her tracks when she saw the machine, and walked out, saying:

'Oh, I usually go to the other branch,'

(referring to a nearby receiving office). Others, with more capacity for denial, would assume that the sight, through the inspection panel, of clothes being 'tumbled' in the cleaning fluid was an advertising gimmick:

'It's the same suit all the time, you can tell it's one they put there specially. It's like the dummy packets in the grocer's and the tobacconist's.'

But plant shops were seen to have advantages as well: the machines were smaller and the shops served a limited area, and therefore there was less chance of contamination. Clothing did not have to be sent to a large anonymous factory miles away:

'You know where it is and you know who's doing it. They're not going to damage it or lose it.'

This argument was used particularly by younger people.

And, indeed, there was some evidence of differences in the clientele of plant shops as against receiving offices. Whenever a receiving office was converted there was always the loss of some previous customers who, like the woman cited above, could not tolerate such a public process and preferred the more intimate transaction and the remote factory. The new customers, often younger, apparently preferred to know where they stood in relation to the cleaning process. The rate at which the new plant shops increased their turnover made it clear that they were taking a good deal of custom from competitors' receiving offices. By no means all of this was attracted by speedier service, which perhaps suggests that the collusive relationship offered by receiving-office staff was an over-response to the fantasies of some of their customers.

PLANT-SHOP STAFF

It is not insignificant that former receiving-office manageresses seldom became successful counter manageresses in plant shops. They were faced, of course, with the problem of subordinating themselves to the shop manager. But a still greater problem was that of adjusting themselves to the customer relationship in the new context. Customer attitudes and the location of organizational boundaries had reinforced one another in the receiving shop to produce a characteristic collusive relationship. Organizationally, the plant shop did not support such a 'good mother' relationship; rather, it enabled the staff to offer a wider range of responses to correspond more realistically to its customers' range of needs. Ex-manageresses who reacted in this new situation by complaining about the standard of cleaning in the plant shop compared with the factory were hardly likely to be judged successful.

Staff attitudes in plant shops were – and had to be – different.

From the point of view of the staff, plant shops had several advantages over receiving offices: first, because the majority of the work coming in was processed in the shop itself, the staff had the satisfaction as a group of completing a whole task; second, by keeping customers' clothes on the premises they could maintain better control over their primary operating relationships – those with their customers; and third, because the whole task was under their own control, they could be granted greater autonomy by their own management and feel that their results were achieved by their own efforts. They did not have to share their successes with the factory. Counter staff appreciated the fact that if a fault was detected while a garment was being handed back, it could often be put right while the customer waited; but in many plant shops there were also scrupulous double-checks, by both presser and counter assistant, to ensure that no spots remained.

As against these advantages there were a number of disadvantages arising from the fact that there was no ready-made protective boundary between the staff and the process: they were a part of it. Cleaning on the premises gave them no escape from the consequences of their actions: they had to accept accountability for what they did to the clothing, and hence to the customer; and they had to carry the responsibility for their own mistakes and to come to terms with the mutual fantasies inherent in their task.

It was predictable, therefore, that staff in plant shops would find it more difficult than those in receiving offices to deal with different grades of cleaning:

> 'If you sell a customer the cheaper clean, you can't deliberately not take a stain out and give it back saying she only paid for the cheaper job. You have to do your best to get the stains out whichever clean she chooses.'

But company policy was the same for both plant shops and receiving offices: two kinds of cleaning at two prices. The cheaper clean comprised the cleaning process by itself; the more expensive service included a special inspection and an attempt to remove stains and marks not taken out by the normal process. We found that staff in plant shops had distorted this pricing policy into an additional speed supplement as the only rational explanation they could give for having two prices. But the company pricing policy included an actual speed supplement as well.

It was perhaps hardly surprising, therefore, that not only the staff but also their customers got confused. Some of the staff in the plant shops tried to deal with the confusion by sending all their cheaper cleaning to the factory, retaining for themselves the 'higher-quality' and the higher-priced work. They thus identified the factory with the cheaper, lower-quality trade, and had to deal as best they could with their guilt both at loading the factory with the less profitable work and at keeping to themselves the higher-quality work which they were less qualified than the factory to do. Even when they could manage to persuade themselves that their work was better than the factory's, they then had to face their customers with what they believed to be the lower quality of the factory work. Some went so far as to say:

'Even if we send the cheap cleans to the factory, we have to re-do them all when we get them back. You can't give them back in the state we get them from the factory.'

Alternatively, they would go to extreme lengths to avoid sending articles to the factory: in one instance, when the plant in his shop was shut down by flooding, the manager chose to take a taxi-load of garments to a plant shop in an adjoining town rather than send them to the factory.

The only plant staff who said they had no trouble with the two-clean, two-price policy were those who, on further inquiry, were found to have avoided selling the cheaper clean at all. In most shop plants we found that only one service was in fact sold, whatever the price charged. They would advise customers against the faster clean:

'. . . but come in a bit later and I'll see if I can't get the ordinary clean put through a bit more quickly for you.'

There was a similar attitude towards retexturing, and many customers received this service without paying the supplement. In some instances this was the realistic solution: during slack periods, if some clothes were to be retextured and others not, it was more economic to put them all through the retexturing process (which required a different cleaning fluid) than to batch them into two part-loads. But, in addition, the staff felt more comfortable about it:

'The appearance is so much nicer.'

In those plant shops in which supplements were charged the discomfort was plain. Staff talked about themselves as 'blackmailers' and 'swindlers';

or they projected their guilt onto the customers and spoke of those who paid a higher price for a non-existent 'better' clean or a supplement for a fictitious speed as 'suckers'.

In general, in comparison with the staff of receiving offices, members of the staff of plant shops had to make relationships at a more sophisticated level. They had to cope with the reality that it was the work of their own primary work group that they were selling. They had fewer defences against the anxieties and problems of the business they were in. As against this, however, because they gave a whole service they could respond as a unit to a wider range of feelings and emotions, and hence as individuals could take different roles. Whereas the staff of a receiving office had to appear as good mothers, those in the plant shop could, and indeed needed to, be seen as good mothers, technical experts, and datable girls besides.

Provided the plant shop was large enough, it could offer an adequate and protected occupation for men, who otherwise found themselves in an equivocal position in what is essentially a female occupation. They could operate the machine and concentrate on the mechanical, as distinct from the cleaning, aspects of the task; or they could act as managers of a business enterprise. As men, however, they could not appear easily in the most important area of activity – the customer relationship. Happily, the manager's help on the counter tended to be needed on occasions when it was least inappropriate: during a rush of business provoked by a special offer (for example, two garments cleaned for the price of one). Customers' ordinary anxieties about cleaning would then be submerged by the characteristic manic state of the bargain-hunting crowd.

MANAGEMENT CONTROLS

The senior managers with whom we worked were in a difficult position. For competitive reasons they had to open plant shops; but property for plant shops was expensive and not easy to find, and, even when found, it took a long time to get planning permission to build and to install the plant. The quickest way to secure new plant shops was to convert those receiving offices that had big enough premises. With each conversion the nature of the service given, and hence the kind of staff required, changed in ways that were not easy to detect.

At the same time, all the evidence that was collected suggested that plant shops and receiving offices tended to attract different kinds of customer, and it was by no means certain, therefore, that the receiving-office trade was a dying trade. In addition, every conversion reduced the load on the factory and caused considerable economic and personnel problems there as well.

Even when these practical problems were partially solved (by taking over several smaller cleaners with their own chains of receiving offices) there still remained the problems of control of what was now a larger and more complex enterprise. What had been a simple organization with clear-cut boundaries between shop, transport, and factory commands now included a large number of quasi-autonomous units, each of which appeared to have its own idiosyncratic relationship to the factory and its services, and each of which pursued its own marketing policy with regard to price and service.

The two kinds of outlet required, in fact, two entirely different kinds of control. Receiving-office manageresses, who sometimes worked on their own and seldom had more than two or three people working under them, predominantly needed personal support. They tended to complain alternately of loneliness and overwork. The company provided this support through local supervisors, themselves women too, who dealt with the more difficult problems arising in the shops and also gave quite direct and practical help. The manageresses were 'mothers' to their customers; the supervisors correspondingly acted as dependable mothers on whom the manageresses themselves could lean. In this way, some sentient grouping was provided within the company to counterbalance extreme identification with customers, but it also confirmed the manageresses' style of behaviour and, if anything, inhibited them from developing more diversified and sophisticated responses to their customers.

Plant shops, on the other hand, provided internal support for their staff and encouraged diversity of response in customer transactions. The essential managerial controls had therefore to be directed to technical standards and to profitability.

Thus it was difficult to accommodate these two types of unit within a single set of controls. A simple instruction that plant shops would conform to company receiving-office policy just could not work; and any attempt to set up two simultaneous policies – a multiple-price, multiple service for receiving offices and a single-price, uniform service for plant shops – would destroy the advantages of flexibility that the plant shops permitted.

The solution that the company attempted in this case was to interpose, in effect, a new set of sentient boundaries by establishing 'sub-enterprises'. The original company with its one central factory became a holding company with a number of subsidiaries. Each served a smaller geographical area, included both receiving offices and plant shops, and was backed by its own satellite factory.

FURTHER TECHNOLOGICAL CHANGE

Since the work described above was carried out, the industry has faced further technological development, and 'do-it-yourself' dry-cleaning establishments are now springing up. The factory, as the repository for the customer's dirty clothes and fantasies about them, has moved not merely into the shop but directly under the customer's control. The primary task of such an establishment has correspondingly altered: it is now to make a profit from providing customers with dry-cleaning facilities. We would predict that with this change many of the problems of organization and control associated with a service industry will have disappeared; but also that the sophistication that self-service cleaning implies will mean that demand will grow relatively slowly.

SERVICE INDUSTRIES AND DEPENDENT RELATIONSHIPS

Through technical change, therefore, dry cleaning may be beginning to escape some of the consequences of being a service industry. But there are many other industries whose primary task entails rendering services to customers or to their property. One type of service – air transport – we shall be saying more about in Part IV. Forms of service vary greatly: some are personal and intimate, some remote and even barely recognized. Hairdressing and massage obviously involve direct physical contact between consumer and service agent; in contrast, traffic control and road-sweeping are remote and, so far as the individual citizen is concerned, largely impersonal. The professions, such as medicine, the law, and the church, could, with little distortion of definition, be included in the service industries.

These industries share certain basic characteristics that have organizational implications. Essentially, they are not concerned with the manufacture of end-products; and the criteria used to judge whether the service is good or bad are not always directly or easily measurable. Even in those industries that are not directly concerned with the person, and in which quality can be objectively measured, the human relationships between the consumer and service agent are often influential. Thus, for example, the work of an electrician who visits a house to maintain domestic equipment is seldom judged solely by the continuing technical efficiency of the equipment; and whether the maintenance contract is renewed frequently depends on whether the agency sends men who are 'nice people to have in the house'.

The closer to the person the service has to be, the more important becomes the human relationship, and the conventions and taboos that surround it. In the extreme, in the medical services, where the life and death of the patient may be involved, there are strict rules of conduct, backed by legal sanction, to govern doctor-patient relationships, and elaborate rituals have to be established to decrease the effects of the anxieties that are inevitable in the task that has to be performed.

All those whose work brings them into contact with the person or possessions of others make a series of dependent relationships with their clients or customers. Any individual who gives himself or his possessions into another's hands has to depend on the other's competence to do what is required. Two major difficulties arise:

(i) 'What is required' is frequently not just a simple demand at the reality level, but includes complex demands at both the conscious and the unconscious levels.

(ii) Dependent relationships invariably arouse anxiety and provoke hostility, whose intensity depends upon the extent to which the anxieties of the earliest and most dependent relationship of all – that between mother and child – are reactivated.

Our conclusion is that anxiety and hostility involved in offering and accepting a service are directly related to the nature of the service and the extent to which it recalls, replaces, or simulates the activities that are the essential elements of the mother-child relationship – feeding, care of the body, and general handling. These activities arouse intense feelings which are both positive and negative: they include love, gratitude, and erotic excitement; also hatred, greed, envy, and frustration. To the extent that these feelings, however unconscious, enter into the service transaction between employees of the enterprise and its customers, they will also affect relations between the import-export system and the conversion system, pose problems of control, and perhaps spill over and reveal themselves in unexpected ways in quite different parts of the organization.

PART III

Disentanglement of Coincident Task Boundaries

Introduction

In Part II we examined some of the problems of boundary control that occur when the boundary of a system of activities crosses enterprise boundaries. To the extent that the membership of the enterprise is too large to act collectively in relation to its environment, representatives have to be appointed to carry out transactions on behalf of the enterprise; and we have now seen something of the dynamics of the relation between the transactional system of activities, the sentient groupings of the representative, and task boundaries within the enterprise. Essentially, this is the enterprise grappling with its problem of being an open system – of being sufficiently responsive to forces in its environment but not so responsive as to lose its coherence and identity.

In Part III our perspective is different. We are still concerned with activity systems and groups and with the control of task and sentient boundaries. But the problem area is not of boundaries that cut across one another; it is of boundaries that coincide and, by doing so, act as constraints on the openness of the system.

The kind of situation we have in mind is shown in *Figure 22*. Theoretically, two tasks, and thus two activity systems, can be identified, but those who carry out the tasks – the human resources of the two systems – constitute a single sentient group. Thus the strength of the sentient boundary of the group is affected by what happens in both activity systems and, by way of the common sentient-group boundary, the activities of each system are affected by those of the other. Structurally, the position is precisely similar to that of an individual occupying multiple roles: that is, in *Figure 22* 'individual' would be substituted for 'group' and 'role' for 'task system'. As we know, difficulties can arise when two roles make conflicting demands upon the individual.[1] Involvement of a group in two activity systems, however, carries the added complication that two different arrays of roles coexist and that roles in the two systems may relate the individuals together in different ways.

[1] R. L. Kahn *et al.* (1964) report recent intensive research in this field.

System conflict does not arise, of course, in conditions of stable equilibrium – in other words, where the environmental forces are tenuous or do not impinge differentially on the two systems. For example, primitive societies often seem to have had closed-system characteristics over long periods. A stable equilibrium was established between the different systems of activity in which the tribal group engaged. In our own society, the teaching hospital has already been mentioned as an example of a twin-task enterprise. Here there is the complication that patients, who constitute the throughput of the curing system, are also part of the resources of the teaching system; and that students, the throughput of the teaching system, are part of the resources of the curing system. But permanent staff fill the dominant roles in both systems and the boundary

FIGURE 22 *One group serving two systems of activity*

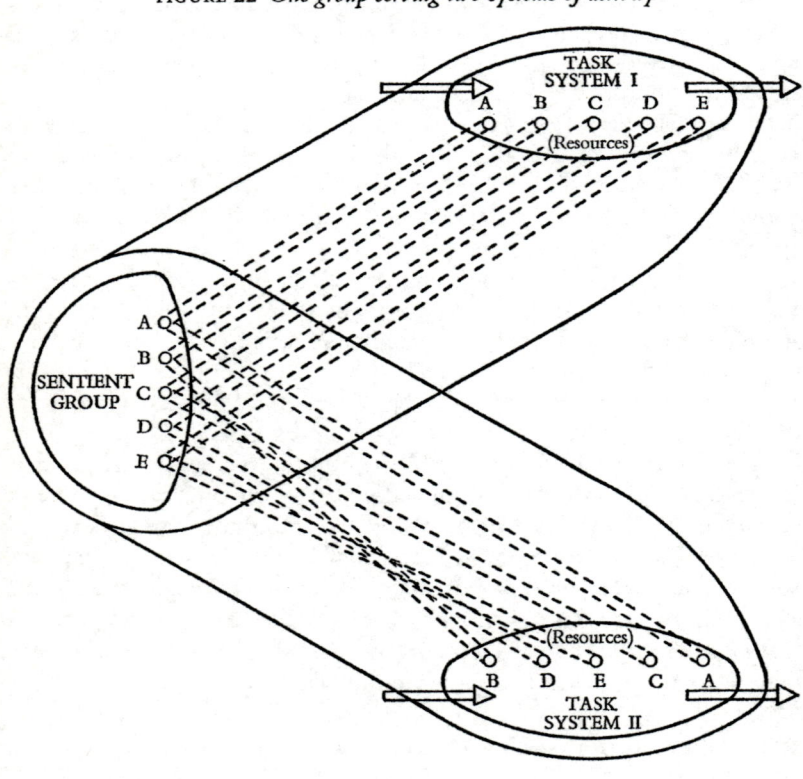

around the teaching hospital as a whole is usually potent enough to maintain a stable equilibrium between the two.

In the two chapters that follow we take the family business as an example of disequilibrium between two systems of activity. Two tasks are placed in increasing conflict through differential pressures from their environments. But often, in our experience, the situation is not seen in these terms. It is felt, initially, as mounting conflict within the family group. Only when the multiple tasks have been clearly identified and their distinctive requirements and constraints spelled out does it become possible to differentiate the controls that each calls for; and only through engaging in this process of analysis can the family group, while not perhaps resolving its conflict, at least confront it more constructively.

CHAPTER 9

The Family Business in Contemporary Society

A family has many tasks. It formalizes the relations between men and women; it provides for the birth and upbringing of children; it houses and feeds its members; it is the primary human group through which social relations are made and maintained. It is the focus of the love and hate, reassurance and anxiety, security and insecurity, that are the fundamentals of social culture. In different societies, different laws, customs, and behaviour govern the roles taken by the members of the family; and family organizations extend all the way from matrilineal and even polyandrous structures, in which the role of husband and father is barely relevant, to the more common patrilineal structures in which, in the extreme, women are regarded, and accept themselves, as inferior to men.

This is not the place to summarize the extensive literature on forms of family organization in different societies. It is enough to emphasize that our own society, however complex in both its material environment and its institutional forms, is based upon the primary human group – the family. In our society, as in primitive societies, the family is the institution that formalizes the relations between the sexes and provides for the process whereby children are born and protected through the long period of their dependence on others.

In this chapter we shall be considering some of the problems created for family businesses by the modern structure of the family and prevailing social values. In the next, we shall be examining some of the consequences of economic and technical change.

There is, of course, still a large number of family businesses in existence, and more are being started daily, but the areas in which they can be successful are diminishing. One can think immediately of small shops, of farms, hotels, and restaurants that are run entirely by family members or by family members with very few employees. Such enterprises have comparatively simple and stable technologies and low capital requirements, and the skills it takes to run them are easy to learn; or, perhaps more accurately, lack of technical skill can often be compensated by the personal service that is given. In many of them, the size of income derived from the business matters less than that the family can 'live off' the enterprise.

In these two chapters we are concerned more with industrial and commercial enterprises which, by their nature, have to adapt to the changing social, economic, and technical conditions of their environment, or fail. Even in the area of the small business, however, mass production – factory farms – and mass distribution – chains and multiples – have led, and are leading, to the takeover or failure of many family-run enterprises. And the successful survivors can seldom support the whole family: younger sons have to seek their fortune elsewhere and daughters are expected to be taken care of by their husbands.

Some family businesses are private, some public, some mixtures of private and public, some wholly and some partly family-owned; but all have the characteristic that the members of one family own enough of the voting equity to enable them to control strategic policy and tactical implementation. In a successful and expanding business, the amount of equity that has to be held to achieve and maintain control may be quite a small proportion of the whole; but if the company is public then the family has to have sufficient to make sure that no single shareholder or group of shareholders can ever become a major embarrassment to family decision-making.

FAMILY MEMBERS IN A FAMILY BUSINESS

In non-industrial societies individuals tend to live, work, and play in small, tight-knit communities. Family life, occupation, and community existence form an interlocking system of mutual dependence; codes of behaviour in all areas of society are often precisely defined and the definitions supported by elaborate rituals. Ritual proscribes deviation, and even such individual deviation as is permitted is regulated. Personal aspiration is limited to the display of superior skill in predetermined callings; and social mobility is for the most part non-existent. Under such conditions wresting a livelihood from the environment is often difficult and life itself often precarious; the integration of family, working, and social activities is essential to the survival of the individual as well as of society.

In contrast, a diversified industrial democracy offers opportunities for alternative ways of life and encourages social mobility. 'Log cabin to

White House' is an acceptable aspiration, and constraints on individual freedom cannot easily be maintained. A major consequence is the increased difficulty, in modern conditions, of maintaining a family tradition of employment. Not only are there more opportunities for competent younger members of a family to escape from family domination, but society is less prepared than it once was to tolerate incompetent performance for the sake of a name. In industry and commerce, society can and does apply both economic and social sanctions that force enterprises either to conform to conditions of employment and yet remain profitable, or to go under.

A name is no longer sufficient. Indeed, a distinguished name can sometimes be a handicap to a family successor, even though he may be of above average competence. The difficulties of the sons of publicly successful fathers are only too well known. There have been, and still are, distinguished families all of whose members appear to make their mark in their chosen profession; but the failure of the children of highly successful parents is the more commonly heard of. There are, of course, added problems when one or more of the family members take public roles that demand particular ways of behaving for the whole family. Notwithstanding personal inclinations or qualifications, the children are brought up in a way of life that imposes special disciplines on them, and deviation from an accepted standard gets more notoriety than it would otherwise deserve. Jessica Mitford (1960) in her autobiography quotes her mother:

' "Whenever I see the words 'peer's daughter' in a headline", she once commented rather sadly, "I know it's going to be something about one of you children." '

Similarly, there are jobs that impose standards of conduct in other areas of activity that make it difficult for their holders to enjoy an ordinary private life of their own.

Family members who take jobs in a family business in a modern industrial society are in a special category: their work, play, and family lives have more integration than is the case with most people, and hence they have restricted opportunities for individual choice. They may not be required to behave with any special austerity in their private lives, but the areas of activity in which they can work out their satisfactions and defences overlap more than they do for other individuals. Because the contexts in which they work and live are so close – and working in a family business involves taking part in decisions on which the family security depends – members of a family who are engaged in the family business are almost inevitably drawn into the family's social life as well; the family credit depends so much on the kinds of friends the members of the family make and are seen with. In modern conditions a family that requires its members to work in the family business and to centre their social life on the family circle is making demands that many find difficult to fulfil. The demand is to turn aside opportunities for self-development and satisfaction by working elsewhere and to hold aloof from social activities that might damage the family image; the demand is to put the family before self.

A family combines all of its members effectively only so long as each of them behaves as if the family will endure in spite of births and deaths, and only so far as all subscribe to their dependence on one another. Each member has to believe that his continuing membership is essential to the other members, and, even more, that their membership is essential to himself. However much he may disagree with other members or disapprove of what they do, he must feel bound to them and they to him. Individual action must be compatible with family aspiration, and individual freedom must be curbed or even denied. Success and disgrace are alike shared.

THE MANAGEMENT QUALIFICATIONS OF FAMILY MEMBERS

In most family businesses there comes a time when some family members fail to satisfy the demands that are made upon them; either they are competent but do not want to take the predetermined roles, or they are incompetent and fail the business. Family pressure, often unconsciously exerted, is to help the family, and because the family depends for its living on the family business, the pressure is towards taking a role in the business whatever individual qualifications or inclinations may be.

Moreover, the question of qualifications and inclinations is seldom one that is raised for its own sake: being a member of the family is sufficient; membership needs no other qualification than birth; family loyalties ensure that the competent will serve and that the incompetent will be protected. Often, both qualifications and inclinations are assumed to depend only on family membership and upbringing. But the management of industrial and commercial enterprises demands experience that cannot be gained and skills that cannot be learned in normal family life – even in a family that owns and runs a family business. Judgements about management potential or competence have to be made within the context of an industrial or commercial enterprise, not within a family. We do not want to suggest that, in other than family businesses, judgements by managers about management potential or competence are necessarily accurate and unaffected by personal feelings or prejudice, but at least they are more likely to be made in an appropriate context. In particular, family attitudes towards incompetent members are seldom realistic: these members are believed to be more incompetent than they are and are over-protected; alternatively, their incompetence is denied and they are believed only 'to require some training and experience' in order to be able to fill the roles expected of them.

In some families, of course, there is a conscious attempt not to put pressure on members to take roles in the family business, and success in other fields is applauded. But even in such enlightened families there can often be detected a feeling that, however great the external success, the family has been let down. Indeed, success in another walk of life is frequently taken to mean that if only those who have succeeded had been less selfish they could have made a valuable contribution to what is essential to the family, the family business. Whatever the outcome, family relationships are affected; and when the pressure has been conscious and the escape determined, grief and guilt are often caused. John Betjeman (1960) expresses the feelings vividly in his autobiography:

> . . . *Most of all*
> *I think my father loved me when we went*
> *In early-morning pipe-smoke on the tram*
> *Down to the Angel, visiting the Works,*
> *'Fourth generation – yes, this is the boy.'*
>
> *'Well now, my boy, I want your solemn word*
> *To carry on the firm when I am gone:*
> *Fourth generation John – they'll look to you.'*
>
> *I was a poet. That was why I failed.*
> *My faith in this chimera brought an end*
> *To all my father's hopes. In later years,*
> *Now old and ill, he asked me once again*
> *To carry on the firm, I still refused.*
> *And now when I behold, fresh-published, new,*

A further volume of my verse, I see
His kind eyes look woundedly at mine,
I see his workmen seeking other jobs,
And that red granite obelisk that marks
The family grave in Highgate Cemetery
Points an accusing finger to the sky.

Even when a family member does not want to escape, or acquiesces in his capture, he often has to live down his family membership when he goes into the family business. The assumption made by everybody outside is that he has got his job on his name and not on his qualifications. The trouble is that, consciously or unconsciously, he often agrees with the assumption. The factors that make for success or failure are so complex that usually only the outstandingly good can take full credit for their success, or the outstandingly bad, unreserved blame for their failure. The precious balm of self-respect and self-esteem is not necessarily easy to believe in when there are no proven external criteria by which judgement can be made. A family member entering a family business today has, as a rule, to be manifestly better than others if he and those with whom he works are to accept his position. Indeed, even those who are manifestly better frequently find it difficult to believe that without the family name they could have done as well as they have done. In short, to be as good as outsiders is seldom sufficient comfort for a family member who tries to make an objective appraisal of his management of the family business. In *The organization from within*, Sofer (1961) describes how the major motive for the reorganization of a family business was the recognition by some of the younger members of the family of problems that had been denied in respect of their own appointments. They wanted some change before their children had to face the same problems.

Part of the self-depreciation that is not uncommon among the family members in a family business derives, therefore, from their feelings of guilt about their exploitation of privilege and the wealth they have acquired. In the United Kingdom in the nineteenth and early twentieth centuries, success in father's or grandfather's business could be a matter of pride; but since the Second World War and the social revolution that has accompanied it, the ideal of equal opportunities for all has perhaps had a greater effect on the members of privileged families than has been fully appreciated by those who press them into management succession.

THE EXTENDED FAMILY IN BUSINESS

One special social and psychological problem of the intermingling of family and business organization arises from the different time-scales of family and business leadership, and from the anxieties surrounding the conflict of emotional climates. A family regarded as an open system has many intakes and many outputs. But if it takes as its dominant output the provision of men as top-level executives for a family business, then its major intakes are male babies at the correct intervals. Acceptance of this view can have serious consequences not only for the rest of family life, but for the family business as well. The strains in a family that has to produce sons to carry on the family line and tradition are only too well known; such a demand distorts the relationships of husband and wife and of parents and children. Not only this, but it imposes additional stresses in the relationships between sons and daughters and inevitably provokes expectations, attitudes, and values that can well be at variance with those of contemporary society.

A nuclear family is, broadly speaking, a three-generation reproduction system with a fifty- to sixty-year cycle. A family that takes as its primary task the production of managers with sufficient skill, experience, and maturity to lead industrial or commercial enterprises cannot produce new generations of them at much less than twenty-five-year intervals. In the United Kingdom of the nineteenth century such a time-scale was usually adequate to fit the needs of most industrial and commercial enterprises, though even in those days there was often trouble with the 'old men who would not give up'. Today, rapid change in technology or markets frequently requires an equally rapid change of leadership (Rice, 1963). Indeed, in some of the newer industries, the time-scale of change demanded, if not obtained, is probably no longer than a decade. The problem is not unique to family businesses, and, though there are many industrial leaders whose capacity to adapt to the changes encountered in both enterprise and environment is unquestioned, there are many others whose inflexibility and inability to adapt their organizations to new conditions have led to takeover bids or disaster. Adapting an enterprise to change is never easy; and it is more difficult when the change involves change of leadership as well. In a family business, when the change of leadership involves the son removing the father before the father is ready to go, it can be well-nigh impossible. Even when the father is ready to retire and there are sons of great competence available, the transfer of power can still be frightening.

Families, of course, often have sons at such intervals as will provide for new blood at more frequent intervals than complete generations; but it is a remarkable older brother who can hand over, and a younger one who can accept, responsibility and authority that have been handed down by the father. An extended family also produces children at more frequent intervals than generations, but by the third or fourth generation the relationships between the members of the extended family are often tenuous, and the family name can confer rights out of proportion to obligations. In such circumstances the advantages to be gained from finding top-level managers within the family are often outweighed by the disadvantages deriving from the rights that family membership gives.

THE VALUES OF FAMILY AND BUSINESS

The driving force of industry and commerce in a capitalistic economy is competition: competition for capital for investment, and competition for customers. Any group can be held together by the identification of external enemies; moreover, the internal environment of an enterprise engaged in competition with external rivals tends to be suffused with the same emotional climate: competition for jobs, for wages and salaries, for status and power. Competition is, of course, offset by co-operation in both external and internal environments: externally, with industrial or commercial rivals in research associations, in the exchange of know-how, and in trade agreements; internally, in the support of enterprise policy against external pressure and in personal and institutional loyalties. But in the end it is competitive success that counts.

In contrast, the driving force in a family is its unity – a unity based on the repression or denial of internal conflict.[1] Competition between members must be kept low. In a family business the internal non-competitive culture of the family and the external reality of competition are frequently incompatible. A family business that is sufficiently successful as a business can sometimes afford to ignore its competitors and maintain a consistent family unity, both in the family and in the enterprise. But

---

[1] At the overt level, that is. In Bion's terms (Bion, 1961), at the unconscious level a group that has identified external enemies tends to mobilize the fight-flight basic assumption; a family tends to be sustained by the pairing and dependent basic assumptions.

any loosening of the family ties through tenuous kinship or any reduction in business success may jeopardize the fragile defence against conflict.

Most of the directors of a family business would almost certainly define its primary task as that of making profits. They often add, and with justification, that the 'profit motive' is not, however, allowed to dominate every decision, particularly decisions affecting security of employment. Their detractors might argue that security of employment is reserved only for the members of the family and for those employees who both accept and respect the family status. While there may be some truth in this for many family businesses, it is our experience, gained from those with whom we have worked, that the concern shown for their employees by the family members of the board of directors is sincere and unselfish. In one firm we noticed a very old man who, whenever we saw him, was sitting on a chair at a doorway between two departments. He was usually asleep, or nodding. When we asked what his job was, we were told:

'His work – well, I suppose it's to draw his wages.'

And when we inquired further:

'He's been here for nearly sixty years. He can't do anything, but it would break his heart if we made him retire. Nominally his job is to inspect the goods as they go from one department to the other. It's not necessary, but it would be a poor look-out if we couldn't keep him on after all he's given us.'

But this very personal concern, as we shall see, can also be a powerful constraint when modernization and expansion are required.

In the next chapter we discuss two import-conversion-export processes: the first, the finding of capital for modernization and expansion; and the second, the recruitment and retention of managers, scientists, and technicians.

CHAPTER 10

Constraints on Growth and Change in the Family Business

Two major difficulties eventually beset the average family business: first, it needs more capital than the family can provide; and second, it runs short of the necessary highly skilled managers.

Most modern industries are competitive and the rate of technical change in them is increasing. Even without expansion, methods of work and equipment have to be modernized more rapidly than formerly, if a competitive position is to be maintained. Modernization, in manufacturing industries certainly, and in other industries frequently, requires greatly increased capital expenditure. In addition, the growing affluence in western society demands expansion of those enterprises that provide goods and services through mass production. Except, therefore, for enterprises that make specialized components for other industries, or work in small specialized markets, growth is usually a condition of survival in modern industrial society. Under these conditions those enterprises that do not expand are at the mercy of those that do, and these, by their greater size and power, dominate the price structure of the market. The smaller enterprises are eventually taken over or go out of business. It does not appear to be possible to stand still. In other words, even to survive, an enterprise in any of the consumer industries has to expand. Expansion also requires larger capital expenditure. Modern taxation limits the ability of any enterprise to continue to finance its increased capital needs from its own surpluses and other savings. Ordinary borrowing is also limited because the recurrent credit squeezes and various fiscal policies cut down the capacity of banks and other financial institutions to lend. Any recourse to other methods of financing usually leads ultimately to the sacrifice of some part of the voting equity.

Highly skilled managers are similarly hard to find. Those who are capable of keeping pace with modern developments and of making the correct critical decisions in the formation and implementation of strategic policy can usually command not only high salaries but also positions of power. If, whatever salaries or stock options are offered, only the members of a specific biological family can attain the ultimate power, highly skilled managers who are not members of the family are unlikely to be recruited, or, if recruited, are unlikely to stay. It does not matter how welcome they are made; if they are treated as adopted children but without the power of succession, they invariably leave.

THE SOURCES OF CAPITAL AND THE CONSTRAINTS OF FAMILY CONTROL

The occasion was a discussion between the virtual owner of a family business and a very able and senior manager who was an acknowledged technical specialist in his own field. The owner was formally the chairman and managing director; informally he was also the sales director, working through a nominal sales manager. The only other members of the board were non-working members of the chairman's family. The manager had been with the company for a long time and, though not a director, had high status and was held in high esteem, and indeed affection, by all the family. He usually attended the so-called 'board' meetings; the only ones he did not attend were those at which the dividend was decided, and the many informal ones that were not recognized as such, at which the family talked about themselves and their aspirations for their children.

The discussion was about the technical developments necessary for the production programme for the following year. Both the chairman (in his informal capacity as sales director) and the manager had been working for some time on the possibility of introducing a new product. The manager was presenting his final plan. He explained his plan lucidly and competently, displayed all his knowledge and experience, and made an overwhelming case for the capital investment required. When the discussion started it was between colleagues who each recognized the other's expertise in his own field; the one in production, the other in marketing. The chairman listened carefully to the production plan and accepted its validity for sales policy. But after some discussion of technical points it gradually became apparent that for some undisclosed reason he did not want to go ahead. The chairman could not easily explain his reluctance, even to himself; and in his difficulty he got confused and the manager became angry. An argument started; at first it was still between colleagues; but in a very short time the manager found himself talking to a managing director who was overriding his technical adviser. As the argument grew more heated the manager found himself talking to a chairman who 'had to discuss it with the board before I can give a decision'. The manager knew at once, of course, that the board was going to be blamed for turning the plan down. He had known his chairman for a long time, and was used to being frank and direct; he became personal, and pointed out, with some force, that the board had neither the knowledge nor the experience to decide. He then openly accused the chairman of using the board as a cloak for his own dislike of the plan. The chairman immediately retreated into his role as owner:

'All right, all right, but it's my bloody money and you're not going to get it.'

The question of who was right is perhaps less interesting than the reflection that, in a discussion about an operating decision, the chairman closed the argument by introducing a role, the power of which could not be matched by the subordinate concerned. The subordinate could hardly avoid feeling that the decision had been made on inadequate grounds and that his work and reputation were going to suffer for apparently irrelevant reasons.

The sources of capital, which is the intake of the import-conversion-export process of investment, are shareholders, banks, and other loan-making agencies; the destinations of outputs are government, which takes taxes; shareholders, who receive dividends; banks, which receive interest on, and repayment of, their loans; and companies in which surplus is reinvested. In most enterprises there is occasional conflict about the raising of new capital and the allocation of profits – whether to reinvest or to pay larger dividends. In a public company with multiple shareholding, the directors have to take into account their shareholders' expectations; at least, if they do not do so, the annual general meeting may become something more than a mere formality. But provided the directors of such a public company do not fear a takeover bid, they are not particularly concerned with the identification of their shareholders or with what the shareholders do with the dividends once they are paid. In a family business, on the other hand, when the shareholders are members of the same family, demands for increased capital and competition between further investment and immediate income are aggravated by intimate knowledge of personal need and concern about expenditure. When the non-working members of a family want to put more wealth into the family business, there is little problem. But when they have deep interests in other activities for which they want all the money they can get, decisions can be difficult. The situation is exacerbated when the activities into which they wish to put their money are disapproved of by the family. Decisions about investment and the distribution of profits are then determined by family relationships instead of by business needs. There are many examples, some sad and some funny, of families broken and businesses ruined as a result of family humours: the son, now head of the family business, who could not control his widowed mother's extravagance because she, with her daughters, had more shares than he; the chairman's dominating wife who insisted on doing 'good' for the reluctant wives of his employees; and the widow who 'milked' the family business to support an organization that was trying to suppress the products of the business.

In any business, whether family, private, or public, the qualification for ownership is shareholding and the power of ownership is directly related to the proportion of shares held, together with the size of the holdings of those who can be relied upon for support in any conflict. In a family business, however, the power of ownership can be reinforced or weakened by the relationships between the members of the family. If the opponents to family power can be identified as outsiders, whether in reality or by unconscious projection, family support can usually be counted on. The projection of hostility onto the outside world is a mechanism whereby the power of ownership can be kept in the collective holding of the family. Any suggestion of withdrawal from the family, therefore, however small, can become a major threat to family unity. Even when the holding that might be withdrawn does not itself cause embarrassment by its size, the very act of withdrawing is a threat to the assumptions on which family unity depends. When the business requires extra capital, the need to buy out even a comparatively small family shareholder can raise financial difficulties; and, still more disturbing, the suspicion that the family might be breaking up can appear as a major disaster.

If there are no formal arrangements – in the sense of a family holding company or some other institutionalized means of carrying out economic planning and investment tactics – decisions about what to invest in and how much are usually taken by those members of the family who work in the family business. Support for their decisions is based, for the most part, on family trust and not on judgements about the merits of the investments themselves. This method serves well when the investments are not large and the results, on the whole, are satisfactory. But modern technologies tend to require increasing capital, and new investments are accordingly larger. Not all members of the family may find it as easy to accept the risk to such a large proportion of their capital, or even worse, their credit.

In addition, if the past rate of investment has assured an adequate income, the need to make larger investments in modernization and expansion may, temporarily at least, reduce it. This can create difficulties when those family members whose wealth is tied up in the family business need to maximize their income for personal reasons. Their support is based on family unity, but family unity, in its turn, is based on the assumption that individual needs are the same as family needs. Conflict between the needs, on the one hand, for modernization and expansion of the business, and, on the other, for personal spending, makes the non-working members of the family begin to doubt both the judgement and the competence of its working members. When non-working members have no means of judging the merit of the proposals put forward about particular investments, they usually appear to be driven to argue about investment as though the working members' need for it were as personal as their own need for income.

In this kind of situation decisions about whether to invest and what to invest in tend to be taken, not because they are necessarily the best business decisions, but because of family feelings, and the attitudes of non-working members towards the working members who are trying to take them. The boundary between an investment task, the operating companies invested in, and the family becomes confused, and control is thereby weakened or lost.

THE SOURCES OF MANAGEMENT AND THE CONSTRAINTS OF FAMILY CONTROL

In a family business, family members who work as operating managers not only have to make day-to-day management decisions but, in making them, have to deal with the stress of investment decisions as well. They operate at investment and operating levels at the same time. In a small business, the making of key decisions at both levels by one man or a small group can be reassuring; but, as the scale of both operations and investment increases, the differences in the kind of thinking required can inhibit decisions at the two levels. Moreover, in relation to other managers who are not part of the family, the additional role of owner-ship with its power can, as we have seen, exacerbate disagreements and lead to endless frustrations. In other words, members of a family working as managers of operating companies always carry at least three roles, and hence have at least three task boundaries to control: ownership, in-vestment, and company operations. Confusion between them can fre-quently lead to unbalanced arguments and inappropriate conclusions.

A time comes in most successful family businesses when they expand to the point at which there are not enough members of the family to fill all the jobs that give power over family investment. And these jobs are not confined to general management: they include technical roles as well. At any one time it is possible to identify a function that can determine to a considerable extent, by the way in which it is carried out, the success or failure of a particular company. For some firms marketing presents the most serious problems; for some, production; for others, buying; for still others, the technical research and development that are required to keep them ahead of their competitors. Families usually assume that overall management will remain in the hands of a family member; and, with increased specialization, they may also begin to feel that a specialist skill that can have a decisive influence on success should be retained in the family as well. Only in this way can they be sure of its use for their own benefit. They appear, therefore, reluctant to appoint the well-qualified outsider.

In practice, however, in a successful family business it is never easy to decide whether failure to appoint sufficiently well-qualified outsiders is because the family will not let go of the positions of potential power or because well-qualified outsiders are unwilling to accept the conditions under which they are expected to work. Our own experience certainly suggests that the suppressed and often denied hostility between family members themselves is a major contributory cause of their reluctance to take on outsiders. But it is seldom easy to make any simple cause-and-effect diagnosis. It is as though the introduction of outsiders might intro-duce a mechanism that would release the latent violence within the family. It is for this reason, perhaps, that many families that see quite clearly the need to introduce outsiders into the business on which their wealth depends nevertheless, irrationally, and sometimes even suicidally, refuse to take the obvious action. As a piece of reality they know that family resources are inadequate, but they fear so much the weakening of family power and hence family dissolution that, at the unconscious level at least, they prefer the disease to the cure. A family that, while remaining united, can produce a management succession and at the same time use its inherent violence to compete successfully in business affairs is indeed both skilful and fortunate.

What is certainly true is that such *technically* competent outsiders as are recruited to family businesses, and stay there, are people who do not appear to want to exploit the power their skill gives them to demand ultimate managerial authority for themselves. They may frequently complain about the stranglehold the family maintains on directorships, at least on the directorships that matter, but we cannot avoid the conviction that the last thing most of them really want is family abdication. Unconsciously at least, they want to be treated like minor, and hence underprivileged, members of the family. But in return for their lower status and their acceptance of the roles they have been assigned, they expect to be looked after not only while they are at the height of their powers, but also when they grow older and can no longer do so much.

Those who are skilful and are content with a dependent position can be valuable members of any enterprise; but their usefulness is limited when, because of expansion or other developments, they have to take initiative and hold independent commands. Inevitably they demand that their decisions shall be endorsed from above, and hence their superiors become burdened with detailed work and, in addition, responsible for decisions about which they can have only a superficial knowledge. This matters less if the superiors can depend completely on their expert subordinates; but it is always difficult for them to discover whether the advice they are being given is the best advice available, or a function of the dependent relationship. They can never be sure that they are not being told what their subordinates think they want to hear.

The predicament is not confined to family businesses: it happens in almost every enterprise, both industrial and non-industrial. It is, however, in a family business that the problem is seen in its most acute form, since the family firm is one that actively encourages the emotional climate of the family. It is a climate in which established relationships are, within limits, more important than performance. Indeed, one of the difficulties of converting a family business into one that is less personally managed is that the managers who have served it well for many years, and to whom responsibility and authority would naturally fall, are seldom people who could succeed in the new positions available to them.

Even family businesses that have introduced elaborate management development schemes, with their concomitant selection and training procedures, often find that their best recruits frequently use them only as a training ground and then move on, usually in their early thirties, into public companies where artificial barriers to promotion are not built into the organization. A major preoccupation among the managers of family businesses is the calculation of the ages and intentions of family members. Sofer (1961), indeed, gives an example of a family member – one who had acquired membership through marriage – who resigned when he discovered that the vacancy on the board, on which he had had his eye for some years, was to be given to his much younger brother-in-law, a direct descendant of the founder. He goes on to point out that an inadequate middle management is inseparable from reserving top posts for the family.

Nor does the offer of directorships, with or without high salaries, necessarily provide sufficient attraction for ambitious and capable men. We have often heard family members say: 'We are prepared to pay them as much as we earn ourselves.' They even forget sometimes that their income from the business is not dependent only on their salaries; or, if they take little from the business in dividends, they tend to ignore that the reinvestment of profits is enhancing their own wealth. They are disappointed and even embittered when the response to their offer is meagre. It is not so much title or even financial reward that the ambitious man wants: it is the opportunity to exercise power. While the real power remains, and looks like remaining, only with the members of the family, he will not stay. In consequence, those who do stay, no matter how high a position they may reach or how capable they may be, are usually people to whom belonging to the family is more important than working in the business. In their make-up is an over-determined need to perpetuate some element of an unrecognized and unresolved childhood dependence.

On the other hand it is, of course, true that managers of operating companies can be effective only if they have the necessary authority to discharge their responsibilities. In most industrially advanced societies, good operating managers are so scarce as to derive power from their scarcity, and the power of owners to lay down conditions that are not agreed by operational managers is, therefore, limited. While the scarcity lasts, the power of ownership can be expected to diminish. When disagreement is unresolved, the final sanction of the owners is to remove capital; that of operating managers to resign. Managers, however, have only their jobs to lose; provided that their loss is not too easily blamed on their own incompetence, they can move to another job elsewhere. For the owners of a family business the application of their final sanction may change their whole way of life.

Today, survival in business depends on the adequate exploitation of current ideas and the readiness to accept new ones. For a family business this means that its successive generations have to be prepared to discard not only what was acceptable previously, but what their own intimate mentors and teachers believe and practise. The rapidly changing technical demands of industry and commerce already place a high premium on managerial quality and skill. The margin of safety is reduced with every increase in capital investment. The time will soon be past when any company can face competition for more than a short time with inadequate managers and technicians. As the speed of technical change continues to increase, so also will the speed of run-down of inadequately staffed companies. If, then, the family business fails to attract good managers, particularly to attract and keep those whose strategic judgement is good, it means that an extra strain is thrown on working family members. The premium on their being successful businessmen is high; if they are going to preserve the top positions for themselves and avoid feeling guilty about the opportunities they have pre-empted and denied to others, then they have to be successful. But this high premium means that their risk-taking decisions have to be taken under conditions that might well be thought to preclude good judgement. It is true that, while both the business and the number of family members participating remain small, the entrepreneurs are free from the responsibility for others' money; but when the family has extended to several generations and the business has expanded beyond the family resources, the corresponding increase in the number who depend for their livelihood on the business intensifies both risk-taking and strain.

SOME ADAPTIVE MECHANISMS

Two of the more usual mechanisms by which families try, sometimes successfully, to retain control of their own businesses have already been adumbrated: the introduction of sons-in-law, and the separation of the organizations for the tasks of investment and the management of operating companies.

To enlarge itself by introducing the husbands of marriageable daughters into its business, as well as into the family, is perhaps the most natural solution for a family to try: it is certainly very common. A difficulty, however, of admitting sons-in-law into a family business is that they have been brought up by a different family, and, though they may well continue the business as a family business, a different family may come to power. Indeed, many successful family businesses have remained successful only by extending the family further than was originally intended, with consequent conflict and disorder among later generations. In contrast, in other cases one cannot but get the impression that the men of the family would rather that power went right outside than that they should risk establishing a matrilineal succession. Moreover, the solution of extending the family depends not only on there being a sufficient number of marriageable daughters to marry the required number of husbands, but also on the preparedness of both daughters and husbands to accept, as a condition of marriage, that the husbands should be both qualified and willing to take roles in the family business. Of late, daughters and their husbands have shown themselves less ready to comply with such conditions than were their predecessors of the nineteenth and early twentieth centuries.

A more sophisticated method of dealing with the problems of family and business is to examine the multiple tasks carried out by the family sentient group, and to devise an appropriate organization for each. If the qualification for ownership is shareholding, then the task organization appropriate to ownership is one that fits the task of initiating and steering investments – an investment trust or a holding company. The qualification for taking a role in such an organization is the ability to take decisions about, and to control, investments. The principal boundaries that have to be controlled are those between investors and what they invest in. Ownership gives the right to determine the conditions in which capital shall be invested or withheld, and the task of investment management is to implement the wishes of shareholders in the light of available possibilities. If no family members are competent to make investment decisions, then the investments can be managed professionally on behalf of a family trust. If, on the other hand, the family gives priority to providing jobs for its members without their having to compete with outsiders, then the kind and scale of business they run may have to be modified to suit their competence. If the maintenance of family unity is given overriding priority, then it may have to be recognized that selling out and giving up the family business are the only solution.

The conclusion is that a modern industrial enterprise can survive as a family business only with the most exceptional of families. But although, in these two chapters, we have taken family businesses to illustrate some of the problems that occur when the boundaries of multiple task and sentient systems coincide, and there is no adequate differentiation of task and sentient groups, these problems are not unique to family businesses. They exist for any group that cannot adequately differentiate between, on the one hand, its task and the resources required for its performance, and, on the other hand, its assumptions about itself as a group and the interpersonal relationships involved. This is characteristic of those institutions whose culture and structure are outdated by changes in their environment. A group or an institution created to perform any task establishes a culture of its own – a set of customs, expectations, and attitudes – that is maintained by the emotional ties between its members. The viability of the culture depends on the effectiveness of task performance, and on the satisfaction of need, including defences against anxiety, that it provides for its members. If the task, or its method of performance, changes without any corresponding change in organization and culture, then emotional ties appropriate to an earlier task or environment persist and interfere with the judgements and decisions that the change demands.

Strong personal ties between the members of the elite of any institution can be a valuable means of supporting and reinforcing its leadership; but they can be disastrous when, because of change in the environment or in the institution, its leadership is no longer effective, and the personal ties lead to inappropriate appointments or to the denial of the need to change.

PART IV

Temporary and Transitional Task Systems

K

Introduction

In Part II we were concerned with transactions between an enterprise and its environment. We used two familiar examples, the job of a sales representative and the task of dry cleaning, to illustrate some of the management control problems that arise when the nature of the task prevents task boundaries from coinciding with, or being included in, the organizational boundaries of enterprises. We saw that organizations derived from typical production systems could not provide adequate boundary controls and that simple management hierarchies gave an inappropriate fit between organization and primary task performance. We also saw that when sentient-group and task-group boundaries could not coincide, special mechanisms had to be introduced to control the relations between them.

In Part III we turned our attention to the control problems that arise when multiple tasks are undertaken by the same group, and when the boundaries of multiple-activity systems and sentient-group boundaries all coincide. We used the management of a typical family business to illustrate the confusion between task definitions and criteria for performance when members' commitment to their family group overshadows their commitment to business performance. We saw that, in conditions of technological and social change, the attitudes and behaviour of members of a group to each other and to the external environment may not only jeopardize the survival of the enterprise, but put such strain on internal group relationships that group survival is also jeopardized.

In Part IV we propose to illustrate the proposition that temporary and transitional activity systems, and their equivalent 'project organizations', form the most appropriate basis for a general theory of organization. The essential feature of a project type of organization is that the group brought together to perform a particular task has to be disbanded as soon as the task is completed. The group as a group has no further *raison d'être* in terms of task performance. An extreme example of this we have already seen in respect of the speciality salesman, whose task is to get an order and to get out. Any prolongation of the relationship based on the task system is wasteful and, from the point of view of task perform-ance, unnecessary.

We shall see, however, when we come to consider research activities, that the theoretically finite life of a project team within a research enter-prise is frequently prolonged as a result of redefinition of its task or of the accretion of new tasks. A research team, either because it has invented a new technique or because its members have become devoted to work-ing together, generates further problems to which it can apply its tech-nique, or which will keep the team intact – irrespective of whether the generated problems are relevant to the overall task of the research enter-prise.

It is sometimes possible to recognize at a particular point in time that the system of activities has changed – that the activities are drawing upon a different intake and working towards a different output – but the boundary between the original and the current task system is blurred or invisible. Thus a major managerial problem is to make these boun-daries more explicit and to exert greater control over them. To accom-plish this, it is necessary deliberately to create task-oriented sentient groups whose boundaries differ from those of the activity systems.

The construction industry provides a further example of a project type of organization – one in which, however, the task-oriented sentient boundaries already exist. The task is much more clear-cut. If the required 'output' is, say, a block of flats or a bridge, the necessary intakes of building materials can be readily prescribed and so, too, can the activities needed to convert the materials into the product. Completion of the project provides a clearly visible boundary. Finishing off, tidying up, and dealing with defects may give room for marginal disagreements in the definition of this boundary, but these are normally overcome by a formal procedure of hand-over to the client or purchaser and by the contractual definition of the construction team's outstanding responsi-bilities after that date.

As a corollary of this greater precision in the definition both of the boundaries of the task and of the activities required to carry it out, the construction industry has to provide organizational mechanisms through which project teams can be formed and disbanded. The integrated, 'package-deal' contracting firm, which incorporates in its own organ-ization architects, quantity surveyors, civil and structural engineers, and similar professional personnel, as well as various categories of skilled and unskilled workmen, is a recent innovation in Britain and still the exception. More normally, the task-oriented sentient groups of the building industry have separate organizational embodiments in the different 'firms' of architects, surveyors, specialist contractors, and so on. Beyond these, and often reinforcing the specialisms of the firms, are the various professional institutes and the different trade unions for craftsmen and unskilled workers.

Thus a specific construction project may mobilize a team consisting of members of different firms of architects, consulting engineers, and quantity surveyors, as well as contractors and subcontractors specializing in piling, structural steelwork, scaffolding, plumbing, plastering, painting, and other building trades. The diverse activities that they contribute to the task pose complex problems of co-ordination. Project management in this sense is often the responsibility of one of the contributory firms, which acts as the 'sponsor' of the project in relation to the client;[1] nowadays the sponsor could be an architect, a consulting engineer, a quantity surveyor, or the main contractor. Sometimes, under a direct building arrangement, an experienced client acts as his own sponsor/project manager.

In contrast to research, where management may have to contend with a stronger sentient boundary around a project team than is appropriate to its task, the problem for construction management is to integrate, for the duration of the project, the activities of inherently fissiparous groups and individuals whose primary allegiance is not to the specific project team. Sometimes it is the firm that is the more sentient, sometimes the professional or craft affiliation: inter-firm mobility is particularly high in this industry.

The firms themselves are committed to different, and to some extent incompatible, primary tasks. For example, the primary task of the architect – whether this is an individual or a firm – is to make a profit by making and 'selling' designs. To this end he will want the product to be a building that demonstrates his architectural skills and thereby attracts commissions from new clients and esteem from professional colleagues. The task of the building contractor, on the other hand, requires him to seek out time-saving and cost-saving methods and to secure the most economic deployment of his labour force. Such objectives may be incompatible with those of the architect. It is then the task of the project manager to mediate among these various considerations and to arrive at an optimal solution. But it need scarcely be said that definitions of 'optimal' will differ. If the architect is also the sponsor/project manager, the resolution he reaches is likely to be quite different from the one that the contractor would reach if the control were in his hands; and neither answer would necessarily be 'optimal' from the client's point of view. 'Optimization' may, indeed, be an over-kind term for what is essentially a process of compromise in which the relative power of different parties within the project team will, in its effect on the characteristics of the final product, be at least as significant as the inherent requirements of the project itself.

We shall use building as our first example; specifically, the building of a new works. In the building of a new works some of the control problems of the construction industry may be simplified if, as in this instance, the 'sponsor' is the client enterprise commissioning the new plant and new factory. The co-ordination of the specialist skills required for building and plant installation is, however, complicated by the need to build and man an organization to run the new works, as soon as or even before the actual construction is finished. Often, members of the client enterprise take part in the design and construction of the plant itself and thus change roles, and role relationships, when design and construction cease and operations begin. More formally, we can state that, as design and construction activity systems cease to be required, the task groups are disbanded. Most of their members move on to other projects but retain membership of their professional sentient groups. But other members of design and construction groups join new task groups in the new works that have different primary tasks, and at the same time lose any temporary membership they might have acquired in the established sentient groups of the construction industry.

Our second example is taken from research enterprises – academic, government, and industrial. We shall see that academic traditions of research work lead to coincident task and sentient groups within academic disciplines, but that the resulting organization is inappropriate in many research enterprises of government and industry and that even in academic institutions research that requires a multidisciplinary approach is frequently inhibited.

The last example in Part IV is taken from the transport industry. In it, we examine the organization of a scheduled airline during a period of expansion and increasing competition. We shall show that flying, by its nature, can be managed only through a project-type organization, and that the organization of ground operations, though usually conceived of as a simple production system with its concomitant management hierarchy, basically requires project management as well. But to achieve this, new forms of organization and new technologies have to be invented.

CHAPTER 11

Organizational Boundaries in the Building of a New Works

Superficially, it might seem that the task of setting up a new works is no different from other construction tasks. A bridge will be crossed by motorists; a block of flats inhabited by families. And, in the same way, new factory buildings will be populated by workers and their management. There are, however, significant differences.

Bridge-building presents the simplest problem. The users of a bridge will travel in a variety of vehicles to a variety of destinations, but all share a common need to cross the bridge. The designers have to provide a means whereby they can do so, in appropriate numbers, safely and quickly.

The local authority commissioning a block of flats faces a more difficult problem. Planners and architects are nowadays well aware that they have to provide more than living-space; they are creating a 'built environment' (Holford, 1965). The way in which blocks of flats are disposed will affect community relationships by encouraging some patterns of interaction and inhibiting others. Internally, the design has to satisfy the common needs of those who will use the flats, while at the same time allowing each family as much flexibility as possible in satisfying its own idiosyncratic needs. The client, however, is a local authority, and except in the rare event that a councillor or official actually occupies one of the new flats, is not the ultimate user. And even in that rare event he does not occupy it as a councillor or official, but as a private citizen.

The enterprise commissioning a new works has a still more complex problem. Its task is not merely to provide an environment but actually to create a production system. The setting-up process is fully complete not when the shell of the factory is erected, nor when the plant is installed, but when the new production system is effectively importing its raw materials and converting them into the products it was designed to make – in other words, carrying out its own operating task.

To achieve its task the new works requires more than plant and buildings; it requires human resources as well. As an ongoing production system it must activate the physical and human resources in a purposeful way. The building of a new works therefore includes:

(a) *Plant design and building:* the provision of machinery and equipment and other physical resources.

(b) *Organization design and building:* the provision of human resources in the form of people trained to occupy roles in the system. Also under this heading is the task of establishing an organizational setting that allows the people to form appropriate groupings within sentient boundaries that reinforce task requirements; and this entails creating a system of technical and managerial controls.

And these two building processes must be related to each other in such a way that the emergent production system achieves an appropriate integration of physical and human activities.

PLANT-DESIGN AND -BUILDING SYSTEMS

Within the construction task, two distinct systems of activity can be identified: design and building. The relation between client and construction systems is shown in *Figure 23*.

Intakes into the design system are client requirements and constraints. Conversion activities deploy technical skills to solve problems posed by

FIGURE 23 *The relation between client and construction systems*

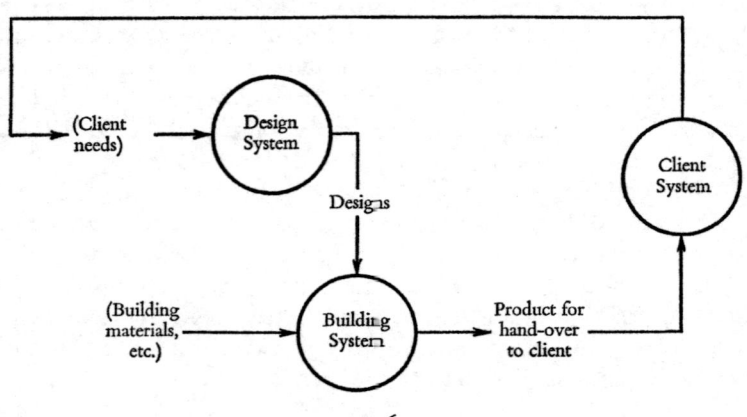

these requirements and constraints. The output is a set of designs that specify the task of the building system and provide the yardsticks against which building activities can be programmed and monitored.

The completed design, then, becomes the control for the building system. It provides blueprints and specifications against which the necessary supplies are procured and converted, by mechanical and manual activities, into the desired end-result. Organizationally, for any complex building, the construction system comprises simultaneous or successive activities provided by different contracting groups whose sentient boundaries cut deeply across the specific construction task boundary. The compromises, however, have largely been made in the design system – this has defined the building task – and the dominant managerial problem in construction is to integrate the activities that the various groups concerned have contracted to carry out. Critical path analysis and similar techniques are now increasingly used as tools to this end.

The relationship between design and building poses complex problems of boundary control. These problems are minimized when there is no overlap in the successive phases of the construction process. In this ideal situation, the design is completed and has been approved by the client, and a full bill of quantities is prepared, before tenders are invited. The selected contractors have accepted comprehensive and precise blueprints and specifications to which they must work, and the fitting together of the various activities by different contractors has been arranged. And nothing goes wrong.

But even in the production of familiar commodities, such as the similar houses of a building estate, such an ideal is seldom realized, and in the building of a new works, never. Construction problems, unknown at the design stage, can lead to modifications in design; and experienced contractors with their specialized skills and resources may be able to make contributions that offer technically superior or more economic solutions to design problems. In addition, the construction of any new plant on a large scale inevitably involves the making of both design and building decisions during building itself. In a time of increasingly rapid technical change it is quite certain that, in the period between the decision to build and the opening of the new plant, new techniques and new equipment will become available. Whether to ignore them and thus avoid interference with design, building, and manning, but accept premature obsolescence; or to introduce them and put up with delays and disputes, is frequently an uncomfortable if not impossible dilemma.

ORGANIZATION-DESIGN AND -BUILDING SYSTEMS

The systems of activity required for organization-building can be seen as basically similar to those for plant-building. The task of the organization-design system is to design the work roles and their interrelationship for the future works. Included within this task is the formulation of all policies and procedures that govern or affect such relationships. The emergent design then becomes the plan against which to regulate the activities of the organization-building system. These are: to recruit and select those who will occupy roles within the future operating organization, to train them for the activities they have to perform, to develop the required interrelations between them, and, more generally, to procure their commitment to the new plant and its task, through appropriate task-oriented sentient groups.

RELATIONS BETWEEN PLANT AND ORGANIZATION SYSTEMS

We can thus identify four constituent task systems in the setting-up process required to produce a new works: plant design, plant-building, organization design, and organization-building. Whether they are recognized or not, they must be carried out. As *Figure 24* shows, these four systems converge upon a fifth, the future operating system, which has its own primary task as an ongoing production system.

As *Figure 24* also suggests, the activities of the setting-up process as a whole have the characteristics of a system in that the outcome – the operating system – is affected not only by the work done within the two designing and two building systems, but also by the way in which these systems are related to each other. We shall try to illustrate this in the next chapter. We shall see, further, that although the operating system is in one sense the end-product of the setting-up process, it is in a very real sense present from the very beginning. Initially in the form of a vision or objective, it constitutes an intake into the plant-design and organization-design systems; subsequently, it becomes a progressively more concrete reality as the plant- and organization-building systems complete their tasks.

Unless, however, the overall project is extremely small, it is unlikely that those involved in the constituent systems will share an identical, comprehensive view of the whole. For most of those in the plant-design and -building systems, the completion of the project will be the end of

FIGURE 24 *Basic model of the setting-up system for a new works*

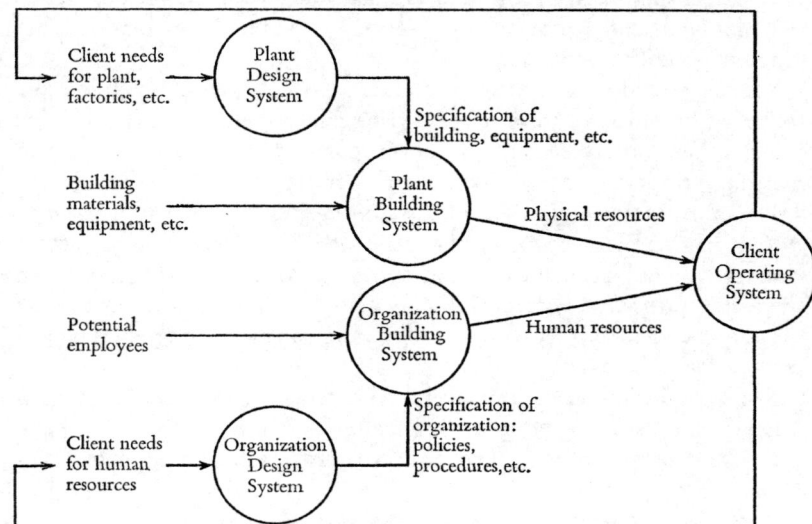

their direct association with it; for most of those in the organization-design and -building systems, on the other hand, the completion of the project is the beginning of the task they have been recruited to perform. In one sense, therefore, the management of the setting-up process can be regarded as an exercise in reconciling different perceptions of the final goal. But the extent of the difference, of course, can vary immensely. At one extreme, the goal may be simply to reproduce a plant and an organization already in operation elsewhere; here the scope for different perceptions is less. At the other extreme, both the technology and the form of organization in the proposed operating system may be new and unfamiliar.

We have said that in an 'ideal' situation – ideal, that is, from the point of view of the building systems – detailed blueprints for both plant and organization would be completed before building started. We have also said that such an ideal is seldom likely to be realized, and have implied that, even if it were, it would be unlikely to provide an 'ideal' solution for the resulting operating system. In the Introduction to Part IV we have referred to the intrusion of the values and beliefs of external professional sentient groups into the plant-design and -building systems.

We saw, however, that in the construction of a new works the 'client' may be the sponsor who acts as co-ordinator between the various activities involved, and hence as controller of the boundaries between the different activity systems.

In such a composite system it is clearly possible to devise alternative forms of organization that relate constituent systems to each other, or insulate them, in a variety of ways. Moreover, an individual or a group may take roles in only one system or in more than one, either successively or simultaneously. To take a simple example, an engineer may move from project work in the plant-design system to construction management in the plant-building system and then to maintenance in the future operating system. We shall need to study particularly closely the consequences of integrating or separating the plant-design and organization-design systems.

Figure 25 depicts an organizational arrangement of the setting-up process which is perhaps the most frequently used in industry. Here, plant design and plant-building have priority. Organization design, which is

FIGURE 25 *A conventional setting-up system*

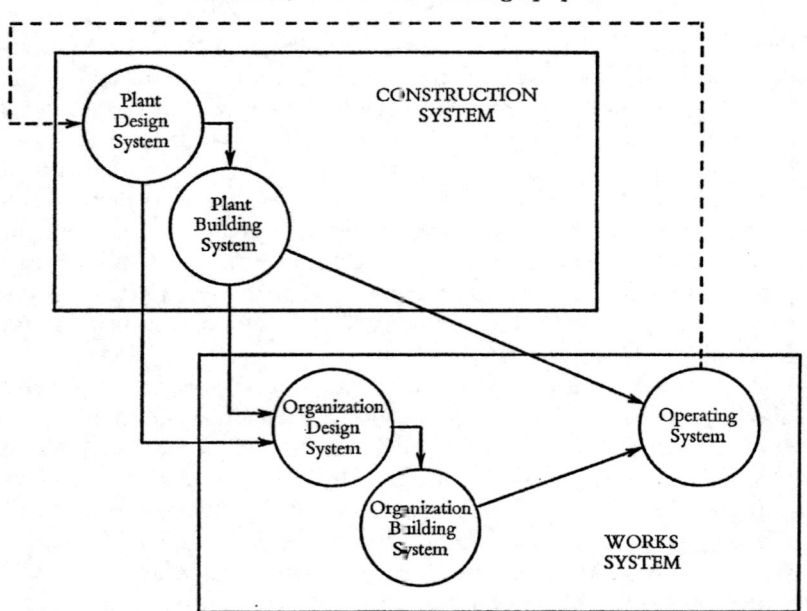

usually the responsibility of the managers who are going to be operating the plant, does not begin until plant design and building are nearly or entirely complete. It is perceived as contingent on plant design. Organization design, in the sense of matching human resources to the pattern of activities in such a way as to ensure effective performance of the primary task and satisfaction of human need, is minimal. It tends rather to consist of adapting already familiar organizational forms and practices to the specific technical constraints that have already been designed into the new situation.

There are several reasons for giving priority to plant design and building. First, the initial decisions required in building a new plant are mainly technical and economic. Second, the costs of a new works are largely costs of plant and of construction. Third, particularly if the works is a large one, the logistic problems of bringing together the materials, the equipment, the variety of construction workers, are considerable; and again, because of the expenses involved, tend to overshadow the problems of designing the future operating organization and recruiting and training personnel for it.

Explicable though it may be, this emphasis on plant design and plant-building and the relegation of organization design and organization-building to a secondary and dependent position can have unfortunate consequences. If plant design has priority while organization is assumed to be uniquely predetermined by the technology, or else inherited, so to speak, from previous works, then any appropriate differentiation of activity-system boundaries and sentient-group boundaries is largely a matter of chance. Unforeseen inconsistencies between the requirements of the activity systems and the social and psychological needs of those who occupy roles in these systems will give rise to processes of accommodation through which the activity systems are distorted, or alternatively, if these are maintained, then human needs will be frustrated. Characteristically, either type of distortion will give rise to a need to strengthen both monitoring processes within the activity systems and managerial controls over activity-system boundaries. In other words, the operating system, once started, will produce its own compromises to overcome conflict between technical and human requirements that has not been dealt with in the design phase. Processes of accommodation are never complete because of the organic nature of an industrial enterprise, which is constantly changing, growing, adapting, and regenerating itself. But if organization design is treated as the dependent variable, or neglected, then the amount of accommodation in the early operating stages will be correspondingly greater and this is likely to lead to lowered standards of performance, not only while the plant is running in, but also later.

If one accepts that the organization of the operating system one is trying to create needs to marry human and physical resources for task performance, then it would seem to follow that such problems can be borne in mind and forestalled in the initial designing process. In other words, by integrating plant design and organization design it becomes possible to take account of constraints and to anticipate and work out many of the problems of accommodation at the early drawing-board stage. We believe that this is both possible and desirable and that some of the adverse consequences of the conventional approach in organizing the setting-up system can be overcome. On the other hand, the integration of plant design and organization design sets up other organizational groupings, which have consequential difficulties of their own.

In the next chapter we propose to examine a specific case, and to analyse it in the light of the organizational model we have discussed in this chapter.

CHAPTER 12

The Building of a New Steel Works

The material for this chapter is taken from a project[1] carried out during the building of a new steel works on a 'green-field' site. It was built by an old-established company, itself the result of an amalgamation of many other smaller companies, which, in the course of the growth and development of the industry, had been overtaken by its competitors in terms of equipment, technology, and expansion. It had been the European pioneer of the continuous production of wide steel strip, and, like most pioneers, had shown the way to its competitors who, entering the field at a later date, had benefited from its experience. Its works, its technology, and its members were ageing.

The company's investment in the new works needs to be considered, therefore, from two points of view: not only was an immense financial investment involved, but also a major emotional investment. The new works on a green-field site would be the means of regenerating the company. The process of building became the repository of the company's hopes for the future. The green field was the one place where (in the words of the managing director) the company could

'build unrestricted and unhampered by site, existing plant, outmoded ideas, tradition and unmovable staff and operatives. It is the one place where no concessions need to be made to costly, worn-out equipment, techniques, technology, or organization.'

Thus the new works was to be not merely new but novel. And two goals were involved: not simply building a works, but rebuilding a company. Both these factors had an important influence on the setting-up process.

Meanwhile, the decision to build the new works was not one that the company could make unilaterally. Location, scale of investment, and timing were matters of such national interest that the decision was

[1] Based on papers by Miller (1962, 1964).

made by the government. This took time and, in fact, three years elapsed before the outline approval for a new works was given.

During this 'decision' period the company's Central Engineering Department had been heavily involved in the formulation of various plans for the new works; it became, in our terminology, the nucleus of the plant-design system. Because the tasks in which it was engaged were so central to the long-term needs of the enterprise, this department also became something of an elite – a tendency enhanced by the fact that it was located some distance away from the company's main works.

FIGURE 26 *The setting-up process in the preliminary phase*

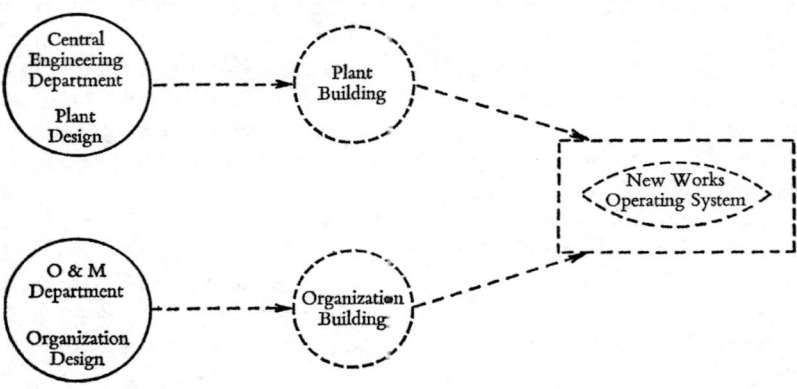

Organization design, on the other hand, had no corresponding focus at this time. There had been within the company a growth of interest in new management techniques: for example, the development of new systems of control, the application of operational research methods, and so forth. But there was no clearing-house through which relevant ideas on organization for a new works could be distilled, corresponding to the clearing-house for plant design that was represented by the Central Engineering Department. In fact, the organization-design system was first activated by the Organization and Methods Department. This department prepared a conventional organization chart for the new works – conventional in the sense that it leant heavily on the organizational structure of the company's existing works. This was accepted as a basis for recruitment of management, i.e. for the first phase of organization-building.

In *Figure 26* the activities in this phase are located on the model of the setting-up process described in Chapter 11.

AN ORGANIZATION FOR THE SETTING-UP PROCESS

As soon as a detailed scheme for the new works had been formally approved and several months before preparation of the site was to begin, a first comprehensive attempt was made to define the structure of management for what we have called the setting-up process. The overall responsibility was to be vested in a committee of management, consisting of the managing director, the company secretary, the chief accountant, and the production controller. This was supported by a major contracts committee. Three main advisory committees were also to be constituted: a technical committee, a staffing and manning committee, and an administration committee. Each of these was supported by a number of subcommittees – working parties which were to concentrate on particular aspects of the design and operation of the new works – and these were to be composed of the best available practitioners and specialists in the company.

At the same time, the head of the Central Engineering Department was appointed general manager (engineering) with overall responsibility for plant design and plant-building. It was also decided that the future general manager (operations) should be appointed at an early date. It was not then contemplated that he would sit on the main technical advisory committee (though when he was actually appointed he did so). In other words, he was not seen as part of the plant-design system; he was seen rather as being concerned only with organization design, organization-building, and operations.

In the meantime, however, a little organization-building was already in progress. The staffing and manning committee was revising and approving the O & M Department's proposed organization chart, and the first appointments to the new operating organization were made. These included a chief accountant for the new works, a commercial manager, and a traffic manager. All three appointments were seen as relevant to activities during the setting-up phase as well as during operations. The position is illustrated in *Figure 27*.

At this time, therefore, plant design and plant-building were being invested with a homogeneous and tightly knit organization, serviced and advised by the technical committee, whose subcommittees quickly be-

FIGURE 27 *Boundaries of the first management organization for the setting-up process*

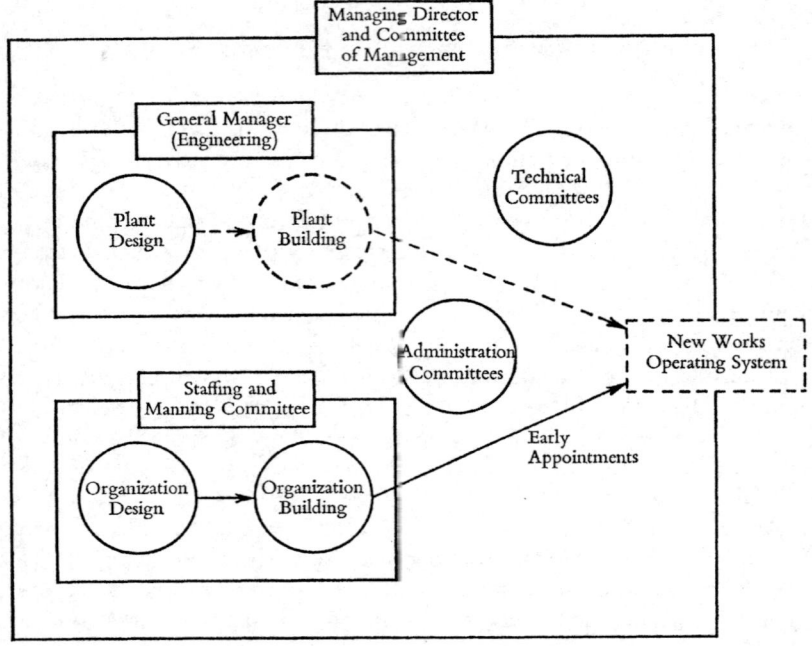

came active. Organization design and organization-building, on the other hand, still remained dispersed.

THE START OF PLANT-BUILDING

Work started on the approach road to the site and on site clearance shortly after the engineering consultants and the first contractors were appointed. Thus roles in the plant-building system, as well as in plant design, were beginning to be activated.

In the meantime, the appointment of the general manager (operations) had a twofold effect: it displaced the staffing and manning committee and the O & M Department from the organization-design and organization-building systems; and it also provided leadership for the nucleus of three administrative managers who had been appointed already. It will be apparent that the latter is an example of a sentient grouping causing an organizational boundary to be drawn inappropriately. In their future roles the three administrative managers and their departments would 'belong' to the general manager (operations); but temporarily their task was to service the entire setting-up system. To the extent that they were contained within the boundaries of a constituent system, their capacity to carry out this task in the supra-system was correspondingly reduced. The boundary changes are shown in *Figure 28*.

FIGURE 28 *Boundary changes in the management organization of the setting-up process on the commencement of both plant- and organization-building*

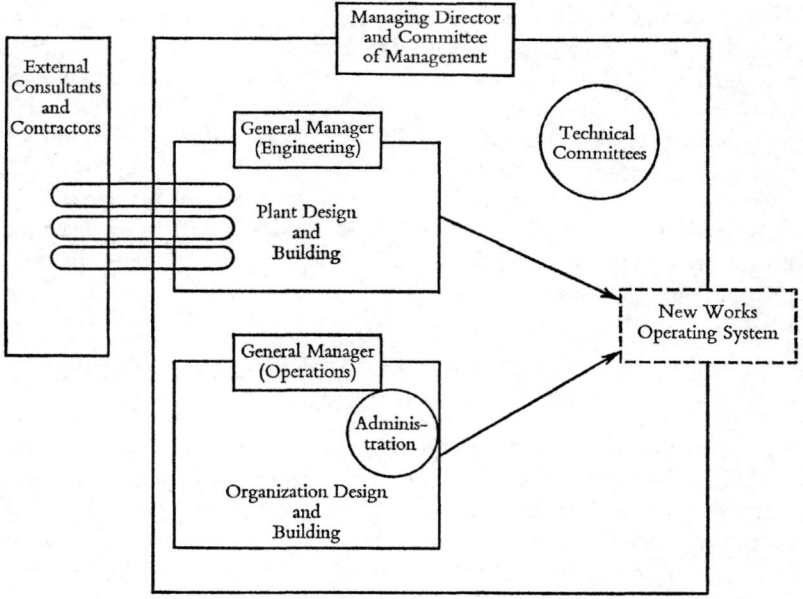

The new general manager (operations) held the view that if the new works was to have a well-equipped, integrated management group in the future, then managers had to be brought in at an early stage. He believed that the teething troubles almost always encountered in a new works were not entirely caused by problems of plant; they could also be caused by problems of management. The notion that management as well as plant needed 'running in' fitted well with the challenge presented by the fresh start on the green-field site. Accordingly, it was agreed that managers should be brought in early and plans were formulated for a series of events through which they would be prepared for their jobs and developed into an integrated team.

Such a notion was obviously a constructive departure from the conventional practice of bringing in operating managers at the last moment, when construction of the plant is nearly complete. It should be noticed, however, that there was also a paradox inherent in this proposal. The future operating-task group was, in effect, to be called into existence in order to design and build itself. This paradox is significant because, although it was not recognized until later, a circular process was involved. The managers were appointed according to an organization chart for operations, and by virtue of this they would occupy roles in organization design. As organization designers, they were expected to develop management philosophies, techniques, methods, policies, and procedures that would take advantage of the green-field situation. But it was not foreseen that in carrying out the task of organization design they might well call into question the conventional assumptions that underlay the chart by which they had been appointed. In other words, either the organization for operations would act as a constraint on organization design or, alternatively, the organization-design activities would threaten the operating organization.

EFFECTS OF CHANGES IN PLANT-DESIGN AND -BUILDING PROGRAMMES

Two major decisions made after work had already started on site clearance served to consolidate the position of the plant-design and plant-building systems. The first was that the construction programme should be greatly accelerated, the proposed construction period being reduced from nearly four years to just over two; the second, that the capacity of the plant being built should be increased by more than a third. Both decisions reflected changes in the external environment. These events placed a premium on rapid decision-making in the plant-design and -building systems by top management. The technical advisory committees faded away, and shortly afterwards even the committee of management petered out. The managing director himself assumed overall responsibility for the setting-up process. But it was not, of course, his only responsibility: there were other works in the company.

Operating managers began to be recruited in larger numbers. The staff and labour relations manager and the education and training manager, both of whom would have major roles in organization-building, were followed by the first few production managers. It was assumed that some engineers involved in plant design and plant-building would eventually take up operating roles as maintenance engineers, but these were not designated at this stage.

Among the more valuable of the original proposals for running in the new management was the notion that study groups of future operating managers should be set up on such topics as costing, budgeting, quality control, production planning, wages, and labour relations; and that when these had done their work they would report back to a policy-making conference, consisting of the overall management group headed by the general manager (operations). Departmental policies would be formulated subsequently and would be contingent on this overall policy-making activity. In the event, because of time pressures caused by the changes in the building programme, these study groups were not established. As a result, although the general manager (operations) tried to create an informal working climate that would encourage free interchange of ideas, each manager on joining inevitably began to think about methods of operation in his own department or sphere of responsibility. The significance of this shift lay in the fact that it increased the extent to which the roles that these managers were to occupy in the future operating system determined what they did in the ongoing organization-design and -building systems. It correspondingly reduced the possibility of using this pre-operating phase to develop novel modes of organization.

Other factors reinforced a tendency towards conservatism. Some of the new managers came from other parts of the company, but many came from other steel companies and even from outside the steel industry. Few of them had known each other before. All were moving into new jobs and most of them were at critical phases in their careers. They were also transplanting themselves and their families into a new locality. This was to some extent, therefore, a period of disorientation in their lives. The new works contained many technological innovations and was of a scale with which few were familiar. At the same time they began to experience the stress inherent in the challenge of the green-field opportunity, particularly in view of the company's immense 'investment' in the success of the new works.

In this situation managers naturally gravitated towards those tasks and positions that seemed relatively familiar and moved away from those in which they felt stranger and less competent. For most of them, organization design itself was an unusual activity and the somewhat unstructured egalitarian culture associated with it generated anxiety. Many of them tended, therefore, to retreat to their operating roles and, on the basis of past experience in their previous jobs, to form relationships with each other as if they were already working in the new operating system. Plainly, however, such a retreat was not possible in reality. One form of organization is seldom appropriate for two quite different tasks. To carry out the task of organization design and building the managers needed to relate to each other in one way; whereas roles in the new operating system would require them to relate to each other in quite a different way. The operating relationships, to which they were endeavouring in effect to retreat, depended on a task that had not yet started. The difficulty was most acute for the production managers, for they found that organization design offered the most intensive and interesting activities to managers of the future control and service departments, who were engaged in formulating systems of costing, developing personnel policies, wages policies, and so forth. When these specialist managers were planning the future activities of their departments, their plans were affecting the whole works. The specialist managers were therefore much more powerful than in a conventional operating situation, and the customary relationship between specialist manager and production manager was in some ways reversed.

This particular problem and its consequences did not become fully revealed for some time. Another problem, however, rapidly emerged soon after the first production managers arrived. It had been assumed that organization design was dependent on plant design. Such an assumption is natural and inevitable in a situation where operating managers arrive only after plant design is complete and plant-building far advanced. But such dependence is not so readily acceptable if the organization designers are already at work when plant design is still incomplete. They begin to discover aspects of plant design that could be modified to make future operations more economic or easier to control. The engineers engaged in plant design had foreseen this as a possible source of conflict but had built a firm organizational boundary around themselves. In any case, they were so busy with the tasks of expansion and acceleration and with the intensification of construction work, that production managers found it difficult even to get plant layouts and designs to study, let alone time to feed back criticisms. Moreover, the abolition of the tech-

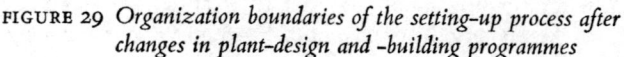

FIGURE 29 *Organization boundaries of the setting-up process after changes in plant-design and -building programmes*

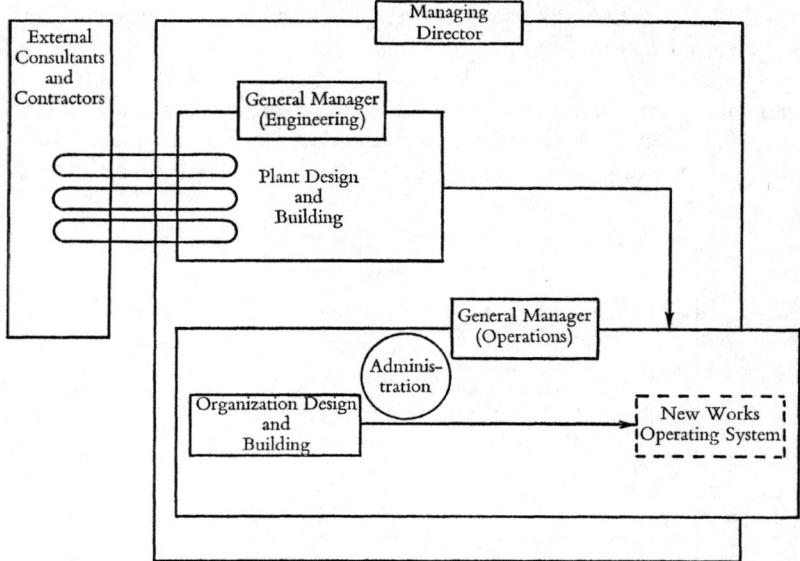

nical committees diminished the contact between the 'engineering' group and the 'operations' group. In the 'operations' group, signs of tension and frustration started to appear.

In addition, the tasks of expansion and acceleration began to present problems of control. Communications between the administrative organization of the general manager (engineering), located in the plant system, and the administrative organization for the setting-up process as a whole, under the general manager (operations), showed signs of deterioration. The position at this stage is illustrated in *Figure 29*.

REORGANIZATION OF THE SETTING-UP PROCESS

At this point the general manager (engineering) fell ill and had to be relieved. There followed the first major revision of the organization of the setting-up process. The Central Engineering Department was reconstituted, and, although most of the engineers who had been engaged on design work remained on site, the department as such no longer had a role in the setting-up system. At the same time, the general manager (operations) was assigned responsibility for the overall setting-up process. A new chief engineer was appointed under the general manager (operations) and it was decided that this engineer would also be the future chief engineer in the operating organization.

Two questions may be asked about these changes. First, how far did the reorganization bring about some accommodation between the activities of plant design and plant-building on the one hand, and organization design and organization-building on the other? Hitherto they had been

FIGURE 30 *Reorganization of the setting-up process*

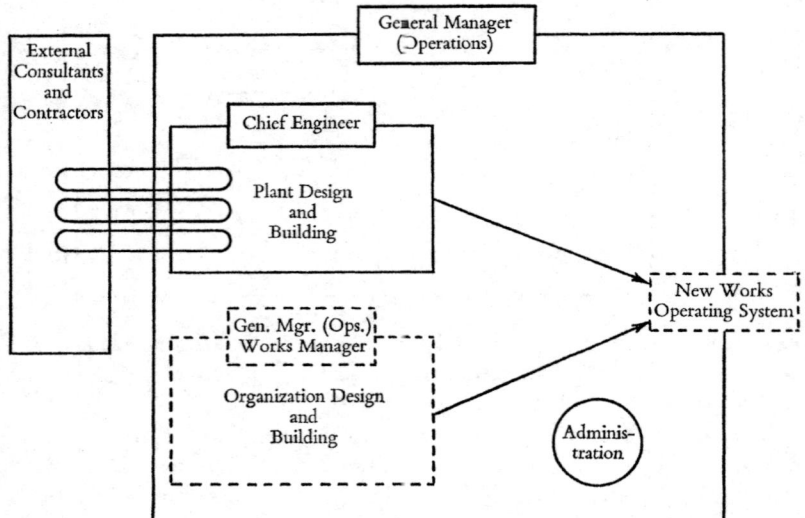

separated from each other. Second, how far did the changes help to clarify the tasks and roles of members of the setting-up organization, and the relations between these and operating tasks and roles?

Ostensibly it now became possible for organization design to affect plant design. And it also became possible for the whole setting-up process to become a single integrated system.

There were, however, difficulties. Some changes in plant design were made, based on the recommendations of production managers, but they were made rather late in the day, and the constraints of time and money, together with the inevitably close articulation of plant-building to plant design, prevented such modifications from being very far-reaching. Second, there continued to be an imbalance between the closely-knit plant-design and -building systems on the one side, with well-defined tasks and a coherent management structure, and organization design and building on the other, whose only structure was inferred from the future organization for operations. Moreover, the organization-design and -building activities at once lost much of the leadership that they had just begun to receive from the general manager (operations), for he was now increasingly involved in the overall management of the total setting-up process. To some extent, his role in organization design and building was taken over by the works manager of the future operating organization. Superficially, this might seem to have been appropriate in that, within the operating organization, his production responsibilities gave him a position parallel and equal to that of the chief engineer. But the organization-design and -building systems were in fact incomplete in that the operating system from which they derived their own organization lacked engineers. The newly appointed chief engineer, himself pre-occupied with construction, was the only exception. Shortly afterwards, two other engineers were recruited specifically for operating roles, and not until some months later were any engineers in the plant-design and -building systems designated for positions in the future operating organization. The changes are illustrated in *Figure 30*.

A few months after the reorganization, two conferences were held, each a fortnight long. These brought together the twenty-five senior managers in the future operating organization under the leadership of the general manager (operations). Their principal task was to begin to formulate the policies according to which the works would be operated in the future. The two conferences inaugurated a long series of planning and training events, which were to culminate in the starting up of the new works.

Such a systematic scheme for running in management was a novel and valuable experiment. In many ways, too, it was a successful experiment. It is worth noting, however, that there were certain features already built into the situation at this stage that prevented it from being wholly successful. In some respects, indeed, the conferences actually helped to crystallize conflicts of task and role that were inherent in the situation that had developed. For example, membership of the senior managers' conferences was based on membership of a future operating organization. Perhaps because this was the basis, their agenda was composed of problems that would arise in steady-state operations, whereas the more immediate problems of the setting-up process – of commissioning, running in, building up production – were scarcely mentioned.

When the conferences were over it was possible to see the emergence of three differentiated sentient groups, all of them linked by a common membership of the future operating system, but each with different aspirations in terms of its ongoing tasks in the setting-up process. They were:

(i) a specialist (service and control) group of managers, committed to tasks of organization design and organization-building;

(ii) an engineering group, committed to plant design and plant-building;

(iii) a production group, committed to future operating activities.

When members of these groups tried to communicate with each other about their common task of setting up the new works, they tended to use frames of reference determined more by their sentient groups than

FIGURE 31 *Sentient-group boundaries imposed on task boundaries*

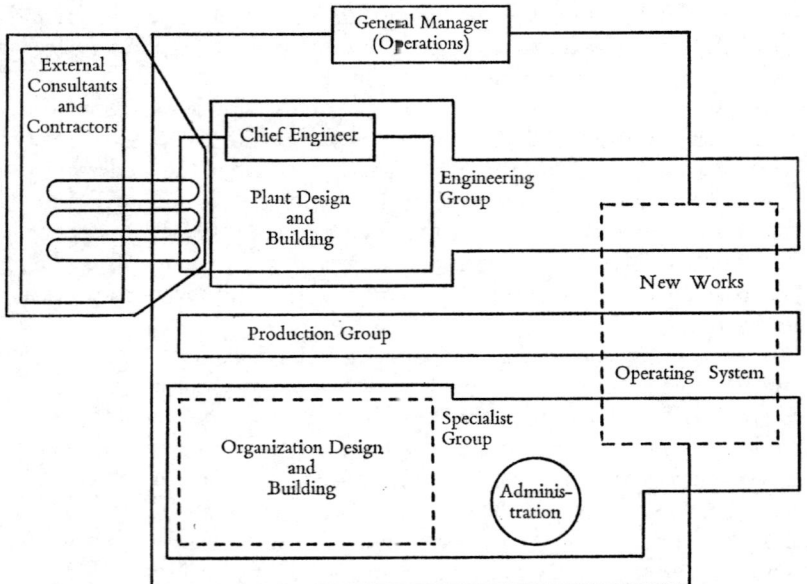

by task requirements. The production managers were, in effect, trying to impose the future onto the present; for they, as we have seen, felt particularly insecure during the setting-up phase. At the same time, both engineers and specialist managers, who were experiencing for once the feeling of being executive rather than advisory, wanted to prolong the power they had obtained during the setting-up phase and to extend it into the future operating period. The sentient-group boundaries imposed on the task boundaries are shown in *Figure 31*.

We leave the case history at that stage, though there were still another eighteen months to go before the beginning of integrated production. The main forces in the field were already set. From then onwards top management, with its understanding of the difficulties, took steps to rectify the relationships and to modify the proposed operating organization so as to produce some workable accommodation between engineers, production managers, and specialists.

CONFLICT RESOLUTION IN TRANSITIONAL ACTIVITY SYSTEMS

Although our analysis has identified factors which perhaps prevented this particular company from realizing all the potential opportunities presented by the green-field site, it would be wrong to overemphasize the negative results. The company, for example, did not meet its extremely tight construction targets; nevertheless, both the completion of the works and the build-up of production to full capacity were fast by any standards except the company's own. Similarly, although the results of the experiment of bringing in managers early did not eliminate all teething troubles, the running-in period was shorter and less difficult than is usual in such circumstances. Many innovations in management methods and techniques were attempted and were successful. Moreover, the setting-up of the new works was accompanied by a resurgence in the other parts of the company.

Some innovations, however, failed. The plan to bring in operating managers at an early stage did not elicit as much commitment to the new operating system as had been hoped. In retrospect it is possible to explain why this happened. We have seen, for example, that the very attempt to secure the commitment of the future operating managers by involving them in organization design meant that the organization-design activities did not have an organization of their own. They were carried out instead through future operating roles. Innovations tended to be perceived as threatening predetermined patterns of power and status in the future operating organization. Thus production managers sometimes defended their future operating roles against change instead of designing change into the operating system. The commitment of the production managers to the operating system was also limited by their feeling that they had been given too little say in the design of the plant: basic features of the operating system were shaped in large measure by factors beyond their control. On the other hand, there was a danger – and this was an engineering view – that if, by virtue of their future operating roles, the production managers had played a larger part in plant design, there too, as in organization design, they might have constrained technical innovations. From the vantage-point of future operations, they would tend to prefer the familiar to the novel and unknown.

Our analysis suggests that, in most processes of institution-building, efforts to secure innovation will conflict with any attempt to secure commitment by involving the future members of the institution in design tasks. The only exception will be in the enterprise in which an individual or a small group, themselves the risk-taking entrepreneurs, can encompass the entire setting-up process. The setting-up task can then be contained within a simple system (cf. Chapter 1). If the task is large enough to require an internally differentiated organization, conflict will arise. Thus if the plant-design system does not include members of the future building system and the future operating system, first the builders and later the operators will be working to designs that they had no part in shaping. Predecessors' actions can then become alibis for current failures. Conversely, if the organization maximizes involvement in the design and building systems of members of the future operating system, innovation will be retarded.

The more general point is that conflict is inevitable in any setting-up process in which the task is to create a system with organic properties. Conflict and the attendant anxieties are likely to be stronger in the greenfield situation, where the heightened expectations at the beginning also exacerbate the ultimate feeling of let-down when – as must be so – the completed task does not live up to all the original expectations. The painful and destructive aspects of the creative process are perhaps easier to bear, however, if they can be anticipated and planned for.

The model outlined here is applicable not only to the task of building a new steel works; it can be applied, for example, to the setting up of a new section in an existing works or to institution-building in non-industrial settings. It enables us to predict and anticipate the different kinds of problem that will arise from organizing the setting-up system in different ways. More positively, it permits us, within limits, to decide where and when to take the inevitable conflict.

Such organizational decisions will plainly depend on specific circumstances, which may preclude some alternatives and encourage others. Consequently, it is not possible to offer a single optimum solution. Four general points are nevertheless worth noting:

1. If innovation is to be maximized, the boundaries of the design systems will require maximum protection. This can be achieved if the design-task boundaries are also sentient boundaries, especially in the earlier stages. The nuclear group engaged in design, in other words, should have a full-time commitment to that task and not occupy (or be specifically promised) roles in building or operating systems. Such protection can also be afforded by making use of outside consultants within the design systems.

2. The activities of plant design and organization design need to be closely co-ordinated. If the number of designers involved is small, the two systems may be integrated within a single command. In a bigger and more complex situation the different groups of specialists involved are unlikely to be accommodated within a single sentient boundary. Strong managerial controls will therefore be required at the level of the overall setting-up system to secure consistency in the design phase.

3. The systems of activity identified here have distinctive tasks and hence distinctive import-conversion-export processes. It follows that they require distinctive organizational forms. If these are explicitly provided, and in particular if each system can be given its own explicit leadership, then managerial controls both at the level of the individual system and at the level of the overall setting-up system will be strengthened and the 'contaminating' effects of multiple role-holding will be reduced.

4. An organic system needs time for growth, not only as a whole but in its parts as well. Imbalance is caused when one constituent system is brought into being more quickly than others. In the calculation of results, the gain obtained by more rapid completion has to be offset by the cost of subsequent disruption.

CHAPTER 13

Organization for Research

We define 'research' as an endeavour to discover facts by scientific study. In this and the succeeding chapter we are concerned with formally organized research work, and include as research therefore attempts to create new knowledge, to extend existing knowledge, or to transfer existing knowledge from one field to another. In other words, we include what are commonly referred to as 'pure' or 'basic' and 'applied' research. The question of the use to which the knowledge is put will be taken up in Chapter 14 when we come to discuss the different approaches to research and the different conditions under which it is carried out in different kinds of institution. The distinction then is between the pursuit of knowledge for its own sake, on the one hand, and the pursuit of knowledge about specific things to be applied for specific purposes, on the other.

Organized research, in any modern sense, started, for the most part, in academic institutions. Gifted workers pushed forward the frontiers of knowledge in their own specialized subjects, initially in the natural sciences and later in medicine; thus the boundaries of the first research institutions were naturally determined by academically recognized disciplines. As knowledge extended, academic disciplines tended to become more specialized. At the same time, as knowledge derived from research was applied to specific practical problems, some 'pure' and all 'applied' research work tended to become problem- rather than discipline-centred. The boundaries of academically recognized disciplines then became less precise and multidisciplinary studies became necessary. The creation of multi-disciplinary teams in their turn required a different kind of management control – one in which decision-making could be based on judgements in more – often many more – than one scientific discipline.

A further complication for the building and organizing of research institutions was introduced as research extended into human affairs. The isolation of the 'problem' was no longer feasible. The nature of the field of study – medical and social – made it impossible always to control the course of investigation, since the 'problem' was 'accompanied' by an individual or a group of individuals. Access to data necessary for the investigation often depended on obtaining permission from the subject, permission that was granted only in return for some benefit. This in turn meant that the field conditions of the research, and hence the data, were changed by the investigation.[1]

In this chapter we propose to examine the import-conversion-export processes for research work and the nature and location of appropriate boundary controls. We shall then suggest a model organization for any research institution. In the succeeding chapter we shall consider the application of this model to three kinds of research institution: university, industrial, and government.

THE DOMINANT IMPORT-CONVERSION-EXPORT
PROCESS OF RESEARCH WORK

The primary task of research work is the creation of knowledge. The basic intakes into the research system are therefore questions; the conversion processes are the thinking, experimentation, and other activities that go on to try to find answers; and the outputs are answers. It is irrelevant whether the questions imported are precisely formulated, or even whether they have been consciously asked; the result of successful research work is the discovery of something that has not previously been known.

In scientific terms, perhaps no question is ever answered except in so far as it gives rise to other questions. In this sense an output may be a reformulation of the problem in such a way that further work can be started; or the output may contribute to the answer to a different question. Or, if it does not answer the question asked, it may throw up new questions that can be asked only as a result of the research work that has been done. Even a nil result may suggest questions to which answers can be found. Indeed, the ability to ask the right question can make a major contribution to creative research work. Inevitably, a large number of the activities of any research institution lead either to 'frustrated outputs', whose by-products are potentially fresh intakes, or to unintended outputs, which are only remotely related to the questions originally asked.

Any research process, in other words, has an in-built tendency towards the formation of a relatively closed system, in which self-generated intakes crowd out intakes from the external environment; and in which answers to self-generated questions are, in their turn, reimported into the system as

[1] Data collection in the natural sciences has not been unaffected by the investigator.

new questions. Research institutions have, therefore, a natural tendency to become increasingly divorced from their environments, and their boundaries to become increasingly impermeable. Apart from the extent to which support may depend on the maintenance of an open system, it is also likely that the institution's capacity for creative problem-solving will decline without the feedback that accompanies transactions with relevant parts of its environment. Certainly, a major problem for the management of any research institution is to steer between the Scylla of creative research activities that are irrelevant, and the Charybdis of relevant research activities that are uncreative.

Outputs of the research process may take many forms – all the way from the publication of scientific papers to the direct application of research

FIGURE 32 *Dominant import-conversion-export process of a research institution*

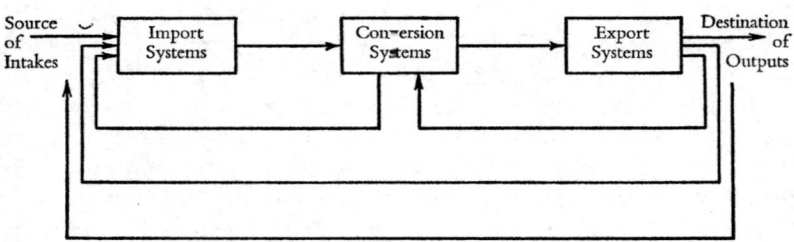

findings to specific practical problems. We suggest that the assumption that must be made, implicitly or explicitly, by any meaningful research institution is that its outputs will have value in human affairs. Even the publication of a scientific paper presumes its use somewhere, sometime, by somebody to solve some problem of human existence.

The dominant import-conversion-export process of a research institution is shown in *Figure 32*.

THE CONSTRAINTS ON RESEARCH WORK

The major resources required for task performance are human – scientists and technologists – and physical – space, equipment, and supplies. The major constraints are the capacity and availability of the resources. There are, in addition, the constraints of time and money – how much has to be invested and for how long, with what hope of a result? – and the social and legal conditions of the external environment – what may be investigated and by what methods within the environment in which the enterprise exists?

If the dominant import-conversion-export process is concerned with finding answers to questions, then the skills and equipment required are ideally determined by the questions asked and the research work needed, rather than by the needs of the scientists or the availability of their equipment. Pressed to its logical conclusion this would imply that, for every question accepted as an intake, the research institution would obtain the requisite scientific skills and equipment and would dispose of them when an answer was found.

The availability of scientists and the cost of equipment act in practice as constraints on such a procedure, as well as on the questions that can be imported with any hope of a fruitful output. Moreover, to secure the survival of a research institution as an institution, as opposed to the setting up of a team to answer a single question, it is necessary to provide opportunities for feedback so that questions can be reformulated and the by-product of one research project harnessed to the solution of the next. Characteristically, therefore, a research institution assembles a collection of scientists and equipment with a capacity to work on a genre of problems. The composition of these resources, though undergoing progressive modification through changes in problem requirements, also tends to limit the range of problems that can be tackled and inevitably leads to their redefinition according to the capacities and needs of the scientists and the availability of the equipment.

The economic, social, and legal constraints will be discussed in more detail in relation to university, government, and industrial research. They affect particularly control over intakes and over outputs. More generally, the more dependent a research enterprise is on its environment for support, the more it has to ensure that questions that are important to the environment are investigated, and the more it has to provide answers from which the environment can benefit. Equally, the more the actual research work depends for its success on access to data within the environment, the more will the environment control what kinds of investigation and what kinds of experiment can or cannot be carried out. Conversely, control over research activities by the environment can be redefined in terms of the extent of the protection a research institution can give to its members and to their work. Degrees of protection can be broadly classified as:

(a) *Complete* (maximum control): the problem is adequately formulated; all necessary data are obtainable by 'laboratory' experiment on unprotected materials or organisms; work on the data and on their interpretation can lie entirely within the boundaries of the research institution; and publication of findings is free of constraint either from the source of the data or from the environment. Most research work in the natural sciences falls into this category, though experiments in the use of nuclear energy or in the development of pesticides are now subject to, or becoming subject to, environmental control.

(b) *Limited* (limited control): the problem is adequately formulated in the laboratory, but the data have to be obtained in the environment, and access to data is therefore subject to environmental control in varying degrees; publication of findings may be subject to clearance by the source of the data; and other applications are dependent on acceptance by relevant parts of the environment. Examples are found in clinical research in medicine, and in most social science research.

(c) *Professional* (minimum control): the problem is inadequately formulated, that is, the presenting problem is believed to be symptomatic of an underlying but unknown cause; the data are doubtful and access is subject to stringent conditions imposed by the environment; where subjects of research are identifiable, publication is subject to clearance by the source of the data; and the application of results is a part of the research investigation. Research workers have to accept professional responsibility for their interventions in the interests of research. Examples are clinical research work that involves actual interference with the subject, and studies of identifiable institutions that involve data whose discovery might be threatening to the institutions or damaging if revealed outside.

MODEL ORGANIZATION: THE OPERATING SYSTEMS

The major operating systems of research organization are those systems through which questions are identified, answers found, and results communicated. The boundaries between the different kinds of system – import, conversion, and export – are frequently difficult to define, since by its nature creative research work involves the self-generation of intakes, and outputs are often papers written by the scientists responsible for the actual research activities. Much of the control over import and export processes is therefore likely to be included in an undifferentiated conversion system. But within the conversion system, whether integrated with or differentiated from the import and export systems, the boundaries of operating systems are determined by the technical conditions necessary to answer a question or to solve a problem. This dominant technological dimension of differentiation is reinforced by territorial differentiation if the data required are to be found only in specific places; and by time differentiation if the investigation demands that data be taken at specific intervals. But when the answer or solution has been found, the operating system, strictly speaking, no longer has any *raison d'être*.

The form of organization that fits the members of a research institution and their equipment to their task must, therefore, be technologically determined and essentially flexible. It must permit groups of scientists and equipment to be formed, modified, and dispersed as research questions are progressively posed, reformulated, and answered. Such an organization can perhaps best be described as a *project-type organization*. The groups so formed are organizationally viable only so long as they are working on the problem for which they have been put together. Once the project has been completed, even if the point of completion is only the reformulation of the problem, then the project team has to be unmade and its members and their equipment have to be reassembled, with or without additions and reductions in terms of new or reformulated problems.

We define a programme as a group of projects that, while being sufficiently discrete from one another to be separately led, are sufficiently close to each other to be parts of a larger integrated programme under common leadership.

The basic model for the organization of operating systems and the minimum managing system – that is, of the executive control system – is shown in *Figure 33*. As in other diagrams, each box represents a constellation of management and leadership activities, not necessarily one individual. Boxes may therefore be occupied by individuals, pairs, or larger groups; and an individual may occupy more than one box. Institutional management may thus consist of an individual whose major task this is, or it could consist of some or all of the programme and project leaders. That is to say, the diagram could represent a single individual research director with subordinates; or an autonomous group whose members not only act as leaders and staff for programmes and projects but also, as a group, manage their own internal co-ordination, and control the transactions of the enterprise with its environment.

It will be seen, further, that this diagram envisages an overall management that might be managing two kinds of operating system: programmes that are internally differentiated into projects, and independent projects, which, though concerned with discrete problems, are not subdivided internally. It is conceivable that, within a major programme, projects might be further differentiated into sub-projects; but a hierarchy with so many levels would probably be inconsistent not only with adequate organizational flexibility, but also with the egalitarian culture generally associated with scientific research.

FIGURE 33 *Operating systems of a research organization*

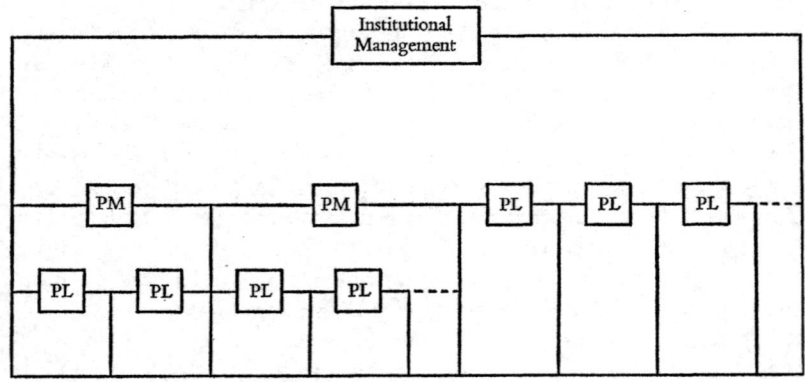

PM: Programme Management   PL: Project Leadership

Thus in the series of sub-systems that compose our basic model organization to fit task performance, none of the boundaries is permanent and members of the institution may occupy roles in more than one sub-system simultaneously.

If the programme and project groups have to be multidisciplinary in character because of the nature of the problem being studied, then individual scientists can become academically isolated. In such circumstances the emergence of 'informal' groups, with a consequent 'informal' organization and communication system, becomes inevitable unless the institution provides for stable sentient groups.

MODEL ORGANIZATION: THE MANAGING SYSTEM

The primary task of the managing system is to control the internal environment of the institution and its transactions with its external environment, in such a way that performance of the research task can be maximized. When support is assured through endowment or other means, and the organism or material under study is not subject to social or legal protection, the primary control may have to take the form of 'avoiding' transactions, that is of protecting the enterprise from interference. More usually, research institutional management has to satisfy the relevant parts of its environment that its performance of the research task is such as to justify continuation of support. This means, among other transactions, maintaining relationships with the sources of support, both scientific and financial. Internally, the managing system has to control, co-ordinate, and service the operating systems in the performance of their tasks. It has to provide the resources and so control them that external and internal requirements are matched.

A central internal problem for the managing system of a research enterprise is therefore to secure the necessary flexibility of the operating systems, the assembly of appropriate scientists and equipment for the various projects that are planned, and their dispersal and reassembly at the end of each project. Almost inevitably, a group of scientists who have worked together on a project will wish to preserve their group after the problem they were brought together to tackle has been solved. This is especially likely if the group has been successful, even though it no longer has any organizational reality for task performance. It can, of course, happen that the desire to preserve the group will be functional: work on the initial problem, for example, may have generated a new problem which is germane to the task of the research institution as a whole, and on which the same group is well qualified to work. On the other hand, there is also the possibility that the work of the group will become increasingly ingrown and the group self-supporting, unconcerned with creative intake or output. From the point of view of control, such a situation is hard to deal with. The standard argument used in research organizations in such cases – that the work may well have a long-term pay-off in unforeseen ways – is usually a rationalization, but is never very easy to rebut.

The same difficulty arises with the assembly of expensive equipment to solve specific problems. Its very existence becomes an argument for further experimental work to justify its organization and retention. Even more awkward, from the point of view of adequate control, is the group of scientists who assemble expensive equipment and develop a new technique to solve a particular problem. Unless they and their management are careful they can become prisoners of their own technique and, in consequence, fail to tackle problems that should be tackled. Instead, they find uses for their technique and its accompanying equipment. With unlimited resources this may not matter very much, and, indeed, in the development of uses for a technique, answers to unforeseen questions may be found; but where research management has to make decisions about priorities in the investment of scarce resources, this prolongation of scientific groups and the retention of their equipment may be, in the long run, destructive. Such situations are not, of course, confined to research enterprises. Many manufacturing companies, having planned and erected expensive factories, have become prisoners of their own technology as well. So enthusiastic have they been in designing their new factory that they have failed to notice that the market for the products it will manufacture is dwindling.

Internally, therefore, an essential part of the control and service of research operating systems is that the organization itself should facilitate the disbanding and re-forming of programme and project groups, together with their equipment. At the same time, a scientist has to maintain his scientific skill. If he is working on a project in his own field, with colleagues in the same discipline, his skill will tend to be strengthened; but where he is working on a multidisciplinary project, which involves him in work with others whose skills are beyond the boundaries of his own discipline, he may need an opportunity elsewhere to preserve or renew the skill he brings as a unique contribution to the project. Similar considerations apply to equipment, particularly when it is scarce or expensive, and can be used for more than one kind of research activity. Its continued use by one group on one project will deprive other projects of its contribution; moreover, the equipment itself may demand so much attention as to employ over-scarce skills in its construction and maintenance.

Management needs to have adequate organizational mechanisms for rescrambling project teams and reallocating equipment and for maintaining adequate scientific skills; scientists require a more stable affiliation to the institution than is obtainable through transient project teams. Both may be secured if every scientist is attached to a 'base' that represents his own specialist discipline. He can return to his base, at least theoretically, when not deployed on a specific project; even though, in practice, there may be no interval between his leaving a disbanded team and joining a new one. Membership of such bases provides scientists with opportunities for support and reinforcement in their own discipline. A junior physicist, for example, may be in considerable difficulty if, as a member of a multi-disciplinary team, he feels that his senior colleagues, who are chemists, are paying insufficient attention to the physical properties of their subject, and are also, because of their seniority, paying insufficient attention to him.

Such bases provide internal manifestations of, and partial substitutes for, real or imaginary external sentient groups. To the extent that they can do this, the research enterprise is able to incorporate some of the commitment that would otherwise belong to external scientific or professional associations. The bases supply scientists with science-centred leadership as a complement to problem-centred management. But the responsibility of the leadership of these bases is also to ensure that the scientific

FIGURE 34 *Model organization of managing and operating systems of research institutions*

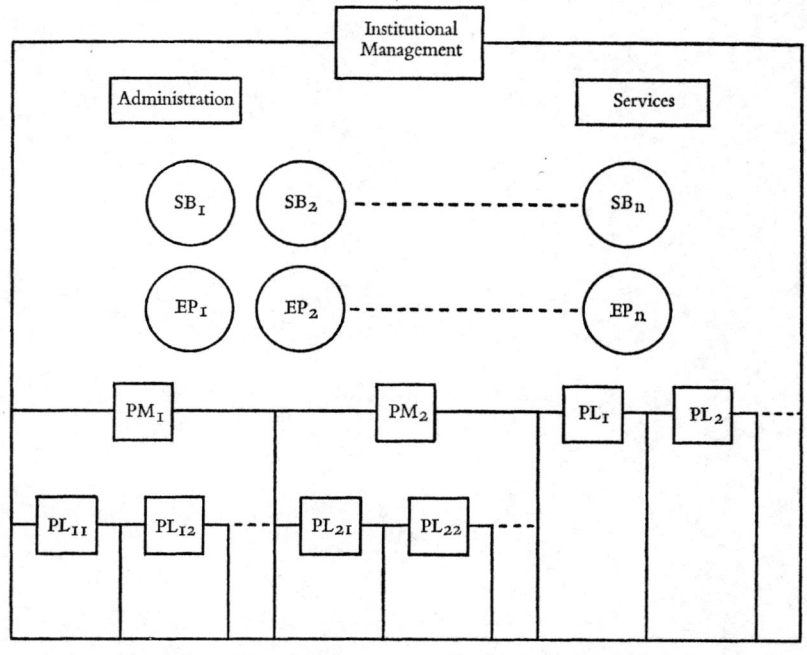

skills necessary for project work are available and properly maintained. Hence the bases offer consultative help to scientists in difficulties in multi-disciplinary project work. That is, the sentient systems are task oriented.

The organizational implication is that an essential control and service function in the managing system of any research enterprise has to provide bases for scientists and, if necessary, 'pools' of equipment. The bases and the pools control the quality of the scientific skill and equipment available, and supply projects with what they need. The model organization of managing and operating systems is depicted in *Figure 34*. Finance, personnel, and general administrative functions have been shown under the general rubric of 'administration', and other possible functions under the title 'services'. These will be discussed more fully under problems of control in the next chapter.

CHAPTER 14

The Control of Research Institutions

A simple enterprise carries out all the activities of importing, converting, and exporting. There is no differentiation of sub-systems, and management – control, co-ordination, and service – is contained in the undifferentiated production system. Such a system is the one-man business, in which the owner puts up his own capital or borrows it on his own credit, buys his own raw materials, works at his own bench with or without assistants, and is his own salesman. Such a system is also the one-man research institution or sub-institution. The scientist gets the necessary financial support on his own 'credit' – in this case his reputation as a research worker – decides what to investigate, carries out his own study, sometimes with students as assistants, and writes his own papers on the findings. The transition from a simple to a complex system originates in the demand for specific and different investigations, involving a necessary enlargement of the field of study, and a consequent need for greater specialization. Or it can occur as the result of a need for different kinds of 'output' to ensure continuation, or increase, of support.

In the growth from a simple to a complex system, the first differentiation is into operating systems, each carrying out a discrete project or programme. This differentiation calls into being a managing system which, since it controls, co-ordinates, and services the operating systems and relates them to the external environment, must be external to all of them. As complexity increases, specialist control and service functions, as well as specialist operating systems, are required. Which functions are differentiated in the managing system will depend upon the extent to which the external and internal environments have to be related to, or can be kept apart from, each other, and upon the capacities of overall research management to match these needs. Whether the functions are differentiated or not, the overall management of any large complex research institution will have to maintain relationships in the external environment with institutions or individuals who provide financial support; scientific and academic bodies that set criteria for the judgement of performance; sources for the recruitment of scientists and supplies of equipment; and consumers of research findings (even if only the editors and publishers of appropriate journals). In the same way, within the institution, overall management must be concerned with the maintenance of scientific standards; the resolution of conflicts between research policy and the private aims of scientists or groups of scientists to pursue other kinds of investigation; competition between projects for limited resources in personnel, money, and equipment; the provision of services in the form of laboratories, computer installations, and the like; and all the administrative paper-work that such activities entail.

RESEARCH MANAGEMENT IN PRACTICE

We have emphasized that, organizationally, it is irrelevant whether overall management of a research enterprise is vested in one individual or several, and whether the individual or individuals concerned act also as programme or project leaders. In other words, the boxes in the organization diagrams represent activities rather than individuals; more than one individual can fill a box and any given individual can appear in more than one box. It is nevertheless true that in research, as in other kinds of institution, the expectation is that a box represents a role that will be filled by one individual, and that this will be his only, or at least his principal, role. In scientific research work this expectation is reinforced by the tradition that 'management' should be in the hands of an eminent scientist whose reputation is such that he attracts brilliant students and thus builds a research institution or sub-institution round himself. The reputation of most research institutions, though nominally in terms of the scientific work they turn out, is frequently highly personalized. The source of attraction is the scientist (or group of scientists) who works in an institution, rather than the institution itself. One has only to think of the changing reputation of different universities in respect of different disciplines to realize how easily traditional status can be lost as a result of the loss of scientific leadership.

The differences between various kinds of research institution – academic, public, and private – will be considered later in this chapter, but, in general, research organization still tends to be modelled on the tradition of the individual scientist. He establishes his name by doing original and creative work as a young man, and then, in later life, becomes the 'manager' of other scientists. In this role he invariably finds himself forced more and more into administration, and into money-raising and similar activities; and this is irrespective of whether he has any managerial or administrative skill, or is good at 'selling' the products of his enterprise. Inevitably, unless he is a genius, the longer he holds, and becomes involved in, such a managerial role, the less personal and direct a contribution he can make to the creative thinking that his own earlier work presumes, and the more out of touch he is likely to be with the thinking and work of his 'subordinates'.

Almost every discussion we have had about the organization of research institutions, particularly about their management, raises sooner or later the problem of how managers can make decisions concerning the scientific or practical value of research projects unless they are themselves pre-eminent in the scientific field or fields in which the projects have to be carried out. It is often said, and more often implied, that decisions about scientific work and judgements about the scientists who do it can be made only by people who are superior, as scientists, to those whose work is under scrutiny. Only three possibilities seem to be envisaged: judgements have to be made by one man; or they have to be made by a team containing, at the highest level, representatives of all the necessary disciplines; or all the scientific members of the institution have to be given the right to make them. While any one of these possibilities may serve for a time, all of them have major disadvantages, and none of them appears to us to provide an adequate model for future research management.

The concept of one man making all the major decisions is very much like the concept of the tycoon in industry: a man who knows everything, takes every important decision, and builds the business round himself and his own personality. But just as, except in the early years of new industries and, again, except in the case of rare genius, the business tycoon is becoming more and more of an anachronism as the leader of large-scale, complex, and specialized industries, so, we believe, is the one-man research institution – with its research tycoon – becoming less appropriate as scientific knowledge expands, as the techniques of research become more specialized, and as the cost of equipment (and scientists) increases.

The idea of a directorate, or other kind of management group, advisory or executive, containing within it people who between them cover all the necessary scientific disciplines at the highest level, can similarly become untenable. Given the multitude of specializations that exist today, such a management group would have to become very large. So far as the social sciences are concerned, for example, we find it difficult to believe that it is any longer possible for a single psychologist to represent all the psychological disciplines; and certainly in psychiatry it seems unlikely that any one psychiatrist would be accepted even as a representative of all disciplines, let alone as superior in terms of scientific knowledge and skill.

The weakness of the third possibility, scientific egalitarianism, is that it denies the inequality in scientists' competence to make judgements about their own and others' work. The more original the work that is being done within the institution, the more likely is it that judgements about it will be uneven. Creative scientists, even if they are interested in others' work, are not notorious for concerning themselves about the problems of its administration or management. The reaction of many of them to the demand that they should be so concerned is to withdraw into an ivory tower of their own making, resenting any management or administrative procedure that they regard – and they so regard most – as an unwarrantable interference with their rights as scientists to conduct their scientific affairs in their own way. But even this situation is not so difficult for research management as that in which scientists who have lost, or never had, creative ability nevertheless expect to be treated as equals when decisions about policy or about the expenditure of scarce resources have to be made. The introduction of the democratic ideal of one man, one vote, into research management invariably leads either to the growth of a differentiated, unco-ordinated series of autonomous sub-institutions or to anarchy.

What we feel is required is a new concept of the major decision-making process. In effect, the critical decisions that have to be made by research management are about investment in research activities. Investment decisions involve judgements about whom to back, to do what, and for how long without demanding results. The judgements are clearly interdependent. Much research work is comparatively straightforward, in the sense that a competent scientist, or a group of scientists if a number of disciplines are involved, can produce answers in the long or short run by the application of known techniques. The problem is adequately formulated, techniques are known and tested, and the subject of study is under complete control. At the other end of the continuum, the question is only vaguely formulated, techniques – and apparatus – for investigation have to be invented, and answers are unlikely without many years' work, if at all. At this level, judgements about competence or the availability of techniques are not enough. Investments have to be made on the basis of belief in the scientist as a creative individual. Such belief will of course be determined to some extent on the evidence of past achievement, but the decision to invest is more often a blind act of faith than those responsible for it would like to admit.

In other words, the major qualifications for research management are a capacity for making investment decisions and the abilities, on the one hand, to protect the investments once made and, on the other, to make ruthless judgements about their results. Whether management is by one man or by a group is then decided by local conditions, though we would suggest that, for an institution concerned with multidisciplinary research, a group may represent a wider point of view than is usually possible for one man. Even this kind of management does not solve the problem of adequate institutional reproduction under conditions of rapid change. Research work, by definition, is a change-producing process, and change-producing processes have a habit of leaving behind those who initiate them. Research institutions must have built into their organization mechanisms whereby their leaders can be changed without damage to the institution and with as little damage as possible to the leaders concerned.

BOUNDARY CONTROLS: INTAKES

The majority of research institutions, except for those whose work is entirely routine, have ongoing work at all points of the continuum from 'routine' to 'creative'; and perhaps most would aspire to be doing more creative work in 'pure' research than they do. Indeed, the prestige now accorded to science and scientific research in the modern world allows many 'scientists' to claim a greater independence and freedom to choose their own projects than their contributions to society would appear to warrant. Generally speaking, so far as the majority of research institutions is concerned, judgements have to be made and are made in two main areas: programmes and projects, and scientists and technicians to carry them out – the major import systems of the institution.

The more precise and contemporary the definition of the primary task of a given research institution in terms of what genre of problems it will tackle, the more precise can be judgements about what projects to import and what to reject. Intakes into a research institution can, as we have seen, originate in the environment or be self-generated. But, given a precise definition of the primary task of the institution, the following questions can be asked:

(a) Where are the gaps in the present programmes?
(b) What programmes or projects are required to fill them?
(c) What resources are, or can be made, available?

In addition, since any worth-while research institution will invariably be able to ask more questions than it can ever hope to tackle, research management can ask which frontiers of knowledge should be pushed the hardest. Or, to put it another way, management can ask what kind of pay-off will best meet institutional needs, and how much pushing of which frontiers is likely to give that pay-off. Some frontiers, for example, have already been pushed a long way and, though pushing them further would undoubtedly be valuable as a contribution to basic knowledge, there may be a chance that a similar expenditure of resources in scientists and equipment in another area could give a larger and quicker pay-off. Clearly, also, it is no good expending small resources in a research field merely to fill a gap, if other research enterprises are investing much greater resources in the same field, and will make their results available.

When judgements are made about scientists' creativity and competence, or promise of these, a number of criteria other than academic qualifications and research experience are generally taken into account, even if they are not necessarily very well formulated. Most sophisticated research managements would recognize that when they select a research worker they make judgements about the quality of the candidate's mind, as distinct from his intelligence level, academic record, or other measurable criteria; his imaginative ruthlessness – whether he can think through to logical conclusions without baulking at any emotional fences on the way; and his capacity to commit himself utterly to a given task to the exclusion of other interests. As one research manager said to us:

'In order to exploit an idea you have to be wholly committed to it, to be confident that you are working on the right track. At the same time you have to be aware that if you are a genius four out of five, if you are brilliant nine out of ten, and if you are an ordinary scientist ninety-nine out of a hundred of your ideas will turn out to be failures. So the statistical probability is that the particular idea to which you are wholly committed at any one time will turn out to be a failure.'

Sophisticated research managers are also aware that the scientist who ranks highly on these criteria possesses the very qualities that can make him an awkward 'subordinate' if, in the interests of the institution, he has to be asked to stop his own investigation and carry out some other work.

Such judgements are additional and do not replace strict scientific knowledge where it is available. But they do suggest that it might be possible to articulate criteria that are independent of specific scientific knowledge, which could be, and indeed are being, used by research managers who have to make investment decisions and selections in disciplines other than their own.

A major difficulty in many research institutions is the nature of the contract they make with their members. Unless the institution can offer its recruits security, it will be unlikely to attract the number and quality it wants. As against this, however, 'permanent' employees who lose their creative ability can become an embarrassment. Because of their contributions and service in the past, they have the right to expect that they will not be discarded, but they may be unable, or unwilling, to fill roles more suitable to their current ability. The problem may be eased if the research institution is part of a larger institution such as an industrial company, a university, or a government department; but in these institutions likewise it can be difficult to find suitable roles for run-down, even if willing, research workers. Indeed, research institutions perhaps provide the most profitable field for the introduction of 'leaving procedures' in contrast to the more usual and elaborate 'selection procedures' (Rice, 1952).

BOUNDARY CONTROLS: OUTPUTS

Few research institutions are independent of their environment to the extent that they do not have to make some form of payment to it for the resources they use. There may be a few that are so well endowed that they do not have to justify their existence by keeping up high standards in outputs; but there can be none that can survive for long without having an output of any kind. As we have seen, the output can take many forms, from the publication of scientific papers to the immediate application of solutions to problems; but it is notable that most research institutions are attached to, or are a part of, larger institutions that are maintained by a different kind of import-conversion-export process. Clinical research in medicine, for example, is usually carried out in hospitals; and hospitals are maintained by ongoing thera-peutic activities and the consequent throughput of patients, or, as in teaching hospitals, by the dual throughputs of patients and medical stu-dents. In the same way, industrial research – whether in an industry-wide association or an individual company – is maintained by the manufacture and sale of products; and university research by a throughput of students, few of whom are students of research methodology. Even research in-stitutions that are nominally independent usually have to engage in some other activity – the manufacture of vaccines or consultancy practice, for example – to supplement any research grants they may receive.

The dependence of research work on a different activity with a different import-conversion-export process is perhaps an inevitable concomitant of obtaining support for institutions whose success depends on exporting the results of originality and creativity. Creativity is neither readily assessed nor easily regulated. Nor can its results often be judged by measurable criteria within any time-span that is useful for investment decision-making (as artists as well as scientists have found to their cost). The implicit assumption appears to be that research work should be supported by the users of its results. Nevertheless, except in industrial and some government research work, the connection between research finding and consumer use is frequently difficult to discern. In these cir-cumstances, both the sponsors of research work and research workers appear to go into collusion to find some other criterion for measuring success. Of recent years, both in the United Kingdom and in America, 'publication' may have assumed this role. We cannot help feeling that publication is in danger of becoming valued for its own sake, with perhaps too little regard for the intrinsic merits of the contents. Among the plethora of scientific publications are some – perhaps this is one of them – that merit, at most, the status of scientific pot-boilers. The ability to write in such a way that editors will publish often seems to be more important than what is written about, and finding something to write about more important than the findings.

In the terms used in this book, control of the import-export boun-daries of research institutions appears to be exiguous, and the appropriate control regions are frequently non-existent. At the import boundary, self-generated, and hence unrecognized, intakes can crowd out intakes from the environment; and at the export boundary the value of outputs is not easily measured. And the difficulties are exacerbated by collusion between research workers and their sponsors. These phenomena will be further examined in relation to academic, industrial, and public research institutions in the next three sections.

ACADEMIC RESEARCH INSTITUTIONS

Of all research workers those established in academic institutions are perhaps the most free to pursue their own research aims. University research work can be characterized as being largely concerned with the search for knowledge for its own sake. The only obligation is to publish, normally (or perhaps nominally?) to enrich university teaching. Although at the operating level, therefore, the import-conversion-export process is the same as for any other research institution, the intakes into the majority of university departments are self-generated. A significant consequence is that those responsible for the management of academic research institutions are usually more aware of the constraint imposed by the scarcity of scientists than of the dominant import-conversion-export process. They are likely, therefore, to regard scientists of the necessary ability or promise as the dominant intake, and their work, whatever direction it might take, as more valuable than the finding of solutions to specific problems. Even in universities some support for research work is 'earmarked', in the sense that it is given for particular kinds of work, e.g. cancer research. More usually, however, it is likely to be given for research in a broad disciplinary field. The relevant environment is the scientific world; the pay-off for management and sponsors is prestige.

In organizational terms this means that, in a university research department, the import and export systems are usually undifferentiated from the conversion systems. Each project or programme 'leader', once appointed, can, and frequently does, set up a self-perpetuating, self-generating system. Provided that a reputable output is maintained in the form of scientific publications or brilliant students, and that some teaching – often the minimum – is undertaken, task and sentient boundaries coincide. In an extreme form this is the traditional way of building a research institution, when the leader of the institution becomes a law unto himself, will brook no interference, and acknowledges no rights other than his own to decide what shall be investigated and how it shall be done. It has to be recognized, furthermore, that a certain amount of this 'freedom' appears to provide a healthy environment for the development of originality.

A considerable disadvantage is that traditional academic research tends, in such a situation, to be compartmentalized and the growth of any one part beyond a comparatively small size becomes improbable without a major struggle for power and an organizational revolution. The processes of overall management, whether conducted by the head of a department or by a professional group, tend to become a catch-as-catch-can contest for resources and an administrative battleground rather than a means of rational decision-making about investment.

Apart from compartmentalization arising from the power struggle, the increase in the number of specializations within broad disciplines is also tending to fractionate academic research work and alienate disciplines from each other. This can have two effects: on the one hand, there is a great deal of multiplication of effort with a dissipation of scarce resources; on the other, when a particular scientist (or a group of scientists thinking alike) gets control, he tends to reject those whose point of view or approach does not fall in line with his own, and creative cross-fertilization is thus constrained.

Moreover, as the status of research work in general, and of university research departments in particular, rises, the status of those whose reputation has been made in this field tends to rise at the expense of those who are responsible for other university activities – for example, the teaching of students, particularly the teaching of undergraduates. There are, of course, individuals who can combine teaching and research, but just as there are competent teachers whose contribution to original research work is negligible, so also there are brilliant research workers who succeed only in confusing or even demoralizing any students they may have. In the same way, as the status of research rises, the criteria for the selection of university staff may also change. A record, or a promise, of achievements in research work can then become more highly regarded than other qualities that might have more relevance for the selection of people who are to be responsible for students' growth and maturation. Unwittingly, the primary task of the university tends to be changed, and the throughput of research scientists consequently tends to outrank that of students as the dominant import-conversion-export process. Undergraduate teaching becomes little more than a 'factory' operation, acting as a ruthless and wasteful selection procedure for postgraduate status. It is, perhaps, small wonder that students in many parts of the world are beginning to grow restive, and that, because they are dependent for grades on university goodwill, their hostility often takes the form of protests against injustice outside the university.

Once research competence has become a main, if not the decisive, criterion, determining the original selection and the subsequent status of university staff, then those who have aspirations to academic careers have to conform to the new standards, and the circular process is reinforced. It may well be that the time has come for a re-examination, and if necessary a redefinition, of the primary task of our universities; if so, it should perhaps be undertaken overtly, rather than come about as a by-product of the re-evaluation of research activities.

INDUSTRIAL RESEARCH

At the other end of the scale is the industrial research enterprise, either a part of a large industrial concern or an association supported by an industry and by government. Its immediate environment is the industry or part of it that it works for. Scientific standing, as such, is largely irrelevant, or at best a kind of 'bonus' for the scientists within the enterprise and an aid to recruitment. For the industrial research enterprise it is not enough to say that its primary task is the creation of new knowledge. To survive, it must create knowledge that results in practical pay-offs for its sponsor. Prestige alone is insufficient. Thus the primary task of an industrial research enterprise must always be closely consistent with the primary task of the sponsoring institution. Since industrial institutions have as their overall primary task the making of profit from the manufacture and sale of products or services, research activities must produce findings that will contribute to profit.

This requisite implies control over the import process to ensure an optimum mix of externally and internally generated problems. Externally, interaction in both scientific and non-scientific fields contributes to problem formulation and solution. Plainly, a research enterprise must remain open to stimulation from relevant scientific disciplines, but interaction with non-scientific fields, particularly the market, is more difficult to manage. The task of industrial research is to invent new products and improve existing ones, and to examine to what extent its work can either extend existing markets or open new ones. But pertinent problems can be formulated adequately only if the research enterprise itself has some interaction with the market its sponsor supplies, either through other existing functions of the industrial institution, or directly on its own behalf. This is essential if there is to be a fruitful matching of scientific and technical resources to environmental opportunities.

What is optimum can to a large extent be determined only retrospectively. Thus research management has to produce enough outputs – acceptable manufacturing or marketing solutions – to satisfy the needs of its sponsor and so guarantee continuing investment in research; but it also has to ensure that heavy pressure for short-term results does not grossly interfere with the work necessary to produce long-term pay-offs.

Another aspect of industrial research management derives from the need to have solutions put to practical effect. A high proportion of unutilized solutions can imply only a discrepancy between research activities and sponsor's needs such as to jeopardize continued investment in research. To the extent that the results of research suggest that new products be marketed or new markets opened – in other words, to the extent that the research enterprise is trying to redefine, or to modify constraints on, the primary task of its sponsoring institution – it is attempting to satisfy needs that are unrecognized rather than overt. It follows that 'outputs' from the research enterprise may require more vigorous 'marketing' than is usually considered compatible with the dignity of scientific work; and not only 'market' research to ensure that problems are germane to latent needs, but 'sales promotion' to ensure that solutions are implemented.

The need to maintain adequate boundary controls between the research enterprise and the environment of the sponsor and his market means:

(a) Selection of intakes, to ensure an optimum project mix.

(b) Monitoring what happens to outputs to ensure utilization. 'We produce the findings, its up to *them* whether they use them or not' is an inadequate output (as, of course, is the 'exporter' who cannot communicate with his consumers).

(c) Control of programme and project teams to ensure that they do not:

　　(i) become imprisoned either by their techniques or by commitment to each other;

　　(ii) work on projects that are irrelevant in terms of pay-off;

　　(iii) pursue 'pure' research at the expense of application.

Few industrial research managements can therefore afford to delegate control of import and export processes to programme and project management. They have either to retain these sub-systems as undifferentiated parts of overall management, or to set up structured sub-systems for the purpose. Equally, because they are depriving leaders and members of project teams of the right to generate their own questions (and to degenerate, if they wish, into closed systems) they will be likely so to alienate the more creative scientists in their institutions that task and sentient boundaries can never be assumed, or should never be allowed, to coincide. Differentiated functions of the managing system to provide adequate 'home bases' for scientists are essential not only as compensations for the scientists, but as a means of reducing commitment to task-system boundaries and of intensifying commitment to sentient boundaries relevant to the task.

Before we leave discussion of the managerial problems of industrial research, something should be said about 'services' – both internally to the research enterprise itself and externally to the sponsoring institution and the consumers of its products. Internal services take the form of laboratories for various kinds of testing, computer installations, equipment-building and maintenance, library and information units, as well as administration, financial control, and, in the larger enterprises, personnel. External services consist of dealing with the sponsor's or its customers' problems – trouble-shooting. For the most part, the activities of these service functions, though often intricate and exacting, are routine – chemical analysis, programming, abstracting, and the like. Frequently, the distinction between service functions and project operating systems is far from clear. All are part of a research institution and as such expect to do research work. As long as the distinction remains inexplicit, and service functions continue to be given research budgets as a sort of consolation prize, they will persist in behaving as though their primary task is to do research and not to give service; and inevitably they will be rated inferior on both counts. A model organization would permit service activities to be judged by service criteria and research activities by research criteria.

The statement of the remedy is easy, the implementation of the consequent policy difficult. First, there is nothing to debar scientists from having more than one role, one in service and another, or others, in project teams; indeed, many creative scientists find relief in having some routine task to which they can turn their hand when they are stuck in their research task. But the obligations of their different roles and the criteria by which their performance in each is judged have to be clearly differentiated. Second, it may well be desirable to have research work done in the service functions, on the functions themselves; for example, on the improvement of the techniques of analysis. Third, contact with the external environment while engaged in trouble-shooting can provide valuable feedback data for use in current or future projects. For all these reasons the members of service functions need a research outlook and some at least should have research ability. The balance is not easy to maintain.

Government research falls somewhere between academic and industrial research as far as scientific 'freedom' is concerned. It is usually more constrained than either by its administrative practices. Because government research departments are spending public money, they are constrained as to the field in which they can work and, if they are on defence work, Official Secrets Acts and the like may deny them publication and even discussion of their findings. On the other hand, because they are not attached to profit-making enterprises, they are usually concerned with longer-term projects than are industrial research enterprises, and have a greater freedom to choose the particular line of investigation they will follow. In effect, their primary tasks are defined with greater precision than those of university research departments, but with less precision than those of industrial research enterprises.

Scientists in academic research have almost complete freedom to work on what they want to work on and to publish results, but, unless they take personal steps to act as consultants on practical problems in industry or government, it is seldom that they see any very direct applications of their findings to practical problems. For many, the process can stultify. Scientists in industrial research, on the other hand, are lucky if the problems they are called upon to tackle are always what they would have chosen for themselves, and only occasionally may they publish; but they have the frequent satisfaction of seeing their findings put to immediate practical use. Scientists in government research have some freedom to choose their line of work, can usually publish unless the work they are doing is classified, and sometimes have the satisfaction of knowing that they have influenced, if not determined, government policy.

Organizationally, government research work tends to be severely constrained by the bureaucratic procedures of its environment. Scales of pay, rank, and promotion are commonly geared to those in other government agencies. In contrast to research workers in universities, it is seldom possible for members of government research establishments to enhance their salaries by doing other work, nor, in contrast to members of industrial research institutions, is it possible for them to obtain the level of salary that can be secured in industry. Accounting for expenditure and justifying the use of equipment frequently take a disproportionate amount of the time that should be spent on more productive work. Nevertheless, the great problem for the management of government research institutions is to avoid their becoming closed systems. The security that government service usually offers, the academic model that so many government research establishments are founded on, the natural tendency of scientists to believe that they know better than anybody else what is important, and the long-term projects they engage in, can all conspire to equate task, sentient, and organizational boundaries. Industrial research enterprises are frequently forced into a project-type organization; government research departments often should be, if only to ensure that their work becomes more relevant to their environment.

CHAPTER 15

Airline Operations: Task and Constraints

Our work in research organizations and in the building of a new steel works was followed by a study of a transport undertaking – specifically, of the growth and development of an airline. This is a large airline engaged on passenger- and cargo-carrying. It operates scheduled services in competition with, and in co-operation with, other airlines, both nationalized and private, subsidized and unsubsidized. In this chapter and the next three, however, we are concerned not with a particular airline, but with an exercise in building an organizational model for the task of running any contemporary airline.[1]

PRIMARY TASK, THROUGHPUT, AND BASIC ACTIVITIES
REQUIRED

The primary task of any commercial airline may be defined in general terms as the transport of passengers and/or cargo by air at a profit. As already stated, 'at a profit' is used as shorthand for 'in such a way as to secure the survival of the enterprise over the long term'. Financially, this means ensuring that revenue (for some airlines, of course, revenue plus subsidy) exceeds expenditure so that there is, in the long term, sufficient capital and credit for growth, development, and the replacement of equipment; and, in the short term, adequate working capital to run the services provided.

The process by which the airline performs its primary task is the transport of passengers and cargo from departure points to arrival points. The dominant intakes are therefore passengers and cargo; the conversion process turns them from departures into arrivals; and the outputs are the same passengers and cargo when they arrive.

---

[1] By saying 'contemporary' we are excluding the possible organizational consequences of the introduction of automatic flying – including take-off and landing. We are concerned with the problems of control in an operation in which aeroplanes still have to be flown by human fliers, on whose skill the safety of both passengers and crew depends.

FIGURE 35 *The basic import-conversion-export activities for a passenger throughput*

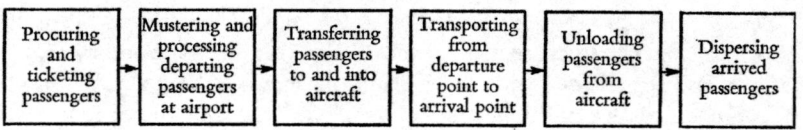

The basic activities required to process passengers through this system are shown in *Figure 35*. A similar diagram, with rather different activities, could be drawn to show the process for cargo. Because a high proportion of airline revenue is derived from passenger-carrying, it is on this aspect of airline activities that we propose to concentrate.

Each of these activities is obviously susceptible to considerable elaboration. Procurement of passengers may require more active marketing – advertising, promotion, and selling – than mere publication of timetables. Mustering departing passengers may call for city terminals and transport between city and airport. Transferring passengers from check-in points in airport buildings to aircraft may involve shepherding them through customs and waiting rooms, making separate arrangements for their baggage, and supplying ground transport from building to aircraft. In the aircraft both passengers and crew may have to be fed and provided with other services during the flight.

PROFITABILITY, SAFETY, AND SERVICE

Safety is a costly preoccupation for every airline. Flying is, or, more importantly, is widely believed to be, inherently dangerous. Civil airlines throughout the world are accordingly governed by law to protect not only the passengers they carry but the people and property over whom and which they fly. Aircraft, aircrew, and engineers all have to be licensed by government agencies; flying height and direction, take-off and landing are subject to government-appointed traffic controls; and the kind of equipment for flying and landing that aircraft must carry is laid down by government orders. All reputable airlines not only obey both the letter and the spirit of the law but, in addition, take their own precautions and lay down strict rules to regulate conditions – regarding the weather and the state of the aircraft – under which flying is, and is not, permitted. As little as possible is left to chance.

It remains true, however, that just as the only 'safe' motor car is one that never leaves a garage, so the only 'safe' airline is one whose planes never leave the ground. Absolute safety – not only in airlines but in any other human activity – is an ideal that can never be achieved. To this extent, airline management has to accept that, for all the statutory regulations, and for all the additional precautions it may take, there is a limit beyond which the multiplication of safety devices and the addition of safety regulations cannot be justified in terms of risk reduction; indeed, they may increase risk. This is because in any human activity there must come a point at which the requirement to utilize yet another device or to observe still another regulation actually adds to danger by distracting those responsible for the activity from what they have to do. Operation of the device or compliance with the regulation occupies their attention and energy, and hence confuses rather than helps them in their task.

Airline management also has to steer an optimal course between safety and profitability. At some point a decision has to be made, explicitly or implicitly, that the reduction of risk likely to be achieved by installing new equipment or issuing new regulations is too small or uncertain to justify the expenditure involved; or alternatively that, because of improvements in technology, operating standards can be relaxed to increase revenue or reduce costs, on the grounds that any added risk is minute. For example, because of improved landing devices certain types of aeroplane may be allowed to land with lower cloud-ceilings than others, or because of built-in reliability some makes and types of engine may be permitted to fly for longer periods without overhaul.

The making of such decisions is likely to pose fewer problems for a subsidized airline, which could presumably, in the extreme, define its primary task as 'to run as safe an airline as is consistent with flying at all'. Such an airline need worry less about the effect on its competitive position of delays and cancellations because of weather conditions or 'technical faults'. Again, decisions of this order may be less critical for a scheduled airline than for a charter company. For such a company, which has to maintain a profit rate in the short term, safety can be a very costly constraint.

In the long term, however, airline safety is essential for profitability: an airline with an unacceptably high accident-rate loses passengers and therefore revenue. Thus, at the strategic level, there can be no major conflict between safety and reliability on the one hand, and profitability on the other. In day-to-day operations, in contrast, as we shall see later, safety and profitability – or, more strictly, safety and the maximization of revenue – are always in potential conflict. Take-off, for example, is governed by the weight that has to be lifted under varying weather conditions. Poor conditions limit pay-load: the greater the quantity of fuel that has to be carried, the fewer the passengers and the smaller the cargo that can be lifted. The amount of fuel taken depends on flying conditions and on the expected weather at the scheduled destination and at alternative landing-points. A 'superfluous' safety margin of 250 gallons of fuel might mean disembarking ten passengers, or the equivalent in freight, and incurring a corresponding loss of revenue.

In the case of any national airline, whether nationalized or not, the public definition of its primary task is commonly in terms of providing a service rather than making a profit. Public demand, often reinforced by government pressure, is for cheap, comfortable, frequent services, with seats available whenever required. But ready availability of seats means lower occupancy, which in turn means either lower revenue per flight or a higher fare per passenger. Similarly, the use of smaller aircraft to carry the same traffic by operating at greater frequencies involves higher capital costs and higher operating costs per seat.[1] Profitability can be reduced if the airline yields either too little to such pressures or too much: a nice judgement is required.

OTHER ENVIRONMENTAL CONSTRAINTS

National airlines in, for example, Britain and France have been under another kind of pressure which may run counter to the requirements of profitability: this is to support the national aircraft industry:

'BEA, as a nationalised corporation, should have the country's aviation interests as a whole at heart, and not merely a thin vertical line of black figures in its accounts.

'It should be apparent to those guiding BEA's fortunes (for whose professionalism I have the greatest respect) that as far as Britain is concerned it is better to have thriving independents, a factory at Weybridge building airliners, mostly for export, and a BEA a million or two in the red, than a BEA making a profit of a million, with no independents and a scar of unemployment at Weybridge' (from a reader's letter in *Flight*, 10 June 1965).

---

[1] For a fuller discussion of the load-factor dilemma, see Milward (1966).

Correspondingly, of course, if the airline accedes to government pressure, buys the costlier home-built aircraft and goes 'a million or two in the red', it is exposed to an equally vociferous outcry about the cost of subsidies and is castigated for operating inefficiently.

Operations of all airlines are controlled by national laws, international regulations, and intergovernmental agreements (bilateral and multilateral), which limit their freedom to operate services and to determine fares. For most airlines such freedoms are also further constrained by membership of IATA (International Air Transport Association) and by specific commercial agreements with other airlines. Such pool and consortium agreements may give an airline the protection that a cartel affords; but the accompanying restrictions may be the price that has to be paid for securing traffic rights.[1]

We have already referred to the external traffic controls to which aircraft are partly or wholly subject between taxying out at the beginning of a flight and taxying in after landing. An additional constraint for most airlines is that airports and terminal buildings are usually owned, designed, built, and managed by other and different authorities, each of which has its own ideas of design and management. It is as though railway companies had to operate from stations none of which they owned and most of which were under different managements, and whose staff had different customs and spoke different languages.

The other major external constraint on airline operations, as all passengers know, is weather. Technical advances are combating this constraint – June 1965, for example, saw the first automatic landing of a scheduled passenger flight – but many years must elapse before all or even most of the disruptions to services caused by weather will be overcome.

A delay due to weather conditions inevitably affects the customer's attitudes towards flying generally and towards the airline concerned; and there is the added difficulty that the conditions causing the delay may not be at his departure point, but at the arrival point or *en route*, or even at the aircraft's earlier departure points. This would matter less if in the meantime the passenger did not see other aircraft, coming from or going to different places and flying different routes, arriving and taking off on time. Rationally, an explanation of the delay is readily comprehensible, but even rational comprehension is made more diffi-

[1] For a full account of governmental constraints and relations with competitors, see Barry (1965, pp. 44–66, 76–9, 82–4).

cult for the layman if, because of different performances on take-off and landing, operating standards vary for different types of aircraft and for the same types on different airlines. It is particularly confusing when the standards are more stringent for the newer types than for the old, or when, because of greater familiarity with route or airport, one captain will fly when another will not.

CONSTRAINTS INHERENT IN THE TASK

Delays, whether attributable to weather or to other causes, have the effect of marginally prolonging the 'shelf-life' of a product which, as someone has remarked, is more perishable than strawberries. For a transport undertaking or for a hotel, a seat or room not occupied is wasted. And, unlike a railway train, an aircraft cannot accommodate standing passengers who might make up for wasted seats on other services. It is a matter of semantics whether one defines the products of an airline as passenger seat miles and cargo ton miles or as arrived passengers and delivered cargo – we would favour the latter definition – but whether one treats the empty seats as unsold products or as superfluous resources they are part of the costs of scheduled airline operations. In a large airline a rise or fall of 1 per cent in load factor[1] can represent £1 million in revenue over the year and the difference between a profit and a loss. And because, in contrast to that in a manufacturing enterprise, the 'plant' – the physical resources required for the conversion process – in a transport undertaking is mobile, each arrival point is also a departure point. Consequently, even a full aircraft that has to return empty achieves only a 50 per cent pay-load. More generally, for an airline as for any transport undertaking, the market is for ever shifting; its potential is a function of aircraft location and flight schedules.

'Mobile plant' creates another constraint: this is the need to standardize operations at the departure/arrival points that it connects. In an airline, where the points are numerous and widely scattered, local differences in law, custom, language, and even climate have to be surmounted in order to achieve the necessary standardization of procedure and adequate communications between the many parts of the enterprise. Administration of the stations by other authorities thus further complicates an inherent airline problem.

But of the constraints intrinsic to the task of a passenger airline perhaps

[1] The proportion of space occupied to space available.

the most significant are those that derive from the fact that the through-put of the process consists of human beings. We consider these constraints here in some detail and will be returning to them later in this and succeeding chapters.

CONSTRAINTS IMPOSED BY THE HUMAN THROUGHPUT

The problems arising from the nature of the throughput can, at least in theory, be considered as falling into three categories.

First, there are problems connected with the requirement that passengers surrender some of their individuality and exchange it for dependence on the airline. As we postulated in Chapter 8, in the light of our examination of dry cleaning, the apparently simple, reality-based, demand that the customer makes of a service enterprise is often complicated by less rational and less conscious demands; moreover, dependent relationships in themselves inevitably arouse anxiety and provoke hostility.

Second, there are problems associated with travelling away from home. It would appear that this is an experience that is dynamically similar to temporary separation from the mother in infancy, and that the frustration and anxiety associated with that early experience are, so to speak, 'stored' in the inner world of the individual. These infantile fantasies attach themselves to and suffuse comparable situations in adult life. Travelling therefore tends to induce anxiety, not necessarily conscious, which is greater than realities might warrant.

The third type of problem is related to flying itself. As a means of transport the aeroplane is relatively new. It is also 'unnatural', in the sense that whereas human beings can, without mechanical aids, propel themselves on land and in water, they cannot fly. And both these factors combine with dramatic reports of accidents, which may kill many people, to evoke a belief that flying is inherently more dangerous than other modes of travel. It is seen as glamorous and adventurous, and frightening as well.

Thus an airline has to contend with the problems of dependence common to all service industries, with the anxieties that people have about travel away from home, and with the still more specific anxieties provoked by flying itself. These last anxieties are probably the strongest and they subsume the others.

It is possible, of course, that the level of anxiety will diminish as flying, like motoring, loses its novelty and becomes more mundane. This is probably happening already: the reduction in the incidence of air-sickness, for example, may not be entirely attributable to the smoother and more comfortable flying conditions in modern pressurized planes, but in part to a wider acceptance of flying as a normal form of transport. On the other hand, a recent study suggests that even among motorists there is a high level of unconscious anxiety, which seriously affects their judgement of reality (Menzies, 1965). It is to be expected, therefore, that in flying as in motoring a number of mechanisms will be used to cope with the fear that it engenders. Moreover, many of the mechanisms, like the anxieties they are created to allay, will be unrecognized and unconscious.

When we postulate unconscious factors we are, of course, exposed to the retort: 'But if anxiety is unconscious, how do you know it exists? And even if it exists, is it relevant?' We derive our postulates from two sources. First, there is the accumulated body of knowledge about human personality, some of which is summarized in Chapter 2; second, there is observable behaviour. Paradoxically, a denial of anxiety is often an expression of anxiety, especially if it is an unsolicited denial. Take, for example, the dry-cleaning customers who asserted that they were not frightened, even though no one had suggested that there was anything in the transaction to be frightened about. The anxiety that they were denying had come from within themselves. More generally, behaviour that is inadequately related to reality, and that the people concerned would themselves acknowledge in other circumstances to be irrational or abnormal, is *prima facie* evidence of the presence of anxiety.

Under normal conditions, passengers' anxieties are to a large extent contained. It is true that passengers can fail to turn up, can get lost between check-in and aircraft, can mishear announcements (not always their fault), and can misread directions; but perhaps this is characteristic of the unpredictability of any human throughput and it is difficult to be sure about attributing such withdrawal to anxiety. Simple manifestations are nevertheless familiar enough: on any flight it is possible to observe some passengers making the sign of the cross when entering the plane or crossing their fingers before take-off.

When a delay occurs for any reason, however, anxiety becomes much more overt. What was an orderly 'package' of passengers awaiting embarkation can disintegrate in minutes into a disorderly rabble: some angrily demanding an immediate alternative, some making their own arrangements, others deciding not to fly but not telling anybody about their decision, and still others sinking into an apathetic, passive with-drawal in which they neither hear announcements nor see messages put on screens right in front of them.

On one occasion, when we were visiting an airport to observe pas-senger-handling problems on the ground, a flight was delayed because the aircraft was grounded by weather conditions at its previous point of call. Most of the passengers had reached the airport before the staff knew of the delay, and were either at the check-in desk or waiting in the departure lounge. There were eighty-four of them. The delay was announced over the public address system and staff at the check-in desk informed passengers there. Several, some of whom had already checked in, immediately left the airport. Two middle-aged, prosperous, and ap-parently highly respectable men carrying briefcases turned on a steward-ess standing by the check-in desk and in loud voices swore at her, using language of which, on reflection, they could not but be deeply ashamed. Within twenty minutes of the first announcement, the staff knew that the delay would be for several hours. They therefore organized two buses to take the passengers to lunch at the most expensive hotel in the city. They hoped that this would be a more agreeable alternative to the issuing of vouchers for lunch at the rather dull airport restaurant. Eight announcements were made about this arrangement, requesting passen-gers to board the buses, and three members of the staff went all round the lounge asking passengers if they were booked on the delayed flight and, if so, inviting them to go to the buses. Forty minutes later the buses left with thirty-seven passengers only. Even while one of the announce-ments was being made – for the fifth or sixth time and very clearly on this occasion – a group of four passengers were heard to complain:

'We're having to wait a hell of a time for this bus that's to take us back';

and ten minutes after the buses had left others were visiting the informa-tion desk to ask when they would arrive. In the meantime, the ground staff managed to get another flight on another route diverted to pick up some of the passengers later in the day, and arranged for another airline with spare seats on a later flight to take the rest. When it was all over – the flights had gone and there were no passengers left behind – only sixty-three had been accounted for.

Observations of this kind suggest that the containment of anxiety is brittle. It is as if passengers have geared themselves to accept that for a limited period they will surrender their independence and tolerate the anxieties of travelling away from home and of flying. But once this time-boundary is breached by a delay, the pent-up anxiety is unleashed and expressed in irrational and abnormal behaviour.

Behaviourally, of course, the different kinds of anxiety are inseparable: they interact with each other. *In toto*, however, passenger anxiety is a major problem for airline management. As we shall try to show, it interacts with and mobilizes the anxiety of airline employees and ramifies through the organization in unexpected and undetected ways.

CHANGES IN THE PRIMARY TASK

With the increased speed and lower cost of air travel, airline operations, particularly those of the short-haul carrier, are becoming far more akin to local rail travel in terms of duration (as distinct from distance) of journey, frequency of service, and complexity of connections. In the meantime, however, the present generation of air travellers has been brought up to expect far more in the way of comfort and service than the rail traveller. In sharp contrast to the latter, air travellers, even though going on what in terms of railway timing would be only a suburban journey, expect to be relieved of baggage-handling, to be fetched and escorted about airports, and to be fed and generally looked after *en route*. Moreover, if any delay occurs for whatever reason, they expect to be provided with free meals and if necessary free alternative transport or overnight accommodation.

Such expectations descend in part from the early days of commercial aviation when it had two quite distinct markets: it provided long-distance services for the very wealthy (and adventurous), and extremely short-distance services (e.g. between Portsmouth and the Isle of Wight) for the man in the street. It has been the objective of airlines during the postwar years to bridge the gap between these two markets – in other words, to get flying accepted as a normal means of transportation available to a majority of the population. The emphasis has been on building up an image of regular, reliable services with few luxuries. There has been a process of scaling down passenger's expectations – of an exotic, exciting experience – and of bringing them into closer conformity with what an airline endeavours to purvey – a quick, reliable service from A to B. This process has, however, been made hesitant by competition between different airlines. When fares and frequencies are limited by statutory bodies and international agreement, then aircraft type, comfort, and other passenger benefits are the only competitive variables left. A reduction in comfort and benefits offered that is not agreed by all can adversely affect competitive status. Initiative by any one airline has thus been curtailed. The only alternative to generally agreed standards would appear to be the introduction of aircraft so superior to competitors' that chances could be taken on a relative reduction in the comfort and benefits offered. At the present stage of aeronautical development no one airline is likely to be able to introduce markedly superior aircraft; and slightly superior aircraft could be expected to give only a temporary advantage.

But competition draws airlines in the opposite direction in other ways as well: for example, to sell more than a service from A to B. By 'selling' destinations (in conjunction with travel agents) airlines have tended to reopen and widen the gap between the expectations of their newer customers and the service they purvey. For customers who have bought an all-in holiday, a punctual efficient service *en route* may be a relatively unimportant criterion of the airline's performance compared with the weather, the hotel, the food, the service, and the beach on arrival.[1]

In other words, although the activities of most commercial airlines can still be embraced by the definition of the primary task given earlier – 'the transport of passengers and/or cargo by air at a profit' – an increasing range of activities may call for a redefinition of the strategic task. This would have the effect of turning the airline company as a whole into the equivalent of a holding company with the primary task of making a profit through investment in transport, hotel, tour, car-hire, and holiday activities. Air transport as such would then become the primary task of one of the subsidiaries.

---

[1] It is also possible that by selling exotic destinations an airline is selling a feeling of adventure and excitement as well, and is thus raising, by other means, the unconscious anxieties of passengers about the journey.

CHAPTER 16

Boundary Controls in an Airline

Figure 35 in the preceding chapter depicted the basic import-conversion-export activities of a passenger-carrying airline. These passenger-processing activities are the airline's transport operating activities and are carried out in operating systems. The organizational boundaries between the operating systems of the airline must therefore occur at points in this process. Moreover, if the organization is to fit primary task performance these boundaries will be drawn at those points, and only at those points, at which there are discontinuities in the process; whether in terms of the technology used, the territory where the process occurs, the time at which it happens, or some combination of these dimensions. At these points boundary controls will be required.

The major discontinuities of the total transport system lie, obviously enough, at each end of the actual flying operation. Flying has its own technology, which differentiates it from anything that happens on the ground.[1] On the ground, the activities concerned with mustering departing passengers and transferring them to aircraft, on the one hand, and with unloading arrived passengers and dispersing them, on the other, have much in common. Departure points for outgoing flights are arrival points for incoming flights; and shepherding and transporting arrivals are much the same as shepherding and transporting departures. Procuring and ticketing passengers may or may not be grouped organizationally with mustering and loading, depending on the extent of marketing activities and on the congruence or incongruence of marketing areas and arrival/departure points.

It follows that, in a simple airline, the basic organizational model would differentiate two major operating systems: a ground system, committed to 'import' and 'export'; and a flying system, committed to 'conversion'.

[1] In a sense it has its own 'territory', too – the air – which also differentiates it from ground activities.

FIGURE 36 *The import-conversion-export systems of an airline*

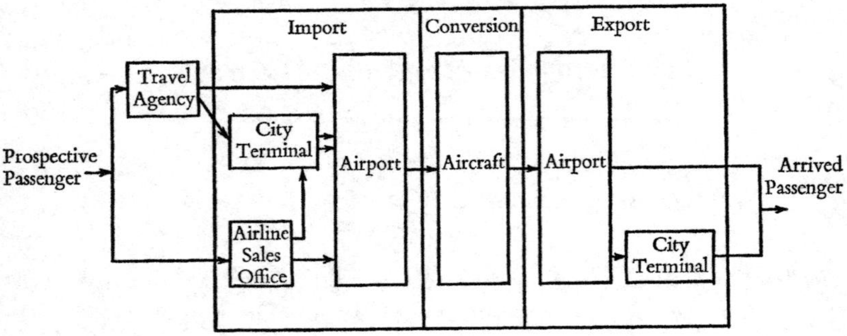

The basic activities of the throughput process differentiated in this way are shown in *Figure 36*.

If operating systems are differentiated, then, as a corollary, a managing system external to these is required. As well as overall management and management of the operating systems, the managing system is likely to include specialized and differentiated control and service functions. In the development of a small airline the earliest functions to be differentiated in this way are likely to be financial control – to measure the results of operations – and planning – to reconcile traffic expectations with the availability of flights. The corresponding basic model organization is shown in *Figure 37*.

Until air transport operations become pure bus services, and passenger-handling at departure and arrival points is therefore not required, the essential operating units within the ground system will consist of a number of territorially differentiated departure and arrival stations. There may be, in addition, a number of selling-points, and still further units which combine selling-points and departure/arrival stations. Seats on any one flight may, of course, be sold at a number of different selling-points; the second-order managing system of the ground organization will therefore have to control and co-ordinate reservations. It will also have to provide services for passengers being mustered and awaiting take-off. The basic model for ground organization is shown in *Figure 38*.

In contrast, within the flying system the basic operating unit is a service-able aircraft, properly loaded and crewed for a flight. Until flying be-comes entirely automatic and the flight deck uninhabited, the management

FIGURE 37 *A basic model of airline organization: 1, The overall system*

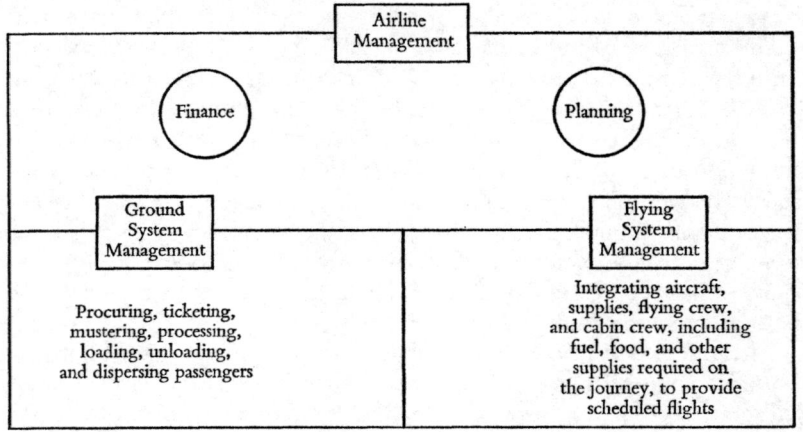

of this unit is vested in the captain of the aircraft. As soon as he starts his engines on the apron he comes under the direction of an authority outside his own company – the air traffic control system. It is this system that gives him instructions about which runway he may use, at what height he may fly, and by what route he must travel while in its area. From the time he starts his take-off, therefore, his own superior management must have

FIGURE 38 *A basic model of airline organization: 2, The ground system*

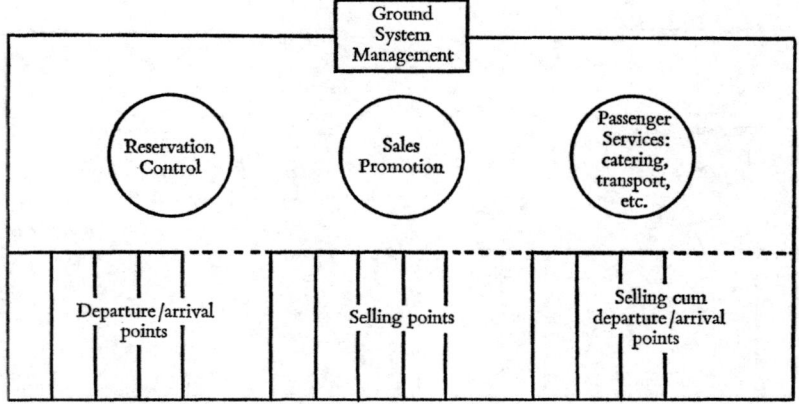

delegated to him full authority and responsibility to make his own decisions about the conduct of the operation. But as soon as the flight has been completed, the particular operating unit – aircraft, flight crew, and cabin crew – has fulfilled its purpose. Although in some small airlines, with few flights, the same flying and cabin crews and the same plane may stay together for some time, even in this very simple case constraints (more fully discussed below) of aircraft cost and maintenance and the limitation of crew flying hours mean that such operating units are constantly being broken up and re-formed. More commonly, in large airlines the same crew members and the same planes seldom stay together for more than one outward and return flight. Indeed, on longer flights, because of limits on crew flying hours, either flight crew or cabin crew, or both, may be replaced, and the flight completed with others.

The model appropriate to this task is therefore a form of project organization. In this terminology, the flight or sector using the same aircraft and crew would be a 'project', and small self-contained networks, with their own flying system, staff, and aeroplanes, would be regarded as 'programmes'.

The major control and service functions of the managing system of the flying organization are thus the provision of pools of flying crew, cabin staff, and aircraft. There may be, in addition, a differentiated supplies function providing catering and other requirements of the temporary project operating units. The aircraft pool must obviously be backed by

FIGURE 39 *A basic model of airline organization: 3, The flying system*

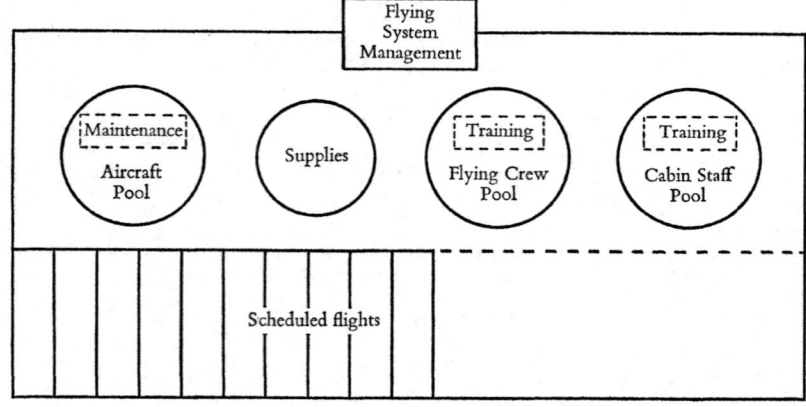

an engineering maintenance function, and the pools of flying crew and cabin staff, similarly, by training functions. *Figure 39* shows the basic model organization for the flying system.

Using this organizational model as a basis, we now examine the boundary controls required in an airline in the light of the nature of its task and the constraints upon it. We consider first the control of the boundary between the enterprise and its environment, and subsequently the control of internal boundaries.

STRATEGIC BOUNDARY CONTROLS

Because flying is, for most people, glamorous, exciting, and dangerous, airlines receive very full publicity in everything they do. If an airline is also a national airline, the press of its own country always gives it particular attention. Any incident, however slight, makes news, and an accident that results in death makes world headlines. The top management of an airline cannot escape notice even when things are going well; when things go badly the full glare of publicity is turned on it and on its activities.

All critical decisions – to open or close a route, to buy new or dispose of old aircraft – have to be made in the knowledge that they will have to be justified publicly. Many such decisions require governmental ratification. A major difficulty is that entrepreneurial decisions, based as they have to be on uncertain forecasts of future traffic, are often difficult to justify in the public arena in advance of their implementation. Decisions to purchase aircraft, in particular, have to be taken many years ahead of their going into service; the capital cost of aircraft is high and their rate of obsolescence in a highly competitive market is fast. When, in addition, a national airline is expected to support its own aircraft construction industry, it may be precluded from making what its top management believes to be the best economic choice available.

The glamour and the hint of danger, the publicity accorded to airline operations, the long time-span of the strategic decisions that have to be made, government and international control of aircraft, airways, and air traffic, the constantly advancing technology of flying, and the continuous attention that needs to be paid to the definition of the primary task that determines the nature of the transactions between the airline and its environment, all mean that a senior member of overall management – usually the chairman, president, or whatever title he carries – cannot avoid being a public figure. His task is so to present the airline to its environment that he can protect the operating systems and their relevant control and service functions from the kind of interference that jeopardizes the performance of their sub-tasks. He has to be perceived as reliable and well informed. To fill this role he has to be, in reality, reliable and well informed. Hence the organization of which he is the head has to be one that avoids long lines of communication. In other words, traditional hierarchies, which, in a large enterprise, might have ten or more levels, are inappropriate for airline management, or, alternatively, there has to be a rapid by-passing communication channel built into the organization.

In practice, top management (the airline management 'box' in *Figure 37*) contains three roles: the public role – to mediate relationships between the airline, government, and the public as a whole; the long-term planning role – to formulate, implement, and monitor airline strategy in the light of traffic development, on the one hand, and technical advance, on the other; and the executive role – to run the airline's day-to-day and week-to-week operations. The extent to which the roles can be taken by different individuals depends on the extent of the airline's operations and, of course, on the experience, qualifications, and personalities of those who fill top-management posts. In a small airline all three roles may be filled by one experienced and versatile individual; but overall management of a large airline is likely to require three people or even more.

In the same way, the functions differentiated in the first-order managing system depend on the extent to which overall management requires specialist help in market forecasting and planning, aircraft procurement, economic forecasting and financial control, personnel management, public relations, and other parts of its overall task of controlling transactions between the airline and its total environment.

MAJOR OPERATING CONTROLS

By major operating controls we refer to the management controls that are exercised over the throughput at the major discontinuities in the import-conversion-export processes. In an airline, the controls may be judged effective in so far as the throughput, whether passenger or cargo, is processed through the system and exported at the required destination without being subjected to any change other than in location.

Strictly speaking, a passenger enters the system when he makes an inquiry about a flight and makes, or does not make, a booking. If he does not book he immediately becomes a 'waste' output, who may or may not subsequently return as an intake. As *Figure 36* shows, for many prospective passengers the import process may begin with a travel agency, which, although it is part of the resources required for the total process, nevertheless lies outside the organizational boundary of the airline. We shall restrict our discussion here, however, to the ticketed passenger who presents himself, at city terminal or airport, for his correct flight. From that time to the time he climbs aboard his aircraft he is, from the airline's point of view, the responsibility of the passenger-handling staff on the ground; in the aircraft, both on the ground and in the air, he is the responsibility of the staff of the flying system; and on disembarkation he once more becomes the responsibility of ground staff, but at a different station.

It follows that, at the day-to-day operating level, four major regulatory activities are required: the first in the import system, concerned with converting individuals arriving at check-in into orderly loads at the aircraft's side; the second at the boundary between the ground and flying systems, to relate loads to seats; the third in the flying system, at take-off, during flight and landing, to ensure 'safe' behaviour; and the fourth in the export system where, flying finished, passengers have to be disposed of promptly and with a minimum of negative reactions.

In a great many respects, of course, the nature of the controls follows rationally from the nature of the process. Basically, controls over quantity, quality, and cost in an airline are comparable to those in a manufacturing enterprise. Our concern here, however, is with factors specific to airline operations and the extent to which these complicate and interfere with control mechanisms and with organizational functioning generally. We have in mind particularly the characteristic that airlines 'produce' their 'products' under the eyes of their customers, and the responsibility and associated anxiety of flying.

RESPONSIBILITY AND ANXIETY

An airline management cannot but respond to passenger anxieties. To quote one authority:

'Management must plan to allay individual fears, and to control group fear. They must plan to encourage the nervous, and comfort the fear-stricken and stop panics. Employees must be trained to avoid giving rise to unnecessary fears. They must be trained to recognise signs of individual fear so that they can behave sympathetically, and ease it. Above all they must be trained to sense the beginnings of group fear so that it can be dealt with before it gets out of hand. Sensible precautions taken openly and in a matter of fact way cause far less fright than strained and covert moves' (Barry, 1965, p. 40).

As the same writer emphasizes, 'however ill-founded his (the passenger's) fears are, the airline must deal with them' (*loc. cit.*); but not all the anxieties are unrealistic:

'Of course, air transport is inherently dangerous, and that fact must never be forgotten' (*op. cit.*, p. 317).

Therefore, airline employees must find ways of coping not only with passenger anxieties but also with their own anxieties, which arise from their responsibilities for passengers in their care. These coping mechanisms should be based on reality:

'The dramatic nature of an airline crash tends to cast an unhealthy spell over the minds of airline officials . . . Having emphasised safety airline managers must then put it into perspective. Thinking about safety does not preclude them from thinking about profitability. Safety and profitability are just as compatible objectives in airlines as they are in any other business' (*loc. cit.*).

This is a valid point. Activities directed towards raising safety standards can be a satisfying means of discharging anxieties. Accordingly, there is a risk that safety precautions may be elaborated to the point at which they become not only uneconomic but also, as we suggested in the last chapter, even dangerous in their multiple application.

In general, if anxiety can be acknowledged it is less likely to distort judgements of reality. The advice that managers should never forget the dangers of air transport is therefore sound. Many managers are able to articulate their anxiety. One senior executive said in conversation, for example,

'My telephone rang at two in the morning, and when that kind of thing happens, I always fear the worst' –

'the worst', of course, being an accident. Or, to quote another:

'The one thing I dreaded when I took this job was becoming involved in dealing with an accident.'

Capacity to acknowledge anxiety does not, of course, mean that it need 'cast an unhealthy spell':

> 'You keep it at the subconscious level: it's always there, but you mustn't let it worry you.'

To the extent that their membership of the airline organization involves any emotional investment, all its employees must carry a share of the responsibility and concomitant anxiety. We would postulate that anxiety is a function of commitment to the organization rather than of delegated accountability as shown on an organization chart. Indeed, the less the actual accountability for safety and the less the personal exposure to danger, the more difficult it is to find activities that provide a rational and realistic way of discharging anxiety, and the more difficult it is, too, to acknowledge and to articulate it. It follows, therefore, paradoxical though it may seem, that those who are overtly least accountable and personally least at risk may be most subject to unconscious anxiety. Lacking rational outlets, this may express itself in dysfunctional ways and in unexpected places. Some of these are explored in Chapters 17 and 18.

CHAPTER 17

Task and Sentient Groups in the Flying System

The jobs of aircrew – of captains in particular – are manifestly the most stressful. They are central to the task of the airline; they carry the immediate risk of flying and immediate responsibility for passengers' safety. It is important therefore to consider by what mechanisms – some deliberately created, others not so and perhaps less obvious – their anxieties are dealt with, how effective these mechanisms are, and to what extent the stress is contained within the flying system or spills over into other parts of the organization.

THE PILOT

The high standard to which aircrew are selected and trained is itself a discharge mechanism. Both flying skills and medical fitness are regularly and frequently checked. Intensive retraining is accepted as standard practice whenever there are changes in equipment or flying procedures. So far as his training or skill is concerned, the individual never gets the benefit of the doubt. Either he satisfies the high standards of competence or he ceases to be a pilot. The risk of losing one's licence is a lurking fear; but, correspondingly, retention of the licence is a substantial vote of confidence.

Sophisticated managers of pilots are very much aware of the stress of flying and of the dangers to which this can lead. Research in aviation medicine and practical experience confirm that

'when anxiety is felt, mental activity . . . is disorganised in greater or lesser degree. This disorder and the disorder of skill should be regarded not as cause and effect, but as complementary aspects of a disorder of the reaction to complex psychological dangers, which the individual perceives to be present in his environment, and which he cannot immediately remove' (Davis, 1964, p. 13).

Or again:

'In certain marginal circumstances – marginal in weather, or workload, or both – it can be shown that any pilot concentrates on the primary task in hand, resulting in a diminishing field of consideration. Thus, at a critical phase of the flight, the commander is narrowing the scope of his thinking to a point where the wider "commander view" ceases to exist – just at the time when the exercise of the widest degree of responsibility is of paramount importance. It is at this point too that if any emotional stress is placed upon the pilot, mistakes are more likely to happen' (Baillie, 1964, p. 20).

Over and over again, reports of aircraft accidents – and in 50–60 per cent of these human error is at least a contributory factor – point to situations in which stress has interfered with a captain's judgement. One such report of an accident arising from an abandoned take-off identifies eleven environmental conditions and concludes:

'Such factors individually are not abnormal in winter operations; cumulatively they may cause a high degree of stress, the effect of which will depend upon the sensitivity of the individual. In this case they may well have contributed to a build-up of tension in the mind of the captain, but the extent, if any, to which this influenced his actions cannot be determined.'[1]

The rate of technical change is rapid. As aircraft become faster, instrumentation and other aircraft systems become more complex, and traffic control procedures in the air become more stringent in regulating aircraft movements, there is a proportionate increase in the probability of pilots' becoming overloaded and making mistakes. To combat this, more rigorous training is not sufficient; nor is

'. . . exhortation to "fly safely" . . . sufficient. Pilots do not like thinking about accidents. If forced to do so they will invariably project their fears and anxieties on to other people and other things by attributing the most likely cause of any accident in which they may be involved to deficiencies in the aircraft, its performance, its equipment, radio aids or other facilities and services associated with the operation. Only very reluctantly indeed would they ever willingly consider the possibility of accident due to their own mistake, error or misjudgement. After all, this is not very surprising because it is surely going

[1] Ministry of Aviation Civil Aircraft Accident Report (C.A.P. 223, 1965), quoted in *Flight International*, 4 March 1965.

against human nature, and certainly the nature of most pilots, to ask them to adopt a defeatist attitude of this sort' (Baillie, 1964, p. 21).[1]

Accordingly, progressive airlines have introduced control cabin procedures which redistribute the work-load in such a way as to provide for double-checking and at the same time leave the captain freer to act as 'the supervisor or manager of his aircraft to the greatest possible extent' (*op. cit.*, p. 24).

Detailed specification of the activities and interaction of aircrew is the more necessary because they constitute such a transient group. Not only are the 'project units', consisting of the aircraft, the aircrew subgroup, and the cabin crew subgroup, being repeatedly broken up and re-formed; but membership of the subgroups too is transitory. In short-haul airlines in particular, it is infrequent for the same crew of captain and co-pilots to be rostered together for more than a few days at a time; often it is only for a few hours. Some airlines avoid keeping the same group together as a matter of principle, on the ground that they are likely to develop short-cuts and other deviations from standard procedures, which could cause difficulty or even danger when individuals did have to be transferred to other crews. All pilots on a particular type of aircraft should therefore be completely interchangeable. Frequent reshuffling is in any case necessary for economic reasons. Statutory regulations, airline policies, and union agreements closely prescribe the individual's flying hours and minimum rest-periods; leave, sickness, and training events intervene; so that if maximum utilization of expensive pilot time is to be secured, rostering has to be on an individual rather than on a group basis. To roster the same plane, aircrew, and cabin crew together continually would be prohibitive.

This does mean, however, that the sentience of the flying group is temporary and limited. The pilot's commitment is not to the task group. The kind of emotional support that an enduring small group can provide, especially in stressful conditions (for example, coal-mining), is thus denied to aircrew.

The significant sentient grouping within the organization is, then, the pool of flying crew. In a smaller airline this may constitute the whole body of pilots; in a larger airline there will be sub-pools associated with particular aircraft types. For many pilots, however, 'pool' membership

---

[1] This closely corresponds to motorists' attitudes and behaviour as described by Menzies (1965); cf. Chapter 15, p. 191 above.

is less significant as a defence against stress than are identification with flying as such and a professional commitment to those who fly rather than to the employing organization.

Towards the employing organization pilots are inevitably ambivalent. They cannot afford to display hostility towards their own immediate flying management, because this is the management that supports the values of safety on which they themselves depend; and most managers are fellow fliers themselves. Union activity, on the other hand, is a less risky outlet for aggression that cannot be expressed in the subordinate-superior relationship. Moreover, in so far as management's formal negotiators are representatives of overall management, rather than of flying management, it is all the easier for fliers' representatives to behave toughly and to cast themselves in the role of defenders of safety in the face of rapacious, profit-seeking commercial managers. One suspects, nevertheless, that pilots are sometimes ashamed of their threats of industrial action; that they do not always respect their shop stewards and would disown them if union activity were not so important as a stress-reducing mechanism.

More generally, we can suggest that the anxieties of aircrew appear to be characteristically dealt with by processes of insulation. The glamour that surrounds the flier in our society – a glamour that in itself provides some defence against occupational stress[1] – is institutionalized within the organization. Pilots are accorded high status and receive salaries that put them on a par with, or above, relatively senior managers on the ground. They are equipped with comprehensive, written regulations that dictate the operating and safety standards to which they must conform. In operational flying they have complete responsibility and authority to decide whether to fly or not to fly, and, if they do fly, how much load they will carry. A captain's right to say 'no go' is respected and usually unquestioned by ground staff. In any dispute with ground staff the captain automatically receives his own management backing. He is

---

[1] It may be speculated that in a similar way in medicine glamour has helped to defend doctors against stress. In this context the recent outbursts from the BMA about pay and conditions of work may be seen as a response to a declining glamour and a search for other supports. Despite the image that TV features and other fiction build up, general practitioners are increasingly perceived by the public as writers of simple prescriptions and referrers to specialists. More importantly, the profession as a whole, supported by other TV programmes, increasingly glamorizes and raises the relative status of the specialist, to the point where the work of the general practitioner is in reality denigrated. The parallel with aircrew and ground staff is suggestive.

encouraged to use his authority to cut through inefficiency and delay in ground handling, and even the passengers the captain meets are in a sense different people. However truculently they may complain to a member of the ground staff about a delay, they invariably accept attentively and submissively a captain's explanation. Passenger-handling staff are inferior in rank, and are not flying. The captain is the man on whom the passengers will have to depend, literally for their lives, within the near future. Unless they believe in his competence and authority, they can only decide not to fly.

THE CABIN CREW

The apparent task of the cabin crew is to look after the passengers during the flight: to provide them with food and drink, take care of special passengers – children travelling on their own, invalids, and so on. In practice, they spend most of their time as waiters and waitresses. The status they are accorded derives, however, from their less obvious but nevertheless very real tasks. Safety regulations demand the employment of cabin staff, trained in emergency procedures, in a fixed ratio to the number of passengers. Thus they would have to be carried even if they had no other function to perform. Their other, covert, task is to reassure the passengers that all is well and that there is no need to be afraid of flying. While they have to be skilful at their jobs, their primary qualifications are a capacity to remain pleasant and helpful whatever the conditions, and the ability, in the fortunately rare moments of crisis, to give passengers precise instructions for their safety. Because they are more 'on view' than flying crew, their behaviour has to be such as to confirm in the minds of the passengers an image of competence and reliability – of the airline in general, and of the particular captain and aircrew on whom they, like the passengers, depend for their safety.

Cabin crew share in the glamour, excitement, and anxiety of flying; but they have far less responsibility for safety than have the crew on the flight deck. The glamour defends them to some extent from the anxiety. As with aircrew too, the cabin crew subgroups are constantly dissolved and reconstituted so that the relevant task-oriented sentient group to which they commit themselves, and which affords them protection, is the total cabin-staff pool. Unlike aircrew pools, however, the cabin-staff pool is not divided into sub-pools that are technically differentiated from each other by aircraft type. Sub-pools that have no technical basis for differentiation are arbitrarily defined and are therefore likely to attract less commitment. Barry notes:

> 'One airline has adopted the device of breaking-up 100-strong "flights" of cabin staff by appointing a number of "aunts" and "uncles", without organisational status, who are expected to work informally among groups of 25 cabin staff' (1965, p. 155).

Partly because such arbitrary groups provide less support and partly, too, because cabin crew do not depend on their own management to support the values of safety to the same extent as aircrew do, cabin crew can afford to be more truculent in direct negotiations.

ENGINEERING

The second major function of the flying system is to provide serviceable and properly loaded aircraft. Service and loading take place on the ground, and, because of the need to refuel, unload, reload, and service at every stop, these functions have to be geographically differentiated. Nevertheless, in terms of technology they belong to the flying system, since without them it could not operate.

The status of the engineering function is determined to a considerable extent by law. A station engineer, responsible for fault eradication and routine checks, has to be licensed, as do those members of his staff who sign the clearance certificates without which the aircraft cannot take off. As a final sanction, the licensed engineer, like the captain, can be prosecuted in the criminal courts if he fails to carry out statutory regulations.[1]

For engineers, as for flying crew, there is a precise and written procedure that must be gone through before every take-off. In addition, specified checks have to be made daily and after specified numbers of flying hours.

Organizationally, engineers on stations always have the right of direct contact with their home base for any advice and help they may need. Indeed, whatever the apparent local organization may lay down, out-station engineers invariably regard themselves as directly responsible to the headquarters engineering department. But because they share with aircrew in a complex technology to which each makes a specific contribution, there is considerable mutual respect between them. Engineers,

---

[1] In practice this rarely, if ever, occurs. Engineers have, however, had their licences withdrawn.

too, have the authority and the responsibility to say 'no go' if they are unsatisfied with the serviceability of the aircraft. Thus problems stemming from the imbalance between the flying group and the rest of the organization do not emerge as conflicts between aircrew and station engineers: this would be much too dangerous.

On an engineering base, however, where major overhauls are undertaken, the problems are more acute. The level of responsibility, as measured by the consequences of a mistake, is high; but by the very nature of the task the base is organized more like a traditional factory and hence has little of the glamour attached to station engineering, and none of that attached to aircrew. On an engineering base there is never a dependent, trusting, and admiring audience of passengers – or even of other ground staff. Nor do the engineers have much, if any, contact with aircrews. To the stress inherent in their task is added the 'overspill' or the residue of conflict between fliers and others that is not worked out elsewhere. It is to be expected that negotiations between engineers on the base and their management, and between management and trade unions, will always, in consequence, tend to be characterized by what on the surface appear as irrational and unreasonable demands. Exchange of staff between base workshops and stations can help, but until means are found of neutralizing the effects of the special position of aircrew, the management control of any engineering base will always be more difficult than the actual problems warrant.

Thus the flying system, and within it the aircrew, represents a powerful and dominating elite within any airline. This creates, between the flying system and other systems, an imbalance which is not adequately portrayed in diagrams such as *Figure 37* or in conventional organization charts. In the next chapter we consider some of the consequences of this imbalance and, in so doing, the particular position of passenger-handling staff on the ground.

CHAPTER 18

The Flying System/Ground System Boundary

We have said that transactions across a boundary and hence the kinds of control required are conditioned by the 'cultures' – the attitudes, customs, and expectations – on each side of the boundary; that the kind of conversion process in the control region depends on the extent to which the throughput that is being regulated is passing from a system with one set of characteristics to a system with a completely different set of characteristics. We have already discussed in the previous chapter the special problems of aircrew, cabin crew, and engineering; in this chapter we shall discuss the other task and sentient groups involved in transactions across the flying system/ground system boundary, and the function – load control – that straddles it.

THE CULTURES OF THE FLYING AND GROUND SYSTEMS

Before we move on to consider the organizational consequences of the imbalance between flying and ground systems, however, one other phenomenon that arises from the nature of the primary task of an airline and from the special position of aircrew should be mentioned: danger creates a culture that encourages personal leadership. Just as a nation at war requires its Churchill, so a ship or an aircraft requires its captain who is expected to rise to moments of crisis – to go beyond technical competence and to produce the extra touch of genius that will convert a near-disaster into a brilliant coup. One would expect a higher premium to be set on personal leadership in an airline, therefore, than in less hazardous industries, and one would expect, too, that this attitude would extend beyond the actual task of flying, where it is most relevant.

On the other hand, a culture that encourages personal leadership also expects that the leader will at times break – or rise above – the rules. This may well be functional on the flight deck and in a chief executive's office. But there are other aspects of airline operations in respect of which personal leadership in this sense is positively dysfunctional and for which bureaucratic forms of organization are much more appropriate. In ticketing, for example, and in accounting activities generally, meticulous attention to detail is required. Standardized procedures are needed throughout the airline and any improvisations resulting from local exercise of 'personal leadership' could be, from the commercial point of view, 'dangerous'. One would expect, therefore, that just as those concerned with flying realistically need mechanisms to insulate themselves from commercial pressure, so also, equally realistically, would those concerned with maintaining bureaucratic procedures require corresponding protection from the 'dangers' of personal leadership.

It follows that any airline may be faced with the organizational problems of containing and reconciling what are, in effect, two cultures. Such problems are especially likely to emerge where the two cultures collide; but if this boundary is 'protected' from the possibility of conflict, overspill is probable elsewhere in the organization – overspill into the engineering base has already been mentioned in the previous chapter. In effect, if the resolution of conflict does not occur in the control region between the boundaries of the conflicting cultures, it is likely to be projected into other regions. But, without very special provisions, it is unlikely that other control regions will be equipped, organizationally or culturally, to deal with the projected conflicts and hence controls will break down more frequently than might otherwise be expected.

THE BOUNDARY BETWEEN FLYING SYSTEM AND GROUND SYSTEM

Overspill into the engineering base would be less if the boundary between the ground system and the flying system was itself not so heavily guarded against expression of the hostility that the powerful and superior position of aircrew must inevitably provoke. The operating boundary is crossed at the aircraft side when the throughput is transferred from one operating system to the other. A number of mechanisms are used to protect this boundary. The most obvious, of course, are the reservations and load-control systems.

Unless aircraft capacity were unlimited, the absence of a reservations system would result in frequent negotiations between passenger-handling staff trying to dispose of their throughput and captains resisting the overloading of their aircraft.

Load control, on the other hand, is a function that guards the boundary by blurring it. Strictly speaking, it is the captain of the aircraft who is responsible for load control – for ensuring that the total weight is within the prescribed limits for the aircraft, that the load is properly distributed around the centre of gravity, and that the fuel carried is appropriate to the weight, to the distance to be covered (including alternative landing-points), and to the prevailing weather conditions (for example, head-winds). But what is commonly called the load-control function is the detailed calculation of the load and fuel data for each flight. Much of the activity is routine arithmetic, and discretion is severely limited, but whoever is responsible for the calculations shares with aircrew and en-gineers anxiety about the consequences of a mistake. He has to face the likelihood that the captain will often rely on the figures and sign the load-sheet without any but the most perfunctory checking. Thus a mis-take in the working could literally be a fatal mistake. But the one who made it would survive. Located, as he often is, within the ground organ-ization, the person (or, at a large station, the whole section) responsible for these calculations can provide an intolerable focus for the anxiety of those passenger-handling staff who want to put the maximum load onto a given aircraft. His sentient groupings are within the ground system; but the values he is called upon to uphold are the flying values of aircraft safety rather than the ground values of maximizing traffic.

Performance of the primary task of an airline requires the assembly of 'packages' of passengers and their baggage at a departure point. It then requires that these be correctly loaded into a serviceable and adequately crewed aircraft before take-off. If providing the aircraft and the crew forms a technologically differentiated system from procuring and mustering passengers, then the amalgamation of packages and air-craft – loading, and its control – would more logically be located within the flying system. This would certainly be a 'safer' organizational posi-tion from which to resist commercial pressures, which is to a large extent what the load calculator on the ground is required to do. A load controller located within the ground system has to be protected by very high status indeed if he is to be in the position to uphold commercial values and to confront the captain with them.

Yet another theoretically possible solution would be to locate this function within a separate operating system, interposed between what we have called ground and flying operations. The load controller would then take over the throughput from the ground system, dispatch a correct load, and return the remainder, if any, to the ground system.

To be able to do this his status would, again, have to be very high.

At all events we can say that this function, especially if located within the ground system, has the effect of blurring the boundary and blunting the confrontation between the ground and flying systems.

Confrontations are therefore relatively rare. This does not mean that captains are not subject to some pressures from passenger-handling staff. The latter may suggest that the captain should change his route and, by making an additional stop, take more passengers and less fuel; or they may point out that another captain has taken off under identical conditions with a heavier load. Captains, however, have the power to make the decisions and if they wish to veto such suggestions they can always adduce justifications in extraneous factors (meteorological reports, air-traffic control, statutory restrictions on flying hours) or in technological mystique. Thus although captains may yield to suggestions of this kind, the amount of 'give' is usually negligible.

In effect, such transactions across the boundary of the ground and flying systems are not genuine bargains. They have the function of exposing aircrew to a glimpse of the pressure under which the passenger-handling system operates. They are a reminder that pilots are members of a commercial enterprise[1] and not just fliers; but it is a reminder under such protected conditions that safety is unaffected. On the other hand, an occasional 'victory' for passenger-handling staff provides some measure of compensation for their constant occupation of the inferior status. It makes an unequal relationship slightly less unequal.

On the ground, staff may tend to magnify their victories. They attribute any change of flight plan to their own influence, and in this way deal with some of the hostility that the unequal status inevitably generates. Too large a victory, however, can raise their unconscious anxiety unbearably, or make them consciously anxious: safety margins may have been eroded. On one occasion a number of passengers were waiting for the only aircraft of the day due to call at a particular airport. The weather was bad. The captain of the aircraft before leaving his previous destination asked for a local weather report. His message was overheard by a member of the ground staff responsible for mustering and loading the passengers. Anxious to get his passengers away, he informed the station of departure that the weather would be clear by the time the aircraft

---

[1] Not that the pressures are solely commercial: ground staff are likely to be more concerned with the immediate problem of dealing with superfluous passengers than with loss of revenue.

arrived. He next heard that the aircraft had taken off. As the time of its arrival approached and the weather did not clear, he became more and more worried, until all he could do was to lock himself in a lavatory and pray. The weather cleared with ten minutes to spare. Even though it was not his responsibility to give weather reports, and the captain had in fact obtained his report through the meteorological office, he declared:

'I'll never do that again – I wouldn't go through what I went through for anything.'

Thus though a captain's decision may make life extremely difficult for passenger-handling staff, they can seldom retaliate without restraint, because they dare not win too well.

In general, therefore, the boundary between ground and flight operations is strongly defended by various mechanisms. The safety/profitability conflict is not fought out there; it is replaced by a pseudo-bargaining procedure. This has the positive effect of preserving safety standards from erosion. On the other hand, it leaves the conflict unresolved. Before we examine the consequences for passenger-handling staff of the lack of conflict resolution at this point, we must turn briefly to the export boundary – the flight is over, the passengers have arrived and have to be disposed of.

Once the flight is completed and passengers have been delivered to the destination to which they have booked, the airline – regarded only as a transport undertaking – has finished its job. The sooner, therefore, the passengers are removed from the system, the better. Anything further that has to be done for them incurs more cost and reduces profit. But it often takes passengers some time to readjust to their different status. They have been wooed by advertising and other devices to book on a particular airline; they have had their baggage taken from them with the assurance that it will accompany them; and on the flight they have been offered food, drink, papers, and other services. At the end of the flight they have been told by a charming stewardess how much their custom has been appreciated and hopes have been expressed that they will travel by the same airline again. Suddenly they are left on their own. Cold impersonal notices tell them where to collect their baggage, ruthless customs officials rifle through their old and new possessions, and, if they are lucky, a notice or another official tells them where to get a bus to the city. Small wonder if sometimes they feel let down or squeezed dry. If, at the same time, the journey from A to B has converted them from citizens into unfamiliar aliens, and as such they are subject to special regulations, the sense of loss and let-down can be severe, depriving them even of their normal common sense. It can react against the airline that has carried them. In many airports, particularly the large ones, in which disposal of arrived passengers is the business of the airport authority, the airline may be unable to control the boundary adequately and have to tolerate the undeserved odium that results.

The situation can be exacerbated if the airline is one that sells inclusive holiday tours, including hotel accommodation and sightseeing visits. If there is a discrepancy between the 'safe, reliable service' from A to B that the flying system purveys and the expectations that the customer is buying, it usually falls to the passenger-handling staff to straddle the gap. If the customer buys a blue sky, bright sunshine, palm trees, golden sands, and blondes in skimpy bikinis, he is likely to complain not only about delays and uncomfortable journeys but about dull skies, stony beaches, and well-covered bodies. Whoever is nearest will catch it. This is never the flying staff and seldom the office from which the original ticket was bought.

PASSENGER-HANDLING ORGANIZATION WITHIN THE GROUND SYSTEM

The activities that make up the task of the passenger-handling staff are mustering passengers and their baggage in aircraft-sized loads; and getting them from the point or points of assembly to the aircraft. The task is inherently centred on departure/arrival points – airports and their ancillary town terminals. Although, even when the weather is fine, passenger-handling staff can never insist on a captain's taking a full complement, they are nevertheless subject to strong pressure from the commercial side of their own ground system to dispose of the maximum number of passengers; and, in the event of passengers' being unable to get into the plane for which they have booked, to pressure from passengers to make alternative arrangements for them. In addition, they are far more exposed to passengers' pre-flight behaviour than are any other airline employees, and passengers' anxiety is likely to interact with and to exacerbate their own.

They work for the most part in buildings provided by other organizations, with all the additional problems that this entails. Abroad, the buildings are frequently owned by competitors, who, however co-operative they might be, are unlikely to be so co-operative as to weaken their own competitive position. And passenger-handling staff have to contend with passengers' irritations over things that have nothing to do with air traffic as such – delays at customs, or even in road traffic before arrival at the airport; inadequate airport buildings or catering; and a host of other, often trivial, but cumulatively annoying disappointments. Where, as in London and other large cities, the airport buildings are not adequate for the traffic through them, some checking-in may take place in city terminals and then staff have to contend with still more possibilities of 'losing' their passengers. The number of boundaries crossed by a typical passenger on a journey from London to a continental city is illustrated in *Figure 40*. At each movement across a boundary there is a chance of passengers' straying – and stray they do. Even if there are no delays, these discontinuities can themselves rupture passengers' brittle control over their anxieties.

In short, the efficient and profitable operation of an airline ideally

FIGURE 40 *Boundaries crossed by a typical airline passenger who checks in at a city terminal for a flight from London to a continental city*

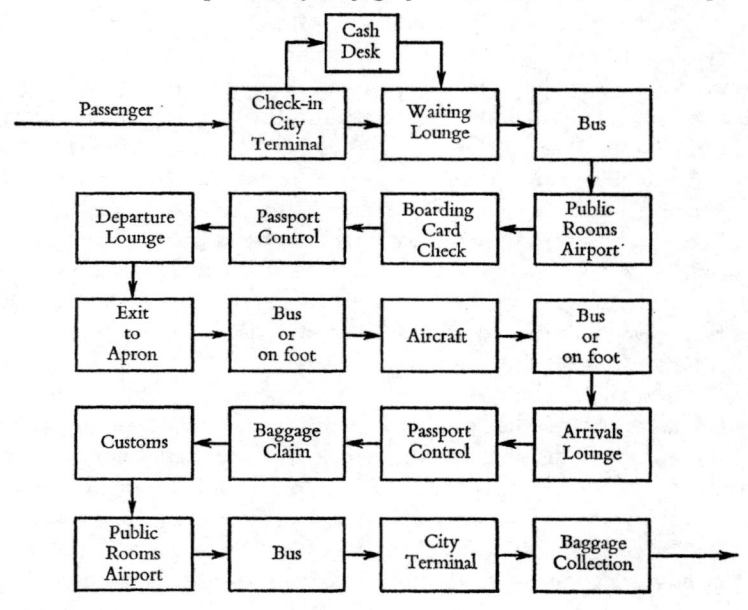

requires passengers to be predictable, uniform, interchangeable units, who will check-in in the appropriate numbers at the appropriate time and will be amenable to being counted, packaged, stored, and transferred to the aircraft in an orderly way. Yet while the pressures for efficiency and profitability are strong, what passenger-handling staff are dealing with is an unpredictable throughput of idiosyncratic individuals over whom they have only intermittent control in an uncertain and anxiety-provoking situation over which they have no control. The very unpredictability of the throughput with which they have to deal makes it impossible to lay down routines to cover every possibility. Passenger-handling staff have to be given authority to exercise judgement and discretion in how they deal with disappointed and anxious passengers – and far more of them are anxious than would ever admit it. But the exercise of judgement and discretion, which can be very satisfying, is usually required only when something has gone wrong: over-booking of the aeroplane, delay, lost baggage, or other major or minor catastrophe. They also have to deal with the effects of changes in policy and procedure which, whether good or bad, are more likely than not to evoke negative responses from passengers, simply because they are changes. Apart from the exasperation that such events can cause, passenger-handling staff can hardly but feel that if other people only did their jobs more efficiently they would have an easier time. They cannot 'get at' flying crews; they should not act out their exasperation and annoyance on the passengers; their only outlets are their own management and other passenger-handling and booking units within the commercial sub-system of their own company. At the same time, those members of commercial sub-systems who never come face-to-face with passengers and for whom the airline is just a commercial operation are not likely to sympathize with expressions of anxiety of which passenger-handling staff themselves are unaware. They realistically need organizational protection from kinds of behaviour, and especially kinds of leadership, that would upset their routines.

On stations where there is comparatively little of a particular airline's traffic, the small working group of passenger-handling staff can provide mutual support, and the group can reinforce allegiance to the airline. On those stations in which selling and traffic boundaries coincide, it is also even possible for sales staff in a city office and passenger-handling staff at the airport to be interchangeable, and the reinforcement can then be maximized by the insight that each is given into the other's problems.

But larger stations have to be manned for twenty-four hours every day of the week; they require large numbers of staff who are generally divided, for economic reasons, into different sections for each of the processes shown in *Figure 35*, and interchange with city sales staff is usually a practical impossibility. Naturally, the duty officers in charge on any given shift have to exercise their judgement and discretion in the handling of day-to-day contretemps of the task; and inevitably, because they are different people, they do so in different ways, emphasizing different aspects of the situation.

In effect, the task group for passenger-handling activities has to be of the project type, groups being formed, disbanded, and re-formed with each change of shift, season, and kind and density of traffic. Furthermore, in a large airport the members of a shift group are widely dispersed. Accordingly, it is difficult to integrate, for example, check-in staff on the import boundary with escort and dispatch staff on the apron; and still more difficult to integrate both of these with staff at the city terminal. Thus the task group on each shift is unwieldy and incoherent, so that members cannot readily experience the satisfaction of a unitary task well done, and at the same time the sections to which individuals belong – check-in, departure lounge, escort, and others – are insufficiently distinctive in their expertise to form quasi-professional bases which could attract commitment and provide support.

The problems encountered in this area, though greater at the large busy airports, seem to be intrinsic to passenger-handling in today's conditions and, until a more sophisticated organization is invented, or the technology of checking-in more advanced – by the use of automation and computers and the redesign of airports – it seems inevitable that maladaptive mechanisms must continue. Three are observable:

(a) Passenger-handling staff behave *as if* their technology were more complex than it is – and thus more comparable to that of flying. This applies, for example, to communication. In aircraft, reserve radios are required and are usually available; but procedures determine which crew member will send or receive specific types of communication on air-traffic control or on company frequencies. On the ground, on the other hand, it is not uncommon to find many alternative types of communication (such as telephone, teleprinter, walkie-talkie, and lamsen tube) being used simultaneously and independently for the same purpose, resulting in a total of information that the organization fails to digest and reconcile.

(b) Passenger-handling staff behave *as if* they had more power than they actually do have – and are thus more comparable with aircrews. Therefore negotiations about changes of route or of fuel-load are treated as though they were bargains between equals.

(c) Passenger-handling management models its organization on that of flying. Thus whereas the organization of traffic activities tends to be based on seniority and rank as on the flight deck, the task, with its unpredictable throughput in dispersed points – check-in, customs, lounge, and apron – demands a far more egalitarian system with widely dispersed responsibilities and authorities.

Some of the bustle and activity at an airport when flights are delayed undoubtedly represents action for its own sake rather than action directed towards a positive goal – it is better to do something, anything, than to do nothing. In other words, the action itself serves as a discharge mechanism for the anxiety, both conscious and unconscious, that is inherent in the job.

THE ELIMINATION OF DISCHARGE MECHANISMS

We have shown that the ground/flying systems boundary is heavily protected in that, in reality, all the power and authority are vested in the flying system, and the flying staff are to some extent insulated against the anxiety inherent in the nature of the airline task. The protection of the ground/flying systems boundary precludes the possibility of working out the hostility that inevitably arises or the unequal conflicts across it. This is likely to 'overflow' into other parts of the airline. One would therefore expect airlines to be particularly prone to types of conflict – whether between departmental groupings or between employees and management – that appear to be largely irrational. It is also possible to suspect that some of the let-down experienced by passengers on arrival is the result of an indirect expression of the resentment felt by passenger-handling staff against both passengers and flying staff.

Some of these problems will disappear as procedures are simplified and technology improves, as check-in becomes automatic and loading computer-controlled. But as the problems disappear, so will the mechanisms they provide for the discharge of stress. There will be fewer boundary relationships into which the unresolved conflict at the ground/flying boundary can overspill. We can therefore expect that difficulties in those that remain – between selling and passenger-handling; between cabin staff and their management; between engineering base and management; between personnel management and other management control and service functions – will be intensified. And as flying becomes more and more automatic, and the flight deck eventually even uninhabited, it is not difficult to predict that very special steps will have to be taken to protect those on the ground who will be responsible for programming and monitoring take-off, flight, and landing.

PART V

The Elimination of Organizational Boundaries within Enterprises

---

R

Introduction

In Part IV we have attempted to establish the basis for a theory of organization applicable to any enterprise. We used both industrial and non-industrial examples to illustrate our proposition that the most general form of organization is what we have called the project type. In this form, activity systems through which the primary task is performed are regarded as temporary and transitional. We have tried to demonstrate that this characteristic demands special control mechanisms that are, or should be, a part of any management organization. We have also tried to demonstrate that in any enterprise the sentient groups of its members have to be identified and differentiated from task groups. When the boundaries of task and sentient groups coincide, special steps have to be taken to introduce innovation; when they do not coincide, relations between them have to be regulated.

However, both 'temporary' and 'transitional' are relative terms. There are clearly some activity systems and their associated organizations and sentient groups that remain unchanged over considerable periods of time. The great religious institutions provide perhaps the most obvious example of enduring activity systems and forms of organization. Under stable conditions, the sentient groups and task groups of an enterprise must coincide if members are to commit themselves to the enterprise and its task. Yet we believe that under conditions of rapid technical and social change, the time-scale of stability will get shorter, and the temporary and transitional characteristics of activity systems will become still more temporary and transitional for most institutions. Even the great, enduring religious institutions are having to face such changes in their environment that their methods of organization are being seriously questioned. The need to discover or to create appropriate task-oriented sentient groups, and to invent control mechanisms to regulate the relations between them and task groups, is a major task of future managements.

Our studies of research organization showed that the individual scientist tends to commit himself primarily to his project team. This probably facilitates the work of the group on the particular project; but unless the organization also provides the team member with a higher-order group with which to identify himself, the task of the project team may be redefined and its life prolonged to the detriment of the overall task of the research enterprise. Managerial attempts to disband and regroup project teams may be perceived as threatening and destructive. One-off construction and institution-building tasks pose the opposite problem in that it may be difficult to secure a coherent project organization to which the individual can commit himself in the face of his stronger identification with the firm of consulting engineers or contractors that employs him or with a professional or craft grouping.

Flying operations provide an example of a project organization in which the specific project group of pilots and cabin crew has an extremely short life – too short to evoke any commitment – and very special measures have to be taken in terms of intensive training of pilots and precise definition of roles and role relationships in order to produce an activity system in which human activities are overwhelmingly prescribed by the requirements of task performance and performance is minimally influenced by the specific membership of the crew. The crew has no time to become a group and, ideally, all captains, co-pilots, and others who operate a particular type of aircraft should be completely interchangeable. Theoretically a flight could be manned, efficiently and safely, by crew members who have never seen each other before and who might never meet again. Given such a task and such technology, the only available type of task-related sentient group with which the individual can identify must have a professional or quasi-professional basis.

Manufacturing industry commonly presents quite a different picture. In one respect, however, it is similar. The human activities required, especially at the machine-minder level, are usually prescribed in precise detail in an effort to integrate them as smoothly as possible with the activities of the physical equipment. These intermeshing activities of people and hardware constitute the primary production system. Such primary production systems are themselves sub-systems of progressively higher-order systems through the co-ordinated activities of which the task of the enterprise (or part-enterprise) is performed. Rigid prescription of activities and roles, as in the flying situation, helps to allow the substitution of one person for another in the task organization without interfering with the effectiveness of the production system.

The major difference lies in the fact that, although such substitutions do take place in manufacturing industry, the task organization and its membership usually have, in practice, considerable continuity over a long period. Social science studies in industry have emphasized the importance of the individual's affiliation to his primary work group and the deprivation and alienation created by technologies and forms of organization that inhibit the building of such groups. It has been observed, however, that groups of this kind often develop supplementary tasks and modes of behaviour which may interfere with the task of the production system to which their activities are primarily intended to contribute. A good deal of research and practical managerial effort has, in consequence, been devoted to the problem of harnessing these primary groups to the wider objectives of the concern.

In some cases a production department provides a ready-made secondary unit of affiliation. If the department is technologically differentiated from other departments in the same works, a segmented form of social structure may arise. Employees throughout the works may make common cause against management; but at least the opportunity exists for an alternative pattern of alliances through which managers and workers within one department can develop a departmental unity and perhaps wage war against other departments. The difficulty is, of course, that interdepartmental strife can inhibit the task performance of the whole enterprise.

This kind of structure has existed in parts of the steel industry, where it is perhaps not accidental that industrial relations, with one or two recent exceptions, have had a more stable history than in many other industries in this country. And in Part V, in which we propose to consider the consequences of a change in technology in a well-established industry with a stable segmented form of social structure, it is the steel industry that we use for our example.

Our thesis is that, although the conventional organization has been able to tolerate quite major technical changes in the past, it is ill-adapted to cope with the consequences of automation. We shall try to show that the introduction of a new technology which transcends established organizational boundaries can disrupt not only established task boundaries, but deeply rooted sentient boundaries as well. We shall also try to show that an organization that provides for amalgamations of activity systems within internal organizational boundaries, which themselves define sentient boundaries, inhibits technological development. A situation appears to be arising in which either past forms of organization must be discarded and new ones invented, or else the full potentialities of the new technologies must remain unexploited.

We should make it clear at this point that the type of automation with which we are concerned here brings together a computer-based 'information technology' with computer control of production operations. Other types of automation plainly have organizational implications. For example, automatic transfer lines, which substitute mechanical for human activities within an operating system, may as a result of affecting the rate or quality of output impinge on other machining or assembly systems quite removed from the one that has been automated. Similarly, it is familiar experience that the apparently straightforward and local application of a computer to stock control can have ramifications on production-planning and marketing policy. More sophisticated computer systems integrating data-handling and process control have consequences of this kind, but, in addition, contain an inherent evolutionary capacity. Because they are able not only rapidly to optimize a large number of variables but also to learn from experience, such systems can allow the enterprise to respond to environmental changes in novel and perhaps unpredicted ways.

The key point to note is that what is involved is not simply a direct impingement of technology on organization. Automation of this kind is likely to produce, or at least permit, a change in the posture of the enterprise *vis-à-vis* its environment. Organizational forms must therefore satisfy both the new technology and the new (and more dynamic) relationship with the environment. And they must also build in the possibility of adaptiveness to match the evolutionary capacity of the computer system.

There is a further problem. The shift from a non-automated system to a computer-controlled system of the kind discussed here is seldom a one-step process. 'Automation' is an ambiguous word, which can imply the *state* of having become automated or the *process* of becoming more automated. A progressive, many-stepped process, in which different production systems and control systems are successively brought under computer control, calls for corresponding 'process' characteristics in forms of organization. These must be able to exploit rather than obstruct the process of increasing automation. At each stage it will be necessary to re-examine the strategic and organizational implications of the new balance of technological and environmental factors.

CHAPTER 19

The Background to the Introduction of Automation

The material of this chapter and the next is derived from a study of a modern integrated iron and steel works with a strip mill (Miller & Armstrong, 1966). The basic flow chart for such a works is shown in *Figure 41*. Each of the five main units of plant has:

FIGURE 41 *Basic flow chart for an integrated iron and steel works and strip mill, showing enterprise/environment and intra-enterprise organizational boundaries*

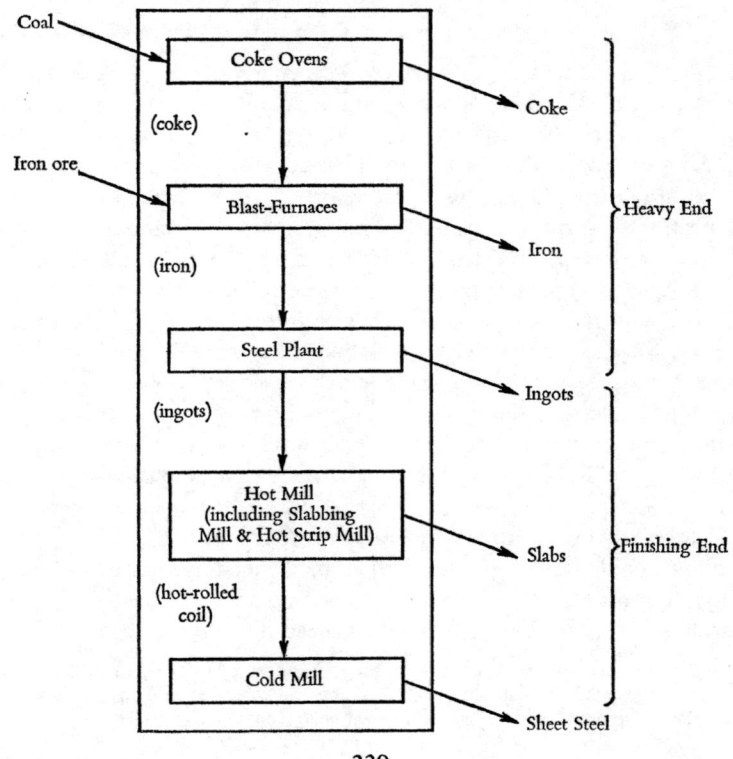

(i) a distinctive technology;
(ii) a discrete product that can be stocked and is at least potentially saleable without being further processed.

The five processes therefore could be – and in the past usually were – carried out independently of each other. Historically, each process has acquired its own experts, its own distinctive modes of working, its own culture. Production expertise has also acquired a mystique, especially in the iron-making and steel-making operations. These offer dramatic and awesome examples of man's mastery of his environment; yet it is a mastery that is not quite complete: occasionally molten metal runs wild and men die. Thus the good iron-maker, it is believed, needs to know more than the chemistry of the process: he must have a flair that will enable him to judge from the sound of the furnace, or through some sixth sense, that something critical is happening.[1]

RIGIDITY OF TECHNOLOGICAL DIFFERENTIATION

This is not to say that major technological changes have not taken place. The modern continuous wide-strip mill, perhaps half a mile long, which converts a thirty-ton red-hot slab into several hundred feet of coiled strip travelling along at thirty m.p.h., is a far cry from the hand-mills and primitive mechanized mills on which most of Britain's sheet steel was produced until twenty-five years ago. Novel techniques of steel-making have been introduced. In iron-making there has been considerable elaboration of the pre-treatment of the ore fed into the blast-furnaces. And in the blast-furnaces, as elsewhere in the industry, big increases in size have themselves created new technical problems to be solved. But all these changes have taken place *within* processes. It could be argued that the traditional technological boundaries have inhibited technical developments that might have breached them. Continuous casting of slabs, for example, which cuts through the boundary between heavy end and finishing, appears to have been used effectively in Russia for wide flat-rolled products for a number of years before it was tried out in Britain. Again, it would seem to the layman that the development of direct reduction processes (which would convert iron ore directly into steel without the need for blast-furnaces) has been inordinately slow.

---

[1] The good miner, too, not only knows the technology of mining; he 'knows' about working underground and can sense what is going to happen when danger is imminent. The conditions are graphically described in Trist *et al.* (1963).

Integrated works, which have brought all the processes together on one site, have until recently eroded unit independence less than might be imagined. Integration certainly allows the blast-furnaces to pass iron to the steel plant in molten form, instead of as pig iron, and reduces the time required to reheat ingots between steel plant and slabbing mill; but at both these boundaries provision also exists for creating buffer stocks of cast or granulated iron and of cooled ingots. Minor or major stocking areas are used not only between all five units, but between sub-units within them as well. Each unit has retained its distinctive technological and cultural identity.[1] Some kind of affinity is recognized between the units that contribute to making the steel ('the heavy end') and between the units that roll it ('the finishing end'); but on the whole the technological and accompanying social boundaries have remained rigid. A unit provides career paths for workers and managers within it and transfers between units are uncommon.

THE CONVENTIONAL MANAGEMENT STRUCTURE

These technological and cultural 'facts of life' are reflected in the conventional management structure (see *Figure 42*). Each unit has its production manager. A works manager is responsible for co-ordination of production for the works as a whole and he is supported, if necessary, by two assistant works managers, one for each 'end'; but it is the production managers who are the repository of expertise on the processes of their units and their statements about what they and their plants can and cannot do are difficult to gainsay.

Figure 42 shows also the location of engineering services and other specialist functions. As the diagram suggests, the chief engineer is often perceived as parallel and equal to the works manager. The mechanical, electrical, instrumentation, and other engineers under him head hierarchies broadly corresponding to the production hierarchy and deploy maintenance staff in each production unit. (Only the mechanical engineering hierarchy is depicted in *Figure 42*.) Since there is no single engineering boss within a production department, but several bosses, the power

[1] To some extent the differentiation is reflected in trade union structure. Blast-furnacemen, for instance, still have their own separate union, and production workers in other units have their separate wage agreements. Increasing technological complexity, however, has brought substantial growth in the numbers and power of the craftsmen, whose wages had been lagging behind those of production workers. Protection of their differentials has somewhat increased the community of interest of the production workers *vis-à-vis* the craftsmen.

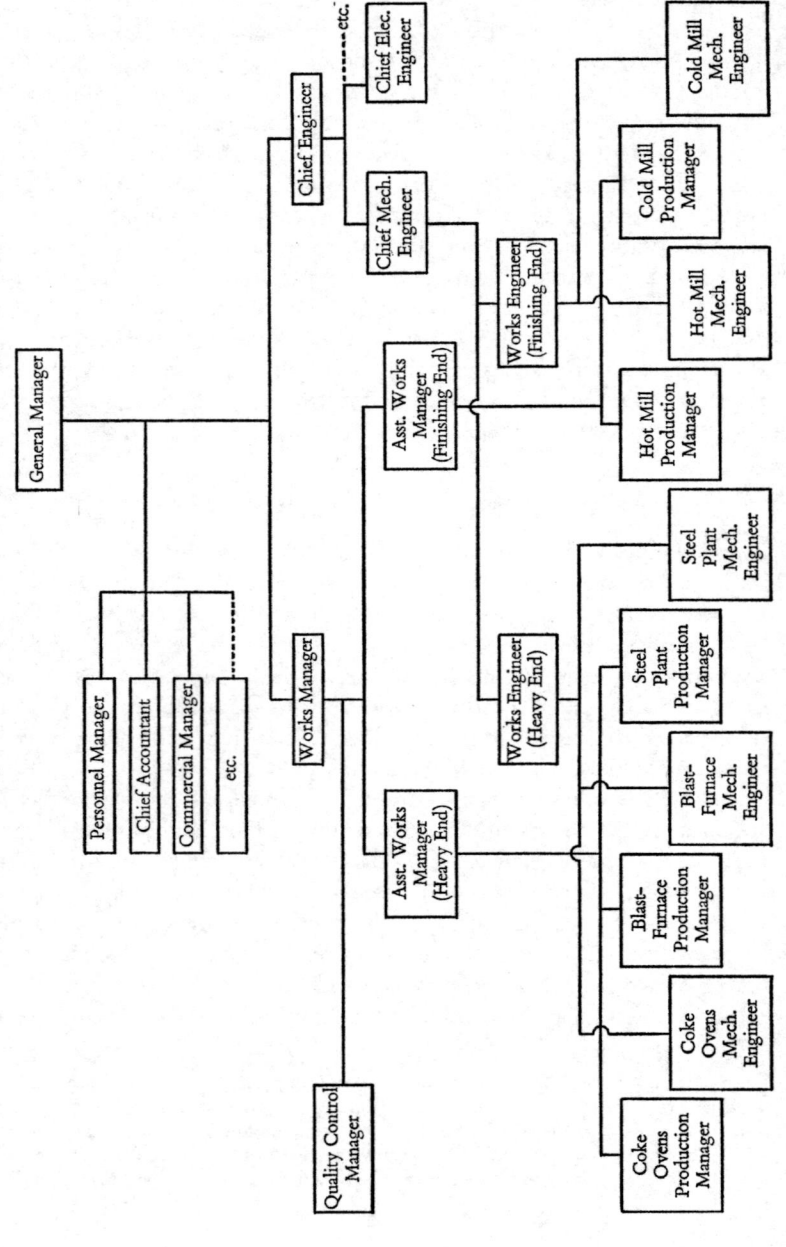

FIGURE 42 *Conventional management structure for an integrated iron and steel works with strip mill*

of the production manager has been correspondingly enhanced. A convention that when plant is running it belongs to the operators, and when it is stopped it belongs to the engineers, helps to define the boundary; but it is not easy for a local engineer to disregard the views of the production manager. His line of appeal is a long one and, as the chart indicates, it is theoretically only at the level of general manager that a local dispute between production and engineering can be mediated.

INNOVATIONS IN A NEW WORKS

Against this background, we now consider the position of a company planning to build a new steel works and strip mill in the late 1950s. The context in which these plans were being framed was changing rapidly and the variables to be taken into account were highly complex. An immense investment was involved and, unless the different variables were adequately appraised, the works risked being unnecessarily obsolescent from the outset. Here we concentrate on a few major variables – which themselves serve to illustrate the interplay between technology and environment and the consequences of this for organization.

Environmentally, a major consideration was the effect of creating substantial new capacity for producing sheet steel. No new integrated works with a steel-making capacity of less than one million tons could be economically viable, and some parts of the plant would be most economically built for a much higher capacity than this in anticipation of future demand. Therefore it was certain that the new works would transform Britain's perennial shortage of strip-mill capacity into a surplus, at least for a time. Instead of being production-dominated, as they had been for twenty years, the company's operations would become market-dominated. Competition would call for greater attention to customer needs and greater flexibility in responding to changes in market demand. The more competitive situation, too, coupled with the heavy burden of interest charges that the capital investment would impose, gave a greater stimulus than before to securing the utmost economy in the use of resources of plant, personnel, materials, and supplies.[1]

[1] In fact, Iron and Steel Board forecasts of sheet steel were so optimistic that the planned capacity of the works was increased after work had already started on preparing the site. Before construction was complete, forecasts moved sharply down again. Even if the optimistic forecasts had been realized, however, it would have taken several years and substantial extra capital investment before the capacity of the new hot-strip mill could be fully utilized.

External changes of this magnitude had obvious organizational implications in their own right. The organization would have to build in the flexibility necessary to cope with the buyers' market. Members of the organization would have to be imbued with the corresponding values and attitudes, which differed sharply from the established production-oriented attitudes that had been appropriate to a sellers' market. New methods of managerial control would also be needed, both to secure responsiveness to customer requirements and to control costs. Such methods were in fact at this time becoming available to industry generally through the development of new and more systematic ways of analysing managerial problems – for example, operational research – and of more sophisticated techniques in quality, production, and cost control. Both developments were supported by great advances in techniques of data-processing.

In production, these same advances were applicable to process control. Most of, if not all, the production processes were amenable to computer control in the foreseeable future. For some – notably the hot-strip mill itself – this was a fairly immediate prospect. In all processes it seemed both feasible and desirable to use the opportunity of the building of a new works at least to take steps in this direction: for example, by partial automation of material-handling and by installation of more advanced instrumentation for measuring and recording, if not actually for controlling. One could go quite a long way in defining the characteristics of an automatic factory, in which process control would be integrated with production and quality control and ultimately, perhaps, with other 'managerial' controls as well.

Thus the company was moving into new and unfamiliar areas, both environmentally and technologically, and the combined effect on organizational requirements was difficult to predict.

In fact, an initial decision on organization was made at an early stage – before all the forces in the field could be adequately appraised and, indeed, before the capacity of the works had been finally determined. The decision was the adoption of an organization chart, on the basis of which managers could be recruited. This chart closely followed the conventional steel-works structure depicted in *Figure 42*.

A second early decision, relevant here, was to introduce modern systems of control in five main areas: production control, quality control, budgetary and cost control, control of manning and wages, and planned maintenance. At the same time, consultants were commissioned to make a study of data-processing requirements. The notion that computer applications might enable these five controls to be integrated was in the air, but the integration envisaged was mainly in terms of centralized processing and of designing primary records and measurements that could be used for more than one of the control systems.

Third, it was decided, also at an early stage, that process automation was 'a good thing' in principle, and that feasibility studies should be carried out to discover where automation might usefully be introduced from the beginning. The hot-strip mill was the most obvious candidate; but in no areas should engineering designs be inconsistent with foreseeable developments towards further automation in the future.

These three decisions were made to a large extent independently of each other. Temporarily at least, for example, process control was seen as the province of the design engineers and quite separate from managerial controls, which were the province of future operating managers. As *Figure 42* shows, the conventional operating organization differentiated production management from engineering at a high level; and, as we saw in Chapters 11 and 12, the organization for setting up a new works may itself produce an even more pronounced differentiation between the two groups.

When the system engineers, who were mainly external consultants, started to plan comprehensive computer applications, they inevitably called into question the conventional distinction between operators and engineers. Their long-term proposal envisaged a hierarchy of computer control along the lines depicted in *Figure 43*. The function of the scheduling computer was to translate customers' orders into weekly production schedules. The functions of the production-control computer were to translate the schedules into piece-by-piece instructions to process operators, or to process-control computers; to receive information about the outcome of these instructions; and to issue further instructions accordingly. The complete installation might take ten years to realize; on this there was no firm commitment and, indeed, some of the process-control applications could be envisaged only in the most general terms. Immediate priority, however, was to be given to the three computer systems enclosed in double boxes in *Figure 43*; the finishing end scheduling computer and the ingot-slab production-control computer were to be operational from the outset, whereas the hot-strip mill process-control computer would not come on line until about a year later because of

FIGURE 43 *Proposed computer hierarchy*

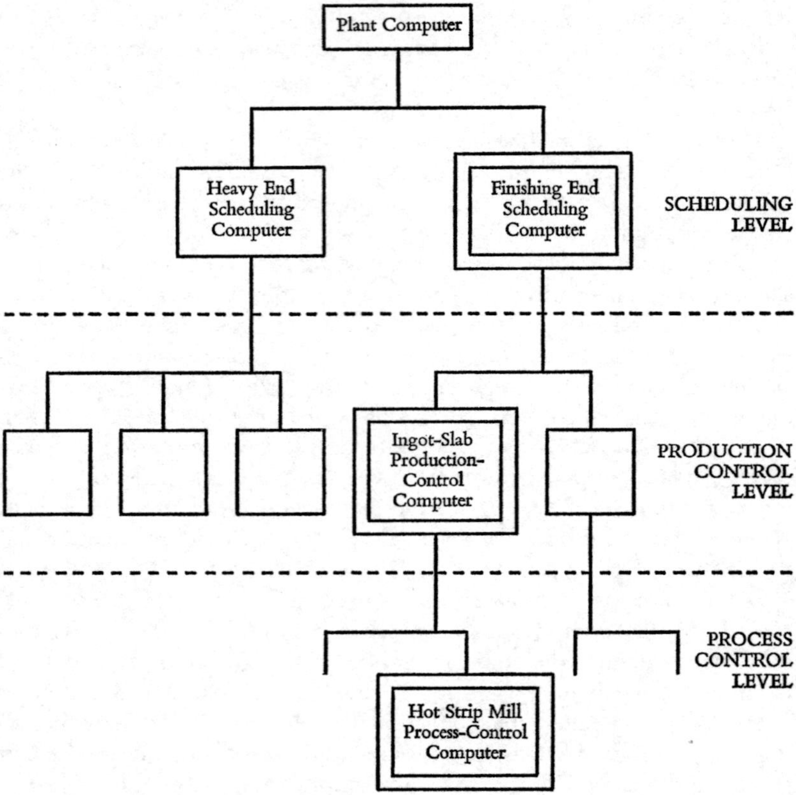

the complex problems of design and installation for what was a completely new application.[1]

As the details of the second and third decisions – on control systems and process automation – began to be worked out, it became increasingly apparent that the conventional structure of management organization, which had initially been adopted without serious question, was not entirely viable in a market-dominated enterprise. The conventional structure had been appropriate for intensive or mass production, carried out in technologically differentiated units operating in a relatively stable

[1] Installation of all three computers was, in fact, delayed.

sellers' market, which offered an assured level of sales and favourable prices. Maximization of production had been the obvious strategy. The basic technology of the new works, with its extremely large blast-furnaces, steel converters, and strip mill, was certainly oriented towards mass production, and operating with long runs at full capacity in a sellers' market it would be highly profitable. For the time being at least, however, it would be operating in a buyers' market with short runs at much less than full capacity; and it was still required to be profitable. This implied still greater weight to be given to the strategies of maximizing customer satisfaction (e.g. through use of computers in scheduling and in production control) and conserving resources (e.g. through other control systems).

These strategies impinged on the conventional management structure in a number of ways.

First, the introduction of centralized controls over manning, wages, and maintenance diminished the autonomy of production managers in these areas and increased the power of engineers and other specialists.[1] Centralized controls invaded the production manager's boundary and at least questioned assumptions about the way in which his department should be run.

Second, the prospect of 'integrated control systems', even if limited to the standardized recording of information and the centralization of devices for data-processing and -transmission, implied a change in the conventional power and status structure by opening a more rapid and complete appraisal of departmental performance to top management.

Third, a major argument for the use of computers for scheduling and production control was a potential reduction of inter-process stocks (and thus of working capital). A sharp lowering of the fences between production departments was thus inevitable. Each manager would be much more dependent upon deliveries from the preceding process and more exposed to the needs of the process following. He would also be involved in more frequent changes in the rate of production and in the product itself.

Finally, the planning of the integrated control system, related as it was to a 'customer satisfaction' strategy, called into question a great

---

[1] Control over manning seemed, at least superficially, to impinge more on production managers than on engineers, since the more complex technology, with greater instrumentation etc., demanded a much larger ratio of engineering to production personnel than in older works.

many assumptions about technological constraints. It emerged that some of these constraints were not imposed by the technology as such but, like the conventional organization itself, were related rather to operating a dominant strategy of maximizing production in a sellers' market. For example, it had always been assumed that orders should be scheduled through the hot-strip mill in such a way as to maximize the life of the rolls through which the strip was run and so minimize time lost for roll-changes. Given a situation in which the mill would be operating at less than full capacity, it became possible to consider measuring the cost of more frequent roll-changes against the gains elsewhere in the total system from greater flexibility in scheduling.

Other accepted constraints seemed likely to evaporate when the application of a computer to quality-control problems retested prevailing assumptions about cause and effect. Quality control for the works as a whole began to be conceived in terms of one massive regression equation instead of as numerous small quasi-independent equations insufficiently related to each other. Developments such as these threatened not simply the autonomy of the conventional production manager, but his monopoly of expertise in his particular field. The mystique that had surrounded many jobs in the steel industry was rapidly dropping away.

CHAPTER 20

The Organizational Implications of Computer Systems

We have shown that a change in the environment, which made a strategy of maximizing production inappropriate, also eroded the power of the production manager and the values underlying that power. Thus even before the new works was operational, the design processes themselves were, in effect beginning to cast doubts on the suitability of the conventional management structure which had been adopted. At the same time, however, both the traditional values in the industry and the basic technological parameters in the new works continued to reinforce the conventional image of the production manager as the key figure, and his department as the significant sentient group for its members. But could this image survive changes that were dissolving the insulation between departments and blurring the definitions of their distinctive competence?

The answer to this question was obscured by the fact that the two newer strategies – maximizing customer satisfaction and conserving resources – which we have so far lumped together in considering their effects, impinged on the conventional system in different ways. They also impinged on each other. Indeed, the two strategies implied two rather different models of managerial control.

MODELS OF MANAGERIAL CONTROL

The strategy of resource conservation implies what we call here a *segmented control system model* of the enterprise. In terms of such a model – exemplified by standard costing techniques – the enterprise is broken down into a number of units (cost centres) for which performance standards are fixed. The assumption is made that units correspond to sub-tasks, so that if every unit attains standard performance this will add up to the attainment of standard performance by the enterprise as a whole. In control-loop terms, each operating unit has its own discrete

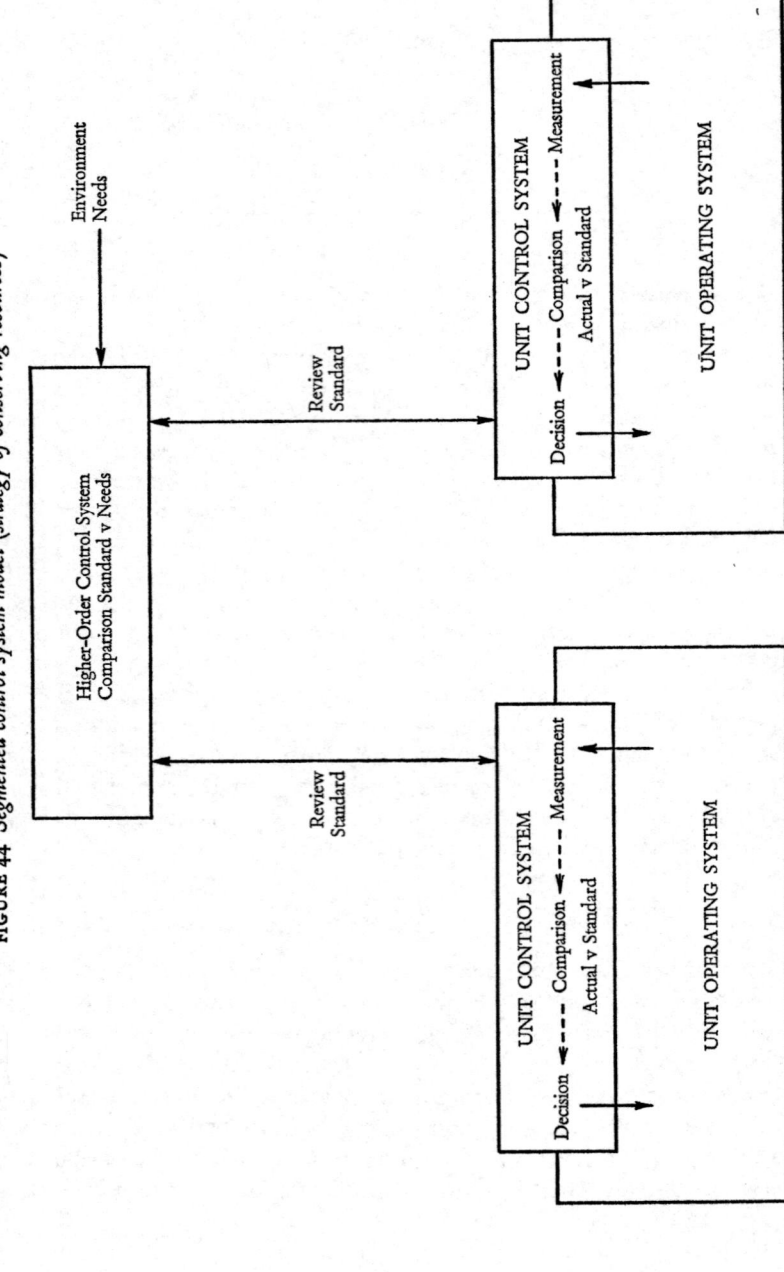

FIGURE 44 *Segmented control system model (strategy of conserving resources)*

control system which measures performance, compares actual performance against standard, and decides what changes, if any, are required
in the operation. Provided the standards are consistent with the unit's
capacity, such a system achieves a relatively stable equilibrium. The
principal task of the higher-order managing system is then to review
standards periodically in the light of changes in the relationship between
internal performance, resources available, and environmental requirements. The very concept of a 'standard' implies that review is relatively
infrequent. This kind of model is depicted in *Figure 44*. (We have used
standard costing as an example, but the model is equally applicable to
other parameters of control such as quality or rate of production.)

The strategy of maximizing customer satisfaction, on the other hand,
implies an *integrated cybernetic model* of the enterprise, which relates the
enterprise as a total system to a changing external environment. Within
this strategy, the concentration of each unit on the attainment of its
own standards might be a serious constraint on the adaptive performance of the overall system. Periodic review of standards is replaced by

FIGURE 45 *Integrated cybernetic model (strategy of maximizing customer
satisfaction)*

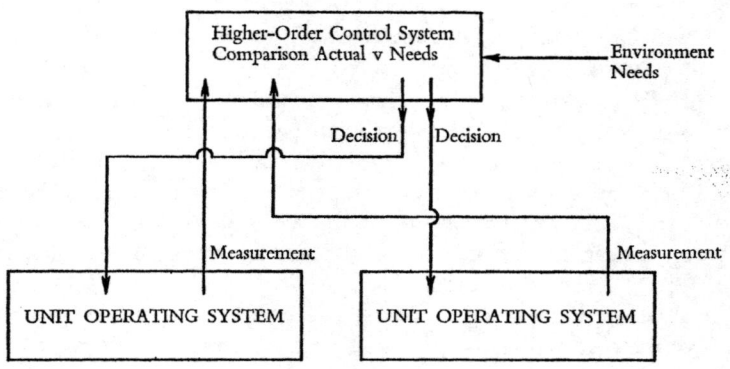

continuous monitoring of the performance of the total system and its
parts in relation to its environment. As *Figure 45* shows, with such a
model the differentiated unit control systems effectively disappear, since
the control loop is no longer contained within the boundary of the unit
managing system.

A computer technology which integrated not only scheduling and production control, but process control as well, would also of course remove the boundaries around the operating systems. Such a computerized overall managing system could theoretically respond immediately to an environmental change by altering the setting on an individual machine. The activity system would be unitary, with no internal differentiation.

THE FIRST EFFECT ON MANAGEMENT ORGANIZATION
OF THE INTRODUCTION OF COMPUTERS

In the particular works discussed here, computer applications tended to be perceived initially as a means of servicing the five unit systems, each headed by a production manager. Computers, it is true, by providing more rapid and comprehensive data-processing, could make controls more effective within the context of a segmented control system model. But the potential 'cybernetic' applications of computers were to some extent obscured by the shape of the computer hierarchy. Drawn as it is in *Figure 43* – and this is roughly how the consultants presented it – the computer hierarchy looked like a homologue or counterpart of the management hierarchy. It suggested orderly movement of suitably filtered information upwards and downwards, and it underestimated the direct and instantaneous vertical and horizontal links that are an integral part of a system that exploits computer technology. It also underplayed the extent to which the boundaries of the computer systems actually departed from the conventional technological and managerial boundaries. For example, the ingot-slab production-control computer would translate production schedules into piece-by-piece instructions for the hot-strip mill process-control computer, thus eliminating the need for a control region between the steel plant and the slabbing mill, and hence for organizational boundaries.

The apparent similarity of the hierarchies, however, tended at first to reinforce the conception that the computer system was little more than an elaboration and extension of the existing control systems. And the operation of the control systems, using as it did the conventional technological sub-units as the units of control, seemed, superficially at least, to reinforce the general shape of the prevailing management structure. Indeed, contradictory to the requirements of the cybernetic model, it made the production department in some respects a more pivotal unit as the locus of decision-making processes that had to take into account and harmonize a more elaborate and complex flow of information from a greater variety of sources than ever before.

In line with this trend, managers of the central specialist departments began to second some of their staff – cost accountants and personnel officers – to production departments, much as engineers had traditionally been seconded.

Consequently, even before the new works came into operation, the role of the production manager, as the person with the technical skill required to maximize departmental production, was almost imperceptibly evolving into a new role of departmental manager, whose predominant task was, it appeared, to operate the control systems in such a way as to meet the various standards laid down. Because this change occurred gradually and because the original production managers stayed on in the newly emerging roles, its full significance was missed at the time. The change was in fact not demonstrated plainly until the works had been in operation for a year, at which point it proved possible to replace a departmental manager by a man who had no technical knowledge of the process concerned. His effectiveness in improving the performance of the department demonstrated beyond doubt that technical production expertise was relatively unimportant to the new role. Even a year before such an appointment would have been unthinkable.

This gradual organizational evolution has been not uncommon in other industries in recent years, for reasons which are fairly clear: industry has become more highly mechanized and control and service functions have become more specialized and complex. In many industries machines have become the producers and the human contribution has become increasingly to service and supplement the activities of the machines. The distinction between production and non-production activities has thus become increasingly blurred. Many of the traditional arcane skills of the production man have been articulated, systematized, and built into the technological system itself. In the face of such changes, it is not surprising that in engineering, textile, and other industries the earlier role of production manager has developed into a role of departmental 'general manager'. Such a manager includes within his command the specialist control and service functions that his operations require. Maintenance engineering is among the functions that may be decentralized in this way; this has even happened in some steel companies in spite of the strong tradition of top-level differentiation of the production and engineering functions.

If the same person makes this role transition, his gain in status may outweigh the devaluation of his specialized production experience. In the steel-works example quoted here, once the production managers had acquired their retinues of seconded specialists and become 'general' managers of their units, the roles of the works manager and the assistant works managers became decreasingly executive and increasingly advisory. There was no need for another level of general management between the departmental managers and the general manager of the works as a whole. After the new works had been operating for just over a year, these three senior roles in the production hierarchy lapsed, leaving the departmental (ex-production) managers to report directly to the general manager.

This gradual organizational evolution had another apparent advantage. It preserved the technologically bounded unit with which employees within the department could identify. The departmental boundary remained as the boundary of the sentient group, differentiating it from other departments. And, in addition, the department now provided a unit of affiliation not only for production workers, as in the past, but for all the engineering and other specialists who contributed to the task of the department. As a sentient group, therefore, the department could become potentially more self-contained, closely knit, and cohesive.

Unfortunately, this apparently desirable result from the social point of view was diametrically opposed to the requirements of the technology. It reinforced boundaries that were not merely irrelevant but inimical to the implementation of what we have called the integrated cybernetic model of the enterprise.

THE DISSONANCE OF TASK-GROUP, ORGANIZATIONAL, AND SENTIENT-GROUP BOUNDARIES

Even if we leave aside the further complication of the introduction of the process-control computers, a computer system for scheduling and production control must, if it is to be effective in reducing the working capital locked up in inter-process stocks and the additional handling cost involved, also correspondingly reduce insulation between one department and the next. Ideally, indeed, inter-process stocks should not accumulate at all. But this presupposes instant reaction to environmental change and no internal breakdowns. Neither is likely, and stocks will accumulate when breakdown in one department makes it unable to import the output of its predecessor; or when, because of the nature of the process, a fall in external demand cannot be translated immediately into modified schedules. Breakdowns in one department will therefore have swift repercussions in others; and interdepartmental conflicts requiring resolution are accordingly more likely to arise. Some stability can be retained as long as it remains possible to work to standards and operate the segmented control system model. But this, too, vanishes as soon as the company is no longer in the happy position of being impervious to market changes, and hence can no longer control transactions with its environment. The resolution of interdepartmental conflict imposes additional pressure on top management. At this stage the communication channel capacity of the human organization gets choked; and the enterprise's rate of response to environmental change is less than is required. But the very existence of the strong departmental groupings – in which task and sentient boundaries coincide – obstructs the exploitation of the integrated cybernetic model that the computers would permit.

In practice, the 'remedy' most often adopted at this point is an attempt to 'strengthen' top management by introducing new posts of controllers, co-ordinators, assistants, or 'assistants to'. Or, even worse, an entirely new level of management is interposed in an attempt to absorb the pressure and to enable top management to pay attention to its primary task – the control of transactions with the environment. Such remedies, however, by interposing additional 'transfer' points in the communication network, either distort communications still more or lead to the proliferation of informal systems. More importantly, they further sanctify the very departmental boundaries that stand in the way of implementing the cybernetic model and so postpone and make more difficult the transition to a more appropriate organizational form.

It must be said at once that it is far easier to point to the failings in existing forms of organization than to devise new forms that are appropriate for increasing automation. So far as a computer-controlled system contains an inherent evolutionary capacity for which there are no precedents in other types of technology, one can be more precise about characteristics that are not suitable than about those that are. For example, conventional 'scientific management' assumptions about division of labour, unity of command, definition of responsibility and authority, and span of control will no longer be useful. Again – and this is perhaps more difficult for us to acknowledge – it will be inappropriate to adopt an organization that secures the motivation and commitment of the individual employee through giving him membership of a group that is associated with a specific technical system. Such commitment can only impede technological change.

Indeed, the one safe prediction we can make is that processes of auto-mation of the kind discussed here will require frequent changes of task organization – much more frequent than we have been accustomed to in the past. Conditions to allow such flexibility have, on the one hand, to provide sufficient stability of expectations and behaviour to enable the necessary tasks to be carried out; but, on the other, must not permit a particular task organization in a particular technical setting to become so rigidly associated with power and status structures and their associated sentient groups that it becomes ossified.

Although these new organizational forms have still to be invented, certain pointers arise from the studies described in the previous chapters. Airline experience shows, for example, that the primary work-group concept of coincident task- and sentient-group organization is not essen-tial to provide the means through which the individual is affiliated to the enterprise. Obversely, if the individual is exposed to frequent changes in work-group membership, in role, or in organization, then he needs some relatively more secure and enduring affiliation to relate him to the task of the enterprise. He must therefore occupy at least two work-oriented roles – one in a task system and the other in what we have called the sentient system.

If the principles of multiple roles and readily dispensable organiza-tional forms are accepted, then a much more flexible approach is possible in the design of organization. We envisage, for instance, a much greater use of the equivalent of the 'scientific' or 'professional' base, not only for specialists, but also for production workers who may have to return at frequent intervals to base for retraining in new skills before being deployed in a new task organization. At the same time, rapid technolo-gical change must inevitably be accompanied by higher mobility. Some enterprises are already having to accept, as a fact of life, that some of the newer scientists and technologists – operational research workers, systems analysts, electronic engineers, computer programmers – are primarily wedded to their crafts and, like their predecessors in guilds, neither want nor need a long-term affiliation to a particular public enterprise. The new technologies are likely to multiply these categories.

If the rate of installation of new systems increases, one would envisage, too, that a growing proportion of the manpower in a manufacturing concern would be there on a contractual basis, deployed as in the construction industry by specialized contracting firms. This trend is already apparent.

PART VI

Task and Sentient Systems and their Boundary Controls

Introduction

In this book we have described a conceptual framework which, we believe, is useful for the analysis and model-building of the organization of any kind of enterprise. The book has two main themes: the first, that a project-type organization, which is appropriate and necessary for temporary and transitional activity systems, also provides the best basis for a general organizational theory; and the second, that such a basis requires the precise definition and control of the boundaries of activity systems and of groups. It requires, furthermore, the reconciliation of two, often contradictory, views of enterprises: on the one hand, the view that the only purpose of enterprise organization is to ensure efficient task performance; and, on the other, that the primary task of any enterprise is to satisfy the needs of those who are employed in it.

We have given examples to illustrate the application of the concepts and theory to particular enterprises of different kinds. None of our data was taken from experiments set up solely for research purposes. In consequence, although each part of the book has its own thesis, which is intended to illustrate a particular aspect of the theory, each example, because it has been taken from real life, is complex and, inevitably, the two main themes have been interwoven throughout. The examples were chosen because we had the data about them. We were not able to seek out particular cases to make specific points. Rather, we had to take what we had and test the concepts and theory in respect of them. We have had to accept that the exigencies of consultancy practice have frequently made it impossible to follow up potentially interesting lines of research; and that the gaining of access to data for research purposes has always involved us in professional relationships with those with whom we have worked. We have therefore been precluded from taking action for research purposes alone.

Nevertheless, we cannot complain about these constraints. A consultancy practice, with its inseparable professional responsibility, has given us access to data that otherwise would have been inaccessible; and we have been fortunate in that our clients have accepted that even the tentative formulation of theories and concepts has contributed to the solution of their practical problems.

In this final part we shall take up again our two main themes, briefly and separately, and consider their application to types of enterprise other than those we have used in the main text.

CHAPTER 21

Task and Sentient Groups

To illustrate the first of our themes we have compared and contrasted different kinds of activity system and made a distinction between the boundaries of activity system, task group, and sentient group – the task group being the group that comprises the individuals employed in an activity system, and the sentient group being the group to which individuals are prepared to commit themselves and on which they depend for emotional support. We have suggested that the endeavour to find task organizations to satisfy human need, while serving as a valuable counterbalance to the machine theory of organization, has nevertheless impeded the formulation of a general theory of organization that is applicable to all tasks. More specifically, we have made the hypothesis that forms of organization in which task and sentient groups coincide may have relatively short-term effectiveness; in the longer term such groups can inhibit change and hence can lead eventually to deterioration of performance and, in consequence, to social and psychological deprivation rather than to satisfaction.

TASKS PRECLUDING COINCIDENCE

We pointed out in Part II that organizational models derived from co-incident task and sentient groups are not applicable to transactions across enterprise or institutional boundaries. If a task system, and hence a task group, straddles an enterprise boundary, it cannot be contained within the organizational boundaries of the enterprise; discrepancy between task and sentient systems is therefore inevitable. More importantly, if managing systems and their accompanying control and service functions are modelled on factory production systems, they tend to give hierarchies that are too simple and too inflexible to fit the complexities of such task performance. We used the representative task of a sales force and the dry-cleaning industry to illustrate this part of our thesis.

In the Introduction to Part II we said that the organization of professional service could also be considered within the same conceptual framework. The characteristic feature of a professional relationship is that it is made between a client (or patient) who wants help and a professional person who gives it, or tries to do so. The activity system through which the help is given has a boundary that encompasses professional and client. On the one hand, the client has to rely on the skill, experience, and integrity of the professional to do what is necessary; on the other hand, the professional has to forswear exploitation of the dependent relationship involved. Implicit in the professional-client relationship is the possibility of failure, with corresponding anxieties, conscious or unconscious, that the client's problems may be intractable and the professional's skills inadequate. The more there is at stake, the more intense the confused and ambivalent feelings associated with the dependence are likely to be.

The sentient groups to which professional men and women commit themselves and from which they draw their support are the professional associations and their related learned societies. Membership is a qualification to practise. And the sanction to practise those professions that are concerned with the lives, liberties, and property of their clients has, in our society, the force of law. Society, in effect, not only defines the boundaries of the task system and of the sentient system, and separates them, but also, through the sentient system, controls professional conduct in the task system.

We have suggested further that the attempts that have been made to devise organizations based on person-centred task systems have ignored what we believe to be the more general case of the task system that is temporary and transitional. We used building, research, and air transport as our examples. The theatre provides another. In the theatre the task group is the cast and other staff assembled for a play. While the play is running, task group and sentient group are, or should be, coincident; but actors have 'the profession' as their superordinate sentient group, to which they can commit themselves whether acting or 'resting', or whether doing other jobs while waiting for parts. Without the profession and the regard in which it is held, both by its members and by the public, it is doubtful if the theatre could survive.

'NATURAL' COINCIDENCE

In the family business, by definition, task and sentient boundaries must coincide. But such a form of organization requires for its effectiveness conditions of stable equilibrium. In conditions of social, economic, and technical change, as we showed in Part III, commitment to the one group, the family, can not only distort judgements about task decisions, but also lead to the disruption of sentient-group relationships. In addition, we tried to show how, as the group increases in size, its relationships become more tenuous, so that it can no longer provide either satisfactory relationships or adequate self-regulation.

We could have used the great religious institutions as examples of enterprises with coincidence of task and sentient boundaries. A church is characterized by its members' collective belief in a deity or system of deities on whom they can, if they are deserving, depend for both spiritual and physical nourishment. But belief in a deity involves belief in some kind of life after death as well. The sentient system of a church, to which its members commit themselves, is therefore unbounded, in that it has no ending. In the spiritual sense there is no export system. Yet many of the tasks undertaken by the Church are performed in activity systems that must have a finite life, if only because in human terms death is an end. As religious beliefs change, and scientific knowledge questions more and more of the assumptions on which they are based, the Church finds it increasingly difficult to reconcile its bounded practical responsibilities for the living and the unbounded sentient system on which its membership depends.

CONTRIVED COINCIDENCE

One of the earliest attempts deliberately to invent a form of work organization in which task- and sentient-group boundaries coincided was in the textile industry (Rice, 1958). The invention, which accompanied the introduction of automatic looms, was stimulated by the need to counter the human deprivation caused by 'job breakdown' and the concomitant loss of a traditional craft skill. The outcome was the formation of internally led, quasi-autonomous, primary work groups. The results showed greatly increased production, higher quality, reduced costs, and, so far as could be judged from their behaviour, much greater satisfaction for the workers.

From this and subsequent experiments and observations we were able to postulate the particular conditions under which such autonomous work groups were likely to be effective:

(a) The task must be such that those engaged on its parts can experience, as a group, the completion of a 'whole' task.

(b) The group must be able to regulate its own activities and be judged by results; that is, there must be a well-defined boundary with a measurable intake/output ratio that can serve as a criterion of performance.

(c) The group has to be of such a size that it can not only regulate its own activities, but also provide satisfactory personal relationships. Trist et al. (1963) have given examples from the Durham coalfield of primary work groups of up to fifty members that have been capable of sustained self-regulation and maintenance. Such examples are rare, however, and in most work situations much smaller groups are required.

(d) The range of skills required in the group for task performance must not be so great as to reinforce external affiliations and thus induce internal differentiation. Nor should status difference in the group be large enough to inhibit internal mobility.

(e) The task/sentient group should not be unique, so that those who become disaffected have no alternative group engaged on a similar task and requiring similar skills and experience to which they can move. Otherwise the investment in the one group is likely to be so great as to distort values and judgements, and the possibility of expulsion so threatening as to be destructive.

This last condition in particular certainly does not hold in the family business. And, as in the family business, the commitment of their members that such groups require for their effectiveness is itself a barrier to accommodating change.[1] In the textile mill already mentioned, for example, the very success that was achieved – both technically and socially – led to such investment by the workers and management in the new task system that, when difficulties arose, they were unable to diagnose faults and to make the necessary adjustments in the system itself. And the strength of the coincident task and sentient boundaries

---

[1] Except perhaps where, as in some mining situations, inescapable external factors, such as the exhaustion of a coal seam, compel disbandment and redeployment. In some instances, the autonomous groups described by Trist et al. may have more of the characteristics of project teams and correspondingly require some more enduring sentient group, such as the local trade union lodge, to prevent over-investment in the transitory teams.

would certainly have militated against further adaptation had a still newer technology of weaving been invented.

Fortunately perhaps, in most of the older industries, scientific and technical invention, and hence the need for radical structural and cultural adaptation, is infrequent; and the time-lag in social invention does not usually do more than delay, or reduce the effectiveness of, the exploitation of the new scientific and technical potential. Recognition of the need for technical and social change is, of course, likely to be correlated with the frequency with which an enterprise has experienced such changes in the past, with the result that the delay can be long and the reduction of effectiveness considerable. Even so, there is undoubtedly scope, in industries with relatively stable technologies, for improvements in productivity by creating socio-technical systems in which task and sentient boundaries coincide.[1]

COINCIDENT BOUNDARIES AND CHANGE

The pace of change is, however, becoming faster and the conditions of 'infrequent invention' certainly do not hold for some of the newer industries, in which, in the extreme, the time that must elapse between product or plant design and manufacture is often sufficient to ensure obsolescence. Nor do they hold for those enterprises into which the more sophisticated data-storage and automatic-control systems can be introduced. In such enterprises, organization must become a readily dispensable tool.

In Part V we gave an example from the steel industry in which the introduction of computers for scheduling and for production and process control had already disrupted not only accepted task-system boundaries but also the associated sentient groups; and, in consequence, had called into question the validity of the location of traditional organizational boundaries and of the associated management roles. Comprehensive data-storage with instantaneous access, the computer programming of routine decision-making, and the building of simulation models to allow the results of alternative strategies to be compared before they are implemented, can lead only to a greater centralization of power and control. The inherent evolutionary capacity of modern computer technology – the capacity of the computer to learn from experience – will rapidly

---

[1] For a preliminary account of a large-scale experiment along these lines in Norway, see Thorsrud & Emery (1964, 1966).

make redundant much of the specialized experience, particularly that of those in middle management and administration, on which so much decision-making has had to rely in the past. Moreover, with this redundancy many established career patterns and their associated promotion paths will disappear. New kinds of organization will provide new roles requiring new skills, and attempts to preserve traditional organizations and traditional roles must inevitably lead to inefficiency and social dislocation.

In the preface we made the point that decisions about change in any enterprise often depend on the attitudes of the existing role holders, and in a settled stable task system their attitudes are likely to be resistant: 'it will last my lifetime' is perhaps a more prevalent attitude than is sometimes thought. The difficulty is that, even if it does, their successors are likely to inherit a bankrupt enterprise; more frequently, however, it fails to last, with consequent conflict, compromise, and chaos.

In industry the invention of a new product can give its inventors several years' start over potential competitors. If the market for the product is lucrative, imitations (even if the product is covered by patents) enter the field. As soon as that happens the inventive phase is over. Thereafter, modification and new applications of the product can give a competitive advantage, but the start gained by such innovations rapidly shortens as know-how in manufacturing and application becomes more generally available. If by this time the market for the product has become a mass market, then mass production – which by reason of its heavy investment in specific manufacturing processes is the enemy of invention and innovation – takes over and inhibits further change until the product itself becomes obsolete.

Institutions tend to follow the same pattern. A new institution in a new field starts up with high hopes and little acceptance. If it survives the early indifference to its outputs (or even attempts to crush it), its ideas and methods gradually become acceptable and it becomes respectable. A new institution can command great investment from its members. Their task and sentient groups coincide. They are prepared to work long hours often for little money because of their belief in their cause. In time, other sentient groups exert their pull – family, other jobs, established professions – and members leave; the remainder may struggle on, but, unless new ideas and new leaders emerge, the institution can easily be submerged and become indistinguishable from its contemporaries. The life-span of an idea, a product, or an institution depends on the field in which it is introduced. It is probably shortest in modern teenage culture, in which it appears to older generations that the acceptance of a sound, a dance, or a fashion is the certain herald of its death.

DIFFERENT KINDS OF SENTIENCE

This brings us to the point that while sentient groups have to have meaning, or else commitment will be inadequate, the sentience may arise in different ways and have different meanings at different times. Sentience is likely to be strongest where task and sentient boundaries coincide and, more particularly, where members share both a common belief in the objective of the group and complementary beliefs about their respective contributions to it. As our work with family businesses demonstrated, beliefs that the contributions of the various members are not merely complementary but indispensable introduce such ambivalent stress into the situation that task performance suffers and the sentience itself is correspondingly vulnerable. At the other end of the spectrum, a group in which every member has a similar role, so that all are interchangeable and each individual is all too dispensable, cannot acquire sentience unless it finds supplementary activities through which members can make individual and complementary contributions. Many groups of semi-skilled and unskilled workers fall into this category. The professional body is in a different category since, although it is largely undifferentiated in terms of the qualifications and the rights and obligations of its members, it is at the same time the powerful sanctioning body that confers on them the right and security to engage in professional relations with their clients. To be effective as sentient groups, the kinds of 'scientific pool' that we have adumbrated earlier in this volume need to have something of this 'professional' quality.

The nature of the sentient requirements is also determined by the nature of the task of the enterprise. An enterprise that carries out a socially reputable task usually has little difficulty in obtaining the commitment of its members; one that is socially questionable will have much more difficulty; and one that is socially objectionable can get commitment only from rebels and deviants. Indeed, antisocial enterprises have to have elaborate codes of behaviour to ensure adherence and, furthermore, have to impose severe penalties for their breach.

In fact, a majority of institutions have had to devise special mechanisms to reinforce commitment. Pension and housing schemes, staff parties, salesmen's rallies, exhibitions, house magazines, are among the more frequently used. But it is notable that welfare activities, sports clubs, and profit-sharing schemes have had a very limited success in industry. Even types of co-ownership, in which employees have had equity voting rights, have proved less attractive than their inventors hoped. The sentient group of ownership has been insufficiently 'professional', usually because the majority of co-owners have not had the experience and skill required to make strategic decisions about relationships with the environment.

One widespread mechanism through which highly structured organizations reinforce both their internal differentiation and the commitment of their members is ritual role-reversal. This may be observed, for example, in an Indian temple festival, when on one day in the year a member of an untouchable caste may be accorded the honour and respect normally reserved for a Brahman. In our own society there is the comparable army tradition that officers serve Christmas dinner to the men. Similarly, during a sale in a large department store, the ordinary selling staff elect managers from among themselves, and the normal managers become staff. But successful mechanisms like these are not easy to invent.

A further point to note is that some enterprises may seek to mobilize more commitment than is necessary for effective task performance. We have known companies in which the cost of a high turnover of staff has been more than outweighed by the flexibility and new ideas that it infuses into the system. Management's desire to reduce turnover and increase loyalty may sometimes be motivated more by a desire to be loved than by the need to be efficient.

What is important is the relative balance of sentience of groups committed to the *status quo* and groups committed to change. Efforts by other workers to replicate elsewhere the experimental changes in weaving cited above often foundered through a failure to create initially a strong sentient group committed to experimentation. It was only such a group that could provide the necessary protective boundary within which innovation could be encouraged to take place. In the case of the loom-sheds already referred to, however, once the new autonomous groups had established themselves, they acquired their own valency and froze into a new *status quo*, and the group committed to experimentation disappeared.

To maintain adaptiveness, the greatest sentience must remain vested in a group committed to change. A recent contribution to the literature on institution-building by Perlmutter (1965) carries the subtitle 'The building of indispensable institutions'. A major lesson from our own work is that the indispensability of the whole institution may depend on building dispensability into the parts. But the sentience of the overall institutional boundary within which this can happen is not easy to sustain. It is here that personal leadership often has a part to play. During a period of critical changes in particular, a charismatic leader who embodies a belief in the future of the enterprise can be a focus of its sentience and correspondingly enable members to withdraw sentience from the parts that need to be dispensed with.

CHAPTER 22

Boundary Controls

To illustrate our second theme we have distinguished between boundary control functions and monitoring activities, and have discussed the various kinds of boundary transaction that have to be regulated. In particular, we have considered the control problems involved in the separation and coincidence of task-group, sentient-group, and organizational boundaries. We have tried to show that inadequate definition of task-system boundaries presents major difficulties in controlling sentient boundaries; and, conversely, that inadequate control of sentient boundaries can lead to the redefinition of tasks and of task systems. We have also tried to show that organizational boundaries that occur at points where there is no process discontinuity can lead only to ineffective boundary control; and, conversely, that points of process discontinuity without adequate regulation can lead to inefficiency or even chaos.

THE PROTECTIVE FUNCTION OF CONTROL

The need for boundary controls to protect the conversion process from interference from the environment and to adjust both intake and output to environmental demands has been demonstrated in the chapters on research organizations and on air transport.

In its 'purest' form, boundary control permits only those transactions between the system and its environment that are essential to performance of the primary task. It admits the necessary intakes, releases the outputs, and maintains and replenishes the resources of the task system.

We have already referred[1] to the strict controls necessary to protect experimental situations, especially those that involve social change. Without protection – diminishing as the experimental changes become more acceptable – interference can lead to 'too early crystallization in social and economic dimensions because of anxiety about the disturbance of traditional patterns' (Rice, 1958).

[1] Chapters 13 and 21. See also Rice (1963).

In the same way, conferences and courses that provide opportunities to learn about the human problems of leadership have to impose strict boundary controls both between the conference and its environment and within the conference between its various events, in order to protect both members and staff during a process that can be stressful (Rice, 1965). The boundaries of the conference itself are protected by the exclusion of all visitors and by the refusal to make reports on participants or to publish anything that could be attributed to any individual. Within the conference programme the specific task of each event is defined as precisely as possible; staff roles and role-sets are also defined and staff members adhere to them. Time, too, is used as a boundary: events start and stop at the times published. Overspill, at least as far as the staff are concerned, is avoided as much as possible. These controls are reinforced by territorial boundaries: staff never enter the members' common room nor members the staff common room; and the uses to which other rooms are put at given times are announced and maintained.

The throughput of a conference or course, like that of any educational institution, is, however, human. No conference management could guarantee to control member behaviour. This is not attempted except by example. All rules are made for, and enforced on, staff. In effect, boundary controls are strict, but they are imposed only where they can be effective.

In other settings, one observes all too often controls being imposed not to protect the task system from interference but to protect management against anxiety. Parameters are controlled not because they are relevant but because they are measurable. Their function is to create an illusion of certainty as a means of coping with intolerable uncertainty.

INHERENT AND IMPOSED CONTROLS

The easiest kind of control to maintain is that over a physical throughput when the transformation in the conversion process never leaves the throughput in an unstable condition. Machine shops in engineering provide an obvious example. The process can be stopped at any time to check the accuracy of the work done and to make any necessary adjustments. Materials or part-processed products do not deteriorate or change in form while the inspection is carried out. More difficult and more dangerous are controls over chemical processes or those that involve unstable materials such as molten metal or atomic reactions. In these processes boundary controls can be imposed only at infrequent intervals and monitoring is the only form of regulation possible at other times. More difficult still are controls over a human throughput. In processes with a human throughput, the throughput has a will of its own which is often at variance with the controlling agency. As we have seen, adequate control is possible only when the dependence involved in the process is fully accepted both by the members of the enterprise and by the individuals who comprise the throughput. Otherwise it is necessary to provide members with the support that enables them to tolerate the uncertainties involved.

We must also recognize that the nature of the controlling agency can radically affect attitudes towards, and acceptance of, the kinds of control imposed. Where, as in religious institutions, the authority for sanctions is derived from a deity, those who believe cannot question the rightness or the wrongness of decisions based on belief. To be engaged on God's work precludes most human interference. There are other spheres, again, in which control is easier to maintain because it is derived from natural sources rather than from human agency. The managers of enterprises concerned with the sea, with agriculture, mining, and the care of the sick, have for a long time exploited their own dependence on 'acts of God', and hence their inability to take responsibility for what happens, as a means of controlling those employed by them.

In chemical processes, in which once chemicals are mixed the process starts and is self-activating, the process itself takes control and imposed organizational controls can be kept to a minimum. Generally speaking, the greater the number of controls that are implicit in the task or its technology, and the more effective they are, the fewer the managerial controls it is necessary to impose. When neither task nor technology provides effective built-in controls, management must devise regulatory mechanisms to ensure that it can manage. Conversely, the greater the number of automatic processes, the fewer the managerial controls that should be required. It is, of course, true that automation often involves more inflexible activity systems; and, since they must be kept going, additional controls may be needed over intake and output. The total system has to live up to its automated parts. In other words, if appropriate boundary conditions are to be maintained, managerial control at the boundaries may have to be increased. This we have illustrated by reference to the steel industry in which we have shown that the introduction of automation allows for more integration between the parts of the process and avoids some intermediate stocks and hence the tying up of working capital. But the elimination of intermediate stocks also demands greater sensitivity to market demand, with correspondingly more frequent adjustments throughout the process.

CONTRACTING OUT

The confusion between task and sentient systems – between task groups and sentient groups – and the problem of differentiating their boundaries and of controlling their interrelations are in some measure simplified by greater differentiation between the sub-systems of complex enterprises. One large oil refinery, for example, directly employs only the few chemists and engineers that are required for its operating activities, and for its technical and financial control functions. All other work – maintenance, transport, and even site security – is contracted out to other enterprises specializing in such services. This is by no means unique. An airline will often arrange for another company to provide its ground transport between city terminal and airport, and at stations away from its base it will commonly contract out passenger-handling, catering, and even load-control calculations and some aircraft maintenance activities. And, of course, the majority of industrial companies import parts of their products from manufacturers who have specialized in the required technology. The trend appears to be increasing: firms of professional architects, civil engineers, and accountants have existed for a very long time, and agencies that provide temporary secretaries have also been available for many years; but they are being added to. It is now possible to make continuing contracts for domestic as well as office cleaning, for canteen catering, long-term car hire, management recruitment, draughtsmen, baby-sitting, and a host of other services that were formerly the normal activities of the enterprise concerned.

Contracting out intakes and services can relieve management of many of the headaches of control of the relationships between different task and sentient groups within the enterprise. In particular, it simplifies the problem of controlling internal sentient boundaries. Against this, however, management faces greater difficulties when what is contracted out is the essential maintenance activity required to keep the process going, or a vital ingredient of the import-conversion-export process by which the enterprise performs its primary task. Management may well find that it has lost control of its own enterprise by giving too many hostages to other managements. We have shown how, in the building industry, even without strikes or stoppages, the major problem is to get sufficient commitment to a project group to maintain any kind of control over the activities of its various parts. With strikes and other kinds of stoppages one group can hold the total enterprise to ransom, as has been demonstrated only too often in the motor-car industry.

Specialization of technology and product in sub-enterprises or separate enterprises can no doubt increase the efficiency of the parts, but until new forms of organization are invented, with activity system, task group, and sentient group adequately differentiated and their interrelations controlled, it is not certain that greater efficiency of the parts will necessarily add up to greater efficiency of the whole.

PERMEABLE BOUNDARIES

Strict boundary controls are especially difficult to maintain in those systems that by their nature have to be more open. Hospitals, for example, find it difficult to control entry into their accident wards or into other emergency services. In general, those institutions and professions that offer help of any kind, physical or spiritual, frequently find that either their intake or their output is intractable to control. Those who come for help tend to be accepted – however hopeless their case – and once admitted are frequently difficult to export. In a study of disasters it was reported:

'The general pattern has been that the nearest hospitals are overwhelmed and the hospitals more remote from the disaster zone receive fewer casualties than their reasonable share' (Raker, Wallace & Rayner, 1956).

And later in the same account:

'At Hospital 4 a staff member who had been appointed triage officer at the time of World War II was alerted by the administrator of the hospital and came to perform this function. So long as he was working at one of the entry points, the flow of casualties was kept in some semblance of order. Several times when there was a lull in the casualty flow he left his post to do other tasks, and disorganization

... became immediately apparent when more casualties arrived' (Raker *et al.* quoting Bakst *et al.*, 1955).

In general, it can usually be demonstrated that more discrimination in admission can lead to greater chances of recovery for the majority; but imposition of the controls to achieve this discrimination demands an exercise of judgement and a decision-making process that run counter to all the training of most of those who manage the institution, particularly if it has a moral or a religious basis. In consequence, from the point of view of society as a whole, far too many resources are often spent on the virtually hopeless, while those who could recover, or even survive, with the minimum of help, go helpless.

In Chapter 3 we pointed out that the introduction of medical services into developing and overcrowded countries can have tragic consequences when food, housing, and other services necessary to sustain the resulting increased population are not provided as well. To advocate only 'balanced' progress is, however, easy when one is not face to face with the suffering that absence of medical care can entail – particularly if medical services are available and others are not. Members of the medical profession cannot just deny the Hippocratic code that has been at least implicit throughout their training. Nevertheless, their failure to control their boundary can result eventually in greater suffering for the very people they save.

DESTRUCTION AND RECONSTITUTION OF BOUNDARIES

Disasters also provide extreme examples of the obliteration of normal boundaries. Floods, hurricanes, earthquakes, or nuclear bombs literally annihilate familiar landmarks by which human life is guided. It has been suggested that behaviour in disaster can be analysed in three overlapping phases: impact, recoil, and post-traumatic stress (Tyhurst, 1951). The first can last from seconds up to one and a half hours; the second from hours to weeks; and the third for the rest of life. In the period of impact, up to a quarter of those affected remain cool and collected, appreciate what has happened and plan recovery; up to three-quarters are stunned, bewildered, lost, and numb; the remainder become hysterical or show other pathological symptoms. In the period of recoil the majority move about aimlessly, seeking shelter without plan or real purpose; they are in a dependent childlike state in which anybody who takes charge and proposes action is followed. In other words, anyone who can replace the destroyed boundaries can assume control of the new boundaries. If, however, in anticipation of disaster, a new set of landmarks and guideposts is got ready – rescue stations, precise directions about evacuation, and so on – and the boundary control functions are manned in advance, casualty rates can be lowered dramatically.

Disasters are fortunately rare, but they serve to emphasize the importance of defined boundaries and of boundary control functions. We have seen that any transaction across enterprise boundaries, an essential process for any living system, involves the drawing, temporarily at least, of new boundaries. And the drawing of new boundaries contains the possibility that the new boundaries will prove stronger than the old. Any transaction across enterprise boundaries has in it, therefore, the elements of incipient disaster, in which not only are essential tasks undone, but sentient systems are destroyed as well.

We can learn something more from the examination of disaster. So far as is known, the actual occurrence of mass panic is rare; but the myth of panic in disaster is strong. The myth, and belief in it, is a mechanism by which stress is discharged and control restored. The destruction of boundaries is so stressful that somebody has to go, or has to be believed to go, to pieces – somebody or some group has to carry the role of panic leader. In more normal situations, religious sects, immigrants, racial groups, delinquents, or other socially condemned minorities can threaten, or be perceived to threaten, the integrity of group boundaries. The preservation and protection of adequate sentient boundaries often depend, therefore, on finding or inventing other groups on whom can be projected the feelings and behaviour that, if retained within the sentient group, would destroy its sentience.

It is indeed very often the charismatic leader who identifies such outgroups and so mobilizes the commitment of his followers. While this is no doubt functional during a period of crisis and individual disorientation, in the longer term it carries dangers of its own. Commitment to the boundary represented by a charismatic leader implies a corresponding withdrawal of commitment to the most important human boundary of all – the individual's own boundary between outside and inside. In the language of Chapter 2, charismatic leadership promotes 'basic assumption' behaviour, and at the level of the 'assumption group' the individual in effect surrenders to the group his ego function.

Long-term solutions to the problem of maintaining adaptiveness to change cannot therefore depend on manipulative techniques. On the contrary, they must depend on helping the individual to develop greater maturity in controlling the boundary between his own inner world and the realities of his external environment.

References

ARGYRIS, C. (1962). *Interpersonal competence and organizational effectiveness.* Homewood, Ill.: Dorsey Press; London: Tavistock Publications.

ARGYRIS, C. (1964). *Integrating the individual and the organization.* New York: Wiley.

BAILLIE W. (1964). Control cabin management – monitored approach; Control cabin management – the double check. (Mimeographed.) London: British European Airways.

BAKST, H. J., BERG, R. L., FOSTER, F. D. & RAKER, J. W. (1955). The Worcester county tornado: a medical study of the disaster. Unpublished report, Committee on Disaster Studies, National Academy of Sciences, National Research Council. Washington, D.C.

BARNARD, C. I. (1948). *The functions of the executive.* Cambridge, Mass.: Harvard University Press; London: Oxford University Press. (First edition, 1938.)

BARRY, W. S. (1965). *Airline management.* London: Allen & Unwin.

BENNIS, W. G., BENNE, K. D. & CHIN, R. (eds.) (1961). *The planning of change.* New York: Holt, Rinehart & Winston.

BETJEMAN, J. (1960). *Summoned by bells.* London: John Murray.

BION, W. R. (1961). *Experiences in groups.* London: Tavistock Publications; New York: Basic Books.

BROWN, W. (1960). *Exploration in management.* London: Heinemann.

DAVIS, D. RUSSELL (1964). Psychological mechanisms in pilot error. In A. Cassie, S. D. Fokkema & J. B. Parry (eds.), *Aviation psychology.* The Hague and Paris: Mouton. Pp. 12–23.

EMERY, F. E. & TRIST, E. L. (1960). Socio-technical systems. In C. W. Churchman & M. Verhulst (eds.), *Management sciences.* London, New York, Paris, Los Angeles: Pergamon.

HERBST, P. G. (1962). *Autonomous group functioning: an exploration in behaviour theory and measurement.* London: Tavistock Publications.

HIGGIN, G. W. & JESSOP, W. N. (1965). *Communications in the building industry.* London: Tavistock Publications.

HOLFORD, SIR W. (1965). *The built environment.* (Tavistock Pamphlet No. 11.) London: Tavistock Publications.

HUTTON, G. (1962). Management in a changing mental hospital. *Human*

REFERENCES

Relations 15, 283–310. Managing systems in hospitals. *Human Relations* 15, 311–33.

KAHN, R. L. *et al.* (1964). *Organizational stress.* New York: Wiley.

KATZ, D. & KAHN, R. L. (1966). *The social psychology of organizations.* New York; Wiley.

KLEIN, M. (1959). Our adult world and its roots in infancy. *Human Relations* 12, 291–303. Reprinted as Tavistock Pamphlet No. 2. London: Tavistock Publications, 1960.

LIKERT, R. (1961). *New patterns of management.* New York: McGraw-Hill.

MCGREGOR, D. (1960). *The human side of enterprise.* New York: McGraw-Hill.

MENZIES, I. E. P. (1960). A case-study in the functioning of social systems as a defence against anxiety. *Human Relations* 13, 95–121. Reprinted as Tavistock Pamphlet No. 3. London: Tavistock Publications, 1961.

MENZIES, I. E. P. (1961). Some psychological consequences of belonging to an organization. Paper given at the Group Relations Training Conference, Leicester University/Tavistock Institute.

MENZIES, I. E. P. (1965). *A note on driving and road accidents.* London: British Safety Council.

MERTON, R. K. (1957). *Social theory and social structure.* (Revised and enlarged edition.) Glencoe, Ill.: The Free Press.

MILLER, E. J. (1959). Technology, territory, and time: the internal differentiation of complex production systems. *Human Relations* 12, 243–72.

MILLER, E. J. (1962). Designing and building a new organization: some lessons of a green-field situation. Paper read at the Manchester meeting of the British Association for the Advancement of Science.

MILLER, E. J. (1964). Social factors in setting up a new works. In Association of British Chemical Manufacturers, *Proceedings of Joint Conference on 'Human Factors and Productivity'*, Brighton. London: A.B.C.M. Pp. 15–35.

MILLER, E. J. & ARMSTRONG, D. (1966). The influence of advanced technology on the structure of management organisation. In *Employment problems of automation and advanced technology: an international perspective.* Proceedings of a Conference held at Geneva by the International Institute for Labour Studies, 19–24 July 1964, edited by Jack Stieber. London: Macmillan.

MILWARD, A. H. (1966). Wasted seats in air transport: an examination of the importance of load factor. The Institute of Transport 23rd Brancker Memorial Lecture.

MITFORD, J. (1960). *Hons and Rebels.* London: Gollancz.

PERLMUTTER, H. V. (1965). *Towards a theory and practice of social architecture: the building of indispensable institutions.* (Tavistock Pamphlet No. 12.) London: Tavistock Publications.

RAKER, J. W., WALLACE, A. F. C., RAYNER, J. F., with the collaboration of ECKERT, A. W. (1956). *Emergency medical care in disasters.* Disaster Study

Number 6. Committee on Disaster Studies, National Academy of Sciences, National Research Council Pub 457. Washington, D.C.

RICE, A. K. (1952). The relative independence of sub-institutions as illustrated by departmental labour turnover. *Human Relations* 5, 83–98.

RICE, A. K. (1958). *Productivity and social organization: the Ahmedabad experiment.* London: Tavistock Publications.

RICE, A. K. (1963). *The enterprise and its environment.* London: Tavistock Publications.

RICE, A. K. (1965). *Learning for leadership.* London: Tavistock Publications.

RICE, A. K. & TRIST, E. L. (1952). Institutional and sub-institutional determinants of change in labour turnover. *Human Relations* 5, 347–71.

SAYLES, L. R. (1964). *Managerial behavior.* New York: McGraw-Hill.

SCHEIN, E. H. (1965). *Organizational psychology.* Englewood Cliffs, N.J.: Prentice-Hall.

SOFER, C. (1961). *The organization from within.* London: Tavistock Publications.

THORSRUD, E. & EMERY, F. E. (1964). *Industrielt Demokrati.* Oslo: Oslo University Press.

THORSRUD, E. & EMERY, F. E. (1966). Industrial conflict and 'industrial democracy'. In J. R. Lawrence (ed.), *Operational research and the social sciences.* London: Tavistock Publications. Pp. 439–47.

TRIST, E. L. & BAMFORTH, K. W. (1951). Some social and psychological consequences of the longwall method of coal-getting. *Human Relations* 4, 3–38.

TRIST, E. L., HIGGIN, G. W., MURRAY, H. & POLLOCK, A. B. (1963). *Organizational choice: capabilities of groups at the coal face under changing technologies.* London: Tavistock Publications.

TYHURST, J. S. (1951). Individual reactions to community disaster. *American Journal of Psychiatry* 107, 764–9.

WOODWARD, J. (1965). *Industrial organization: theory and practice.* London: Oxford University Press.

ZALEZNIK, A. & MOMENT, D. (1964). *Casebook on interpersonal behavior in organizations.* New York: Wiley.

Index

Index

academic research institutions, 177–9
  output of, 177
  and primary task of university, 178–9
  and selection of university staff, 178–9
accidents, aircraft, and pilot, 205
activity
  definition of, 5
  maintenance, *see under* maintenance activities
  operating, *see under* operating activity
  regulatory, *see under* regulatory activities
  systems, *see under* systems of activity
advertising, 51
advertising function, location of, in model sales organization, 70–1
airline
  conflicts within, 220–1
  constraints on operation of, 186–93
    human, 190–3
    inherent, 189–90
  contracting out by, 265
  early days of, 193
  and environment, boundary between, 199–200
  national, 199
  primary task of, 187
  personal leadership in, 211–12
  primary task of, 184–5
    changes in, 193–4
  and safety, 185–7
    and profitability, 186–7, 202
  see also airline management, airline organization
airline management
  and engineering base, 210
  and passenger anxieties, 202–3
  and pilots, 207
  roles of, 200
airline organization
  major operating controls in, 200–1

management systems of, 196, 198–200
  and passenger anxieties, 202–3
operating systems of, 195–9
  flying, 196–8, *see also* flying system
  ground, 196, 197, 211, *see also* ground system
antisocial enterprises, sentience in, 259
anxiety
  and airline management, 201–3
  and airline travel, 190–3
  of ground staff, 214–15
  of pilot, 204–5
ARGYRIS, C., xiin, 271
ARMSTRONG, D., 229, 272
'assumption' group, 18–19, 20, 268
automation, 228
  and computers, 228
  and control, 264–5
  and conventional organization, 227
  of new iron and steel works, 235
    and changes in task organization, 246–7
    effect of, on management, 236–7, 242–4
autonomous work groups, 255–7

'bad patch', in career of speciality representative, 60
BAILLIE, W., 205, 206, 271
BAKST, H. J., 267, 271
BAMFORTH, K. W., xiin, 273
BARNARD, C. I., xiin, 271
BARRY, W. S., 188n, 202, 271
BENNE, K. D., xiin, 271
BENNIS, W. G., xiin, 271
BERG, R. L., (267), 271
BETJEMAN, J., III, 271
biological analogy of enterprise, 3–4
BION, W. R., 18n, 114n, 271

277